KEEP
CALM
AND
LOG
ON

KEEP CALM AND LOG ON

YOUR HANDBOOK FOR SURVIVING THE DIGITAL REVOLUTION

GILLIAN "GUS" ANDREWS

THE MIT PRESS   CAMBRIDGE, MASSACHUSETTS   LONDON, ENGLAND

Library of Congress Cataloging-in-Publication Data

Names: Andrews, Gillian "Gus," author.
Title: Keep calm and log on : your handbook for surviving the digital
   revolution / Gillian "Gus" Andrews.
Description: Cambridge, Massachusetts : The MIT Press, [2020] | Includes
   bibliographical references and index.
Identifiers: LCCN 2019029673 | ISBN 9780262538763 (paperback)
Subjects: LCSH: Online social networks. | Internet--Social aspects. |
   Human-computer interaction.
Classification: LCC HM742 .A65 2020 | DDC 302.30285--dc23
LC record available at https://lccn.loc.gov/2019029673

10 9 8 7 6 5 4 3 2 1

Dedicated to the memory of Dr. Frank Moretti

The imprint of your mind is all over these pages; this is your book.
We all miss you fiercely.

Contents

Acknowledgments

First and foremost, thanks are owed to my editor, Gita Devi Manaktala, and my agent, Jeff Shreve, for understanding the vision of this book from the beginning and enthusiastically and supportively working to get it out into the world. I'm still astounded that this ended up at the MIT Press; I can't imagine a better home for it. Thanks to you both. Thanks also to Maria, Marge, Susan, Katie, Catherine, Nicholas, Elizabeth, and Mary for their patience with the outsize demands of this book on design, publicity, and online publication.

This book draws heavily on the work of a handful of organizations and individuals whose contributors I am indebted to:

- Tactical Tech, level-up.cc, Internews, equalit.ie, Safer Sisters, and Simply Secure, who have done so much of the curriculum and usability improvement legwork reflected in the chapter on security
- Crash Override and Feminist Frequency for carefully curating tips on how to survive doxxing, SWATting and other harassment
- Amelia Acker and her work on identifying fake accounts
- Catherine Price, whose excellent handbook *How to Break Up with Your Phone* has been near to hand as I've written this
- the Poynter Institute for journalism resources
- Fairness and Accuracy in Reporting (FAIR), for its work over the years documenting the effects of media monopoly
- the Association of College and Research Libraries (ACRL), whose "Framework for Information Literacy for Higher Education" is the underrecognized engine driving the chapters on trust and information systems (I am of the opinion most educational standards at all levels should be thrown out entirely and rebuilt with this wise, efficient statement of the goals of education as their foundation)
- Brian V. Street, whose work on literacy helped me understand writing and power

- Model Mugging and Day One for their insights into intimate partner violence
- Safer Nudes for doing work almost nobody else has done to make room for sex positivity in this space
- our long-gone, recently rediscovered, honored ancestor, the Institute for Propaganda Analysis (IPA)

Also the Media Education Lab, with special thanks to Renee Hobbs for continuing to nurture and grow the media literacy community, and pointing me to fantastic resources in doing so, including the IPA and the ACRL framework. Not to mention Renee's enthusiasm for my projects over the years. I hope this book is half as useful to the media literacy community as all their work has been to me. Thanks also to Elizaveta Friesem for great discussions.

James Grimmelmann and Kyle Hodgson for being early cheerleaders for this book and my career, and serving up an effective kick in the pants to pitch this idea at a critical juncture.

Finn Brunton continues to be the only one who can reliably pull me out of my termite-mound-building writing process and spark brand-new excitement about this stuff, and I am deeply grateful for his continued help.

Glyph, for so many sage insights over the years, especially "software ships broken." His honesty and humility help me support others who struggle with technology.

Jessamyn West, for her exemplary devotion to doing respectful and supportive tech support, and her championing of librarians as leaders in this space.

Everyone on the "Keep Calm and Log On" mailing list who passed on useful thoughts, particularly Sarah, Steph, Nick, Nathalie, Catherine, Elaine, Matt P., and Mom. And Mrs. Lahorgue and Mrs. Wilson. I can't believe I'm still accidentally starting drama with my elementary school teachers at my age. I love that you're still here to keep me honest and cheer me on.

All of the supporters of *The Media Show* over the years: this book was the next step, so thank you for believing in those first weird puppet steps.

Lindsay, Devayani, and Ryan, for fielding my questions about how we value the authority of religious texts across various traditions. Special shout out to Stribs for providing inspiration with your "Doubt" essay.

Adriane, for feeding me and putting up with my writing-related dysfunction around the house.

Emmanuel, Greg N., Matt B., Mike C., Rob, and the gang from HOPE and Off the Hook, without whom I would have no foundation for digital security and rights.

My West Point folks, Ed, Greg C., Natalie, and Tanya, whose perspectives have broadened mine and whose continuing commitment to thoughtful expansion of filter bubbles is humbling.

Particular shout-out to the Internet Freedom Festival folks whose concern with disinformation sparked an overhaul of my chapters on trust: Christopher, Javier, Elodie, Wafaa, Sean, Slammer, and Trinh. And the rest of my IFF peeps; Bernard, Jon, Tawanda, Rose Regina, Griffin, Jessy, Dragana, Seamus, Gaba, Sandy, Pepe, Samir, Matt M., trimephalam, and oh my goodness there are entirely too many of you to name, I love you all. And An, who provided additional thoughtfulness on the contemporary social media landscape and helped me understand what the book-promoting process would be like.

Cade, Lester, Sara, Andy, and Philip for their work on the security curriculum at ThoughtWorks, from which I also learned a great deal.

The brothers Q, for making vital space. My gratitude is undying.

Various teachers deserve acknowledgment for their impact on my thinking about the stuff in this book:

Frank Moretti, and his lifelong intellectual partner Robbie McClintock, for making space for the peculiar Communications in Education department at Teachers College and leading its most thoughtful efforts. The most idiosyncratic parts of this book contain their DNA, and their care for my growth as a thinker. And also, for his support for the life of the mind and its evolution over human history: dear Nate Feldmeth.

Hampshire College. *Hampshire Freaking College*. If you like how this book weaves disciplines together, please please *please* go make a donation to Hampshire, if it is still around at publication time; its continued existence is in question as I write this. Without Hampshire's unique curriculum, I would not have been raised to turn the mechanisms of knowing upside down and inside out so we could see them better. I would not have gotten my panoramic overview of academic disciplines if I hadn't started at Hampshire. This line of thinking would be impossible without Hampshire.

Zeva Lahorgue, Roger Ipswitch, Dave Kerr, Tom Gardner, and Nina Huntemann for my early understanding of the media industry. Don Pember's thorough, even-handed media industry textbook continues to guide me in my understanding of what I want to accomplish, nearly thirty years after it was assigned to me.

Ellen Meier urged us all to look harder and smarter at how technology adoption happens, and radically transformed my approach to working toward change. If there are effective recommendations in this book, it's partly thanks to her.

Hervé Varenne, who is a constant encouragement to disassemble surprising human social patterns to their most rudimentary components.

Chuck Kinzer, who at one point challenged me that it was cognitively impossible that everyone should ALWAYS question EVERY text ALL the time; while I'm still quixotically working to prove him wrong, his curiosity about new technologies and other research traditions brought some of the material here into my net.

Ray Coppinger (and subsequently Bruno Latour) for blowing my understanding of science wide open.

The family tree is the first teacher. My father taught me how scientists do; my mother taught me how social researchers do. My grandmother, Dawn Cobb, insisted I know how to write, opened the door out of high school, and pushed me to go further.

Thanks to Mark Lusk, the Alvin Ailey Extension, and the piratical women of Fogo Azul, for helping me keep mind and body together. Musical thanks go to the proprietor of Urban Grind in Galway, Ireland; Shane Mesa for the soundtrack to Mother 4; and the countless YouTubers who curate collections of video game music—y'all provide the most effective soundtrack for staying focused and drowning out city noise pollution.

This has been a WS joint. Thank you for having my back.

Introduction: Surviving the Digital Revolution

They told us the digital revolution was going to do great things for us.

Everything would be more convenient, with the world at our fingertips. We'd have more access to things we needed. And it would just be *fun!*

Revolution sounds good, right? In school, we may have been told in glowing terms about the revolutions that happened in our nations. We learned that the Industrial Revolution, which made it easier for people to get food, clothing, and goods, improved our lives. The consumer revolution that followed, and the appliances and gadgets it produced, made housework easier.

So, why doesn't the digital revolution feel so great?

Maybe you feel overwhelmed by the sheer volume of stuff to keep up with, now that your device goes everywhere with you. Like you're always "on," and your device keeps interrupting you. Like you lose hours down the Internet Hole without even knowing where that time has gone.

Maybe you're exhausted by "fake news" or the disinformation that seems to be floating around everywhere.

Or how negative everything seems to be online—people fighting, talking politics, wringing their hands about the latest outbreak of violence.

Maybe you're worried about identity theft, or privacy violations.

Maybe you've been harassed or stalked online.

Maybe you just secretly feel like you're not as good at digital stuff as everyone else, and you'll never catch up.

I'm going to let you in on something many of us have forgotten about revolutions:

Revolution means everything changes: Who's in control. What we do at work, and who gets to do it. Whether there are any jobs to be had at all. Whose information gets trusted, and whose gets dismissed as fake. Which spaces are safe, and which have suddenly become dangerous. Revolution affects how we feed ourselves and where we live—and whether there's enough food and housing to go around. It even affects how we relate to our loved ones. All of these changes make it feel like we have to scramble to keep up.

This World War I poster encourages support for civilians behind firing lines. *Source:* US National Archives and Records Administration

The fact is, a revolution is a frightening thing to live through. It means people get hurt—our loved ones, and those who are least able to fend for themselves. You're not alone—and you're not wrong!—if you are scared or worried by what's going on in the news, in your bank account, and in your digital devices these days. This is what it feels like to live through a revolution. Frankly, it doesn't feel great.

There have been plenty of books talking excitedly about how the technological revolution will supercharge business. This is not one of those books. We're past the time for hype and excitement. What we need now is a survival handbook.

There are also plenty of books telling us about dangers on the internet, or what not to do online. This isn't one of those books, either. Ultimately, we still need to live our lives, and we can't just give up the internet and our phones. What we need are skills to protect ourselves.

This book is for us regular people, who just want to spend time with our friends and family, keep a roof over our heads, feed our kids, and do a good day's work: For those of us who feel overwhelmed by our digital lives—maybe have even already given up on social media, and gotten rid of our online accounts. Who worry the tech revolution is moving so fast we'll struggle to keep up in our jobs. Who are worried this revolution may not be making life better.

This book is a guide to living through the digital revolution without getting trampled.

Be Prepared

Let's take heart in one thing: we are not the first people in history to live through a time of radical upheaval and change. If our ancestors had not lived through revolutions, both technological and political, we would not be here! During times like these, we can look back to examples of the work they did, together, to survive and thrive. In this book, I'll tell stories about things ordinary people have done throughout history to cope with revolutions and wars. Let's see what advice we can take from them.

You Might Be Asking . . .

"What's with the art?"

Throughout this book, I make use of photos and art from the Great Depression, World Wars I and II, and other moments when communities have come together to cope with social upheaval—because, like I said, we're not the first ones to go through a revolution. In those eras everyday citizens were under threat from forces beyond their control. And yet they contributed to health, security, and conservation efforts to keep their communities running and safe.

In the Great Depression and World War II, US states called on citizens to put in extra effort to keep their communities functioning. WPA poster by Louis Hirshman. *Source:* Library of Congress website

The art that governments commissioned to communicate messages to citizens during that time is a reminder that we're not the first ones to live through massive upheavals. It's also a reminder that whether or not they fought in battle, all our ancestors had roles they played in keeping their communities safe and well cared-for.

Aside from giving us examples of community action in hard times, the illustrations in this book show how art served as *propaganda*—information spread by governments to influence their citizens. I'll talk more about propaganda throughout the book, and especially in chapter 10.

Even young citizens during the two world wars stepped up while the world tore itself apart around them. Youth groups were called on to contribute to their communities' survival. Girl Scouts suspended cookie sales and collected scrap metal instead, sending valuable resources to the front. They set up first-aid stations to help in case of air raids. Boy Scouts were called on to watch telephone lines, water reservoirs, and railway stations in case of tampering, and delivered all-clear messages to their communities after air raids. Scouts also watched the seas for approaching ships, ran messages between posts, and saved their pocket money to support hospitals and orphanages. President Franklin D. Roosevelt turned to the Boy Scouts first to help put up posters that informed communities about conserving resources, volunteering for the war effort, and protecting secrets from Axis spies. Why? The Scouts were already known and trusted by their communities.

We can follow the same patterns Scouts did during the wars to find ways to contribute to our communities during cyberwarfare today. We need to watch for people who try to cause trouble in our digital communities and make sure that we pass along critical messages from trustworthy, knowledgeable sources. And we need to conserve resources.

Communities have traditionally trusted Scout groups because they are organized, and the mission of these organizations is to help young people grow up ethically and live good lives. Even today, in the Central African Republic, the Boy Scouts have emerged as a surprising source of stability in a country wracked by fighting. Their solid organizational skills have helped their tens of thousands of members come together across religious divisions and poorly connected cities to administer vaccination programs and even negotiate the release of hostages by armed groups.[1]

As I was researching the history of what Scouts have done in times of unrest, it occurred to me that in the digital revolution, it can be useful for us to have by-laws, as Scout organizations do, to focus us on how we can do best for our communities. The Girl Scout Law, for instance, asks girls to pledge to be honest and fair, considerate and caring, courageous and strong, responsible and respectable. Boy Scouts are asked to do much the same.

I was a Girl Scout when I was a kid, so I learned all that. What sticks in my mind most about being a Scout isn't Scout Laws, though—it's the fun stuff, and the stuff I'm proud I learned to do: build a campfire, take

Even today, Boy Scouts in the Central African Republic
are trusted to organize and spread information.
Source: Will Baxter

care of a horse on the trail, flip over a capsized canoe, and lead younger girls in silly camp songs (my favorite part).

But my Scout leaders knew that the things we learned to do would help build the qualities of the Scout Laws in us. Leading songs made me considerate of the little ones. Riding the trail made me courageous. "Be Prepared" was the Scout Motto, and that meant being prepared for *anything*, whether we found ourselves alone in the woods or speaking in front of our local government.

If you were a Scout—or a Guide, or 4H member, or part of any group that helped you face challenges—remember what you managed to accomplish that you didn't expect you could. And remember how kids in Scouting organizations have helped in hard times for decades. This book, like your old *Scout Handbook*, will suggest a bunch of activities to help you navigate the worst parts of living through the digital revolution.

What guides these activities? I've come up with the following "Keep Calm Scout Laws" to use as themes throughout the book. Try saying them to yourself. Are there any ideas that feel new? Which ones feel useful?

- I am genuinely living through an information revolution. And revolutions don't always feel good.
- Mentally preparing for life online can help me keep calm and understand what's really going on.
- It helps to look for the helpers.
- Understanding what technologies actually do to my brain can help me break patterns that aren't helping me live my best life.
- Even the little changes I make to my life online can make me safer and happier.
- The struggles I have with technology are not my fault. And I'm not stupid.
- My digital life may feel unimportant in the big picture, but it's important to *me*.
- Control of my digital and media life should be *mine*.
- I talk to different people in my life in different ways. It should be up to me to decide who I want to talk to, how, and when.
- Trust, and the information we trust, belong to us. They are resources we build in our communities, together, for each other.
- If something digital is not doing work for me *right now*, I can turn it off.
- If I didn't ask for something my device is giving me, I should make it go away.
- Security happens because of my behavior, not someone else's, and not because of a gadget or app.
- If I can understand where my own opinion comes from, I will be better prepared to protect myself from people who want to manipulate me.

- Likewise, if I understand how communities decide what information to trust, I will be better prepared to identify bad information.

You'll notice that a number of these laws are about working on your own mindset. This may seem like navel-gazing: If it's the world that's going crazy, why are we looking inside ourselves?

Frankly, in an "attention economy" and an "information revolution," our minds, attention, and beliefs *are* a resource. Just like scrap metal, rubber, paper, and food that Scouts were called on to conserve during the two world wars, our attention and trust are now scarce commodities. We've only got so many hours in a day to spend staring at a screen and trying to make sense of the world around us. There are more and more demands on our attention.

Corporations, politicians, and governments are fighting for every scrap of our trust and our opinions they can get. And some of the ways they

Boy Scouts in Newtown, Wales, UK, collecting paper for recycling during World War II. *Source:* Geoff Charles.

want to use them might cause unexpected damage not only to us, but also our communities and our democracies.

In this book I will delve into a forgotten history of how communities have prepared to defend their mental resources in past times of crisis. And I will explore how mindfulness, an idea that comes from meditation, may help us understand where our attention, opinions, habits, and trust are going.

Keep Calm

The inspiration for this book's title is a British government poster from World War II that has enjoyed a revival as an online meme. In 1939, when Germany was threatening to bomb the United Kingdom, the Ministry of Information developed a series of posters with the goal of encouraging British citizens not to give up when faced with the destruction of their cities. "Keep Calm and Carry On" was one of them.

At the time, there was some cynicism about the posters. The war still seemed far away. Some people thought the message was patronizing in the face of a mortal threat. Ultimately, this was propaganda: the government wanted people to maintain a particular attitude, and it circulated these posters, aiming to ensure that attitude.

But within the idea of "keeping calm" in a time of crisis, there is a nugget of truth. According to a range of experts in psychology, education, and even religion, maintaining calm and understanding our own reactions to difficult situations can help us survive by making better decisions:

- If we identify information that is frightening and understand where it comes from, we can lower our stress levels.
- If we notice we are distracted, we can get our attention back on track.
- If we understand why we feel helpless, we can work to build skills we may be missing.
- If we understand where our gut reactions and opinions come from, we can overcome biases that might make us fall for fake news.

Source: UK government

In the opening chapters of this book, I'll discuss the reasons why media and technology upset us and stress us out. Throughout the book I'll present exercises we can do as we interact with media and technology, to maintain our cool and keep our wits about us. These exercises will help you identify your own reactions, so you can reflect on them and change them.

About Mindfulness

So, how do we keep calm?

When it feels like bombs are falling all around us, it is important for all of us to maintain calm around ourselves. Without it, we might make decisions that make our situations worse. This is where mindfulness comes in.

What is mindfulness? Jon Kabat-Zinn, the founder of the Center for Mindfulness, describes it as "paying attention, on purpose, in the present moment, nonjudgmentally." Specifically, paying attention to what you are thinking. Not beating yourself up over what you are thinking; not grabbing on to a thought and trying to fix it, or rolling it over and over in your mind. Just noticing a thought, and being aware that it's *just a thought*. It may not be the truth.

One of my favorite quotes, by Shunryu Suzuki, sums up what it is like to be mindful, treating your mind as if it were a house on a summer day:

Leave your front door and your back door open.
Allow your thoughts to come and go.
Just don't serve them tea.[2]

By now many people are familiar with the idea that paying attention to our thoughts and feelings can reduce our stress and anxiety and help us enjoy our lives more. Some people may have encountered mindfulness through therapy, some through exercises like yoga or meditation, or some through spiritual practice.

But mindfulness isn't just spiritual! There's a lot of science to support the claim that if you can notice and name thoughts and feelings that occur to you, you will be better able to stay calm and keep your head.

Believe it or not, research shows that just naming an emotion you are having—and not necessarily out loud, it can just be in your head—makes you more able to overcome that emotion. When Matthew Lieberman, a psychologist at UCLA, ran studies imaging the brain's response to emotions, he found that naming an emotion or writing it down actually changed which part of the brain was active.[3]

Our brains have a "fight or flight" center that kicks in when we are frightened or sense danger—a primitive part of the brain we have in common with many animals. Our brains also have a number of circuits that handle other emotions, like pleasure, disgust, and excitement.

But when you say "I'm angry," or write about how you are sad, you are accessing the neocortex, the layer of your brain that kicks in when you use language. The neocortex is the part of your brain that takes the time to analyze. When it takes over, the primitive, reactive brain cools down, and so do your emotions.

So some people might tell you "Just think positive!" and encourage you to repeat phrases that will make you be happier. But when you're actually experiencing negative emotions—fear in particular—it's more effective to name those emotions, to make your rational brain kick in and calm you down.

Scout Law: "Mentally preparing for life online can help me keep calm and understand what's really going on."

Regardless of what overwhelming flood of scary items showed up in your social media feed or the news today, there are a couple of mindfulness activities you can do to help you maintain your composure:

- Decide on a goal before you log on, pick up your phone, or turn on the TV. Being clear about this may help you keep from bingeing or getting distracted. It may even keep you from absorbing bogus information as you aimlessly wander around the internet.
  - Decide *what are you trying to do*: Check in with a particular friend? Are you just trying to relax? Do you want to learn something? Write down your goal to stay accountable.
  - Decide *how long* you want to be on: Setting a timer can help.
- Are you getting distracted from your goal? Don't beat yourself up; just notice when it's happening, and go back to what you meant to do. Noticing, rather than beating yourself up, can make it easier to get back on track.
- Just observe. Don't act on your emotions. Let them pass over you. If there's really something to be done, you will be in better shape to do it after you've processed what you're feeling for a little while.

This idea that mindfulness can not only help calm us down but also protect us from bad information may seem to some people like New Age hogwash. So you might be surprised to learn that even back in 1938, on the eve of World War II, a group of teachers and journalists recommended a form of mindfulness as protection against propaganda—as a way to help civilians survive floods of misleading information. Political groups and governments were trying to sway people's opinions with fake news, just as they are now. That story, and the method these teachers and journalists used to fight fake news, starts in part III of this book.

"But I'm Just Not Good at Technology"

It's helpful to pay attention to one more thing as you prepare yourself to cope with the stress of the current digital landscape: How do you feel about your own technology skills?

If you're a so-called millennial, you may have been told that because you're a "digital native" who grew up with technology, it just comes naturally to you. This may make it harder to grapple with moments when you feel other people are succeeding wildly at social media while you fail, or when you have social anxiety because you'd rather text than talk to people in person, or when your devices or connection stop working and you can't figure out why.

If you're older, you may have given up trying to be as good at technology as the young folks, and have thrown up your hands in despair, letting someone younger or more skilled fix a problem.

Regardless of what generation we're part of, many of us fall into a position of helplessness when it comes to dealing with the technology in our lives. We let someone else take charge of our thorniest technology problems—fouled-up Wi-Fi or devices that are running slow—because we believe we're "just not good at technology."

Remind yourself that your struggles with technology are *not* because you are stupid or bad at technology. This is an important part of the mental preparation you'll need online. Many physical self-defense techniques stress that in order to defend ourselves physically, we have to defend ourselves mentally. And self-confidence is not just important to self-defense. It's also important to learning.

So let's take a moment to think about reasons why we may not feel confident with technology.

I

KEEPING CALM

1

No One Is Born "Good at Technology"

If you're feeling especially hopeless when you're struggling to get social media to "work" for you like they do for other people, to get your phone or laptop to do your bidding, or to learn a new tech skill, some nagging ideas may be getting in your way. Have you ever heard or had ideas like these?

- Some people are just naturally good at technology, but I'm not one of them.
- I'm too old for this tech stuff.
- Men are better with technology than women are.
- Technology just isn't something my people *do*.
- Everyone here is better with the internet than I am. I don't belong here.

I've got news for you:

There's no scientific proof behind any of that. It's just not true.

There *is* scientific evidence that if you believe that some people are "smart" or "naturally good at" things, you will likely perform *worse* at those things. If you change your attitude to believe that you can *improve* your skills with practice and work, your performance is likely to improve.

"I don't belong here" thoughts are often a sign of "impostor syndrome" or "stereotype threat." These cause us to doubt ourselves, and worry that everyone else can tell we're faking it and we shouldn't be in our job or social group. (This happens *a lot* to those of us who are women or people of color trying to break into tech-heavy fields, programming in particular.) These thoughts can actually get in the way of us getting work done, by distracting us and slowing us down. And again: *they're not true*. Let 'em go. Find someone who can remind you how much progress you've made.

Nobody, and I mean NOBODY, is born "good at technology." There's no scientific evidence for it. Using technology requires language skills—and no human infant is born speaking. It requires small-motor hand movements—and no babies are born good at using their hands. These things develop over time. Sure, the earlier in life you pick up a mouse or a cell phone, the more time you will have to practice and get good at it. But that doesn't mean people who have spent time developing such skills are *naturally* good at technology. (I'm looking at you, millennials.) They're *historically experienced with* technology.

If you practice more, you will get better. Don't believe me? Try making a note in your calendar or diary of things you learn about your digital life—your security, privacy, skills, and ability to cope with tech-related stress—and moments you realize you can do things you couldn't before. Just keeping track will give you more confidence that progress is possible.

If you haven't had much time to practice, you're in good company, I promise. The vast majority of people alive today didn't learn how to use technology in school.

Think about it. Suddenly you have these new things called "personal computers" (and later "mobile devices") out in the world, by the billions. Teachers don't know how to use them—they haven't had time to learn. So who's going to teach the billions of people who now have these devices in their homes and offices? For the past fifty years or so—not more than a couple of generations—we've had this chicken-and-egg problem of billions of people who need to learn about digital technology, and a tiny number of people who have the know-how to teach them.

So we're all of us learning as we go—millennials and older folks alike. It's not just you. Almost all of us have bumbled along outside of the classroom, sharing tips with each other, picking up ideas from TV and websites, and inventing our own ways of doing things as we go along. Learning about technology outside of school is *normal*. It's not somehow inferior.

Nobody has a "perfect" idea of what they're doing with their laptop or phone. (And anyone who pretends they do is mostly blowing hot air.) Accept that learning about technology is a part of living through this part of history. Sometimes that means you're going to feel dumb or ignorant. It's OK. You're not alone.

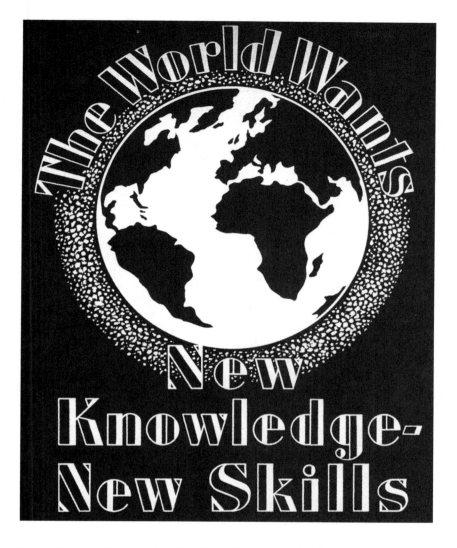

During the Great Depression, the Works Progress Administration
supported Americans by training them in new fields.
Source: Work Projects Administration Poster Collection—
Library of Congress

People with disabilities—including dyslexia, ADD, or even colorblindness—face more challenges with technology than most people. Most technology designers are young, healthy people (and frankly, young men outnumber young women in the field). They generally don't think about people with failing eyesight, mental limitations, or arthritic hands.

When you run into software or a device that *is* designed to meet a wider range of physical needs, you can tell, right? Larger tech companies often staff an accessibility expert, whose job it is to make it clear to developers that their design choices may make digital life hard for people with limitations. The work these experts do is pretty cool! They make developers test the software while wearing weighted clothing, for instance, or with their fingers taped so that they can't move easily. They make them use a screen reader developed for blind users or wear special glasses to simulate vision problems. This quickly drives the point home in a personal way that has turned some developers into passionate advocates for accessibility. (Try turning on a screen reader for an average website sometime. It'll make you want to go yell at designers who make sounds or videos load automatically on a website.)

A poster that circulated among software designers pointed out that we *all* face the same challenges using technology at some point. The poster pointed out that holding and tapping on a phone can be a permanent challenge for someone who's had an arm amputated, a temporary one for someone with a broken arm, and a momentary inconvenience for someone holding a baby! One person might have permanently limited vision, whereas someone else's eyes might be blurred and teary because of a temporary allergic reaction that makes it hard to see. Technology designers ought to be planning for these cases. It benefits all of us. There's no reason why technology should make us feel incompetent or less-than because of our limitations.

How to Keep Calm and Log On

Scout Laws: "The struggles I have with technology are not my fault. And I'm not stupid"; "Control of my digital and media life should be mine"; "Even the little changes I make to my life online can make me safer and happier."

The good news is that most of your devices and their software allow you to customize certain settings to make a standard device more comfortable for you to use. Somewhere under "Settings," "Controls," or "System Preferences" you should be able to customize your device in the following ways:

- Speak to your device instead of typing or tapping
- Have your device read text to you
- Have captions for audio or video
- Use a game controller or other easy-to-move switch to control your device
- Enable special keystrokes or gestures that let you zoom in on part of the screen
- Change the color, remove the color, stop extra movement, or change the font on screen so you find it easier to focus and read
- Change the size of the pointer so you can see it more easily

When trying out these options, keep track of where you made the change, so you can go back and undo it if it ends up not working for you. Also, only change one thing at a time before testing out what the change does. For more information on these options, check **keepcalmlogon.com.**

And one last thing—don't let anyone make fun of you for the font you use on your system or device. Comic Sans is a font that many tech snobs make fun of—they think it looks silly, like phony handwriting—*but Comic Sans can actually make it easier for dyslexic people to read!*[1] (If you're finding this font easier to read than the font in the rest of this book, it may be because it's typeset in Comic Sans.) The shape of the letters makes it less likely that dyslexia will tumble them around in confusing ways.

So if Comic Sans or some other font makes it easier for you to use your device, do what you gotta do! There are actually special fonts designed for dyslexics that may make reading easier—like **OpenDyslexic and Dyslexie**. Courier is another widely available font shown to be easier for dyslexics to read.[2] How's this sentence working for you?

So here's your mantra for getting around the thoughts that are slowing down your digital learning:

It's not that I'm bad at technology. I've just had some bad experiences. I'll get better with practice. I deserve to do well with digital stuff as much as anyone else does.

Let me dissect a few of my own bad experiences with technology, where I lost confidence and doubted myself.

Your Struggles with Technology Are Not Your Fault, and You're Not Stupid

Starting in 2013, I worked for an organization that helped journalists and human rights workers around the world protect their digital communications from censorship and snooping by their governments. From day one, this felt incredibly scary. I'm good at talking to people and learning about how technology is working for them, but my boss wasn't going to let me *talk* to these tech users. Over lunch on my first day, he snapped at me, saying that I couldn't be in touch with the people we were training. "You'll get them killed," he growled. My stomach sank as I started to get the impression that digital security was *so serious* that I wouldn't even be able to use my best skills to do my job. I was going to be working with one hand tied behind my back.

To communicate with these people, we were instructed to use—meaning use ourselves, in the office—the very same email tools and system software we were supposed to be training *them* to use. (In the tech industry, this is referred to as "eating your own dog food.") And that security software was incredibly hard to use. Often, this was because it just didn't work right. One day, my laptop refused to unlock with the password I had set to keep it encrypted and protected from prying eyes. I tried rebooting over and over, tried half a dozen passwords—my coworkers were getting on with their day, meetings were coming up and I literally couldn't even start my work. The clock was ticking. I was stressing out. If I couldn't unencrypt my disk, *all* of my work was lost—nobody would be able to unscramble my machine and get my work back.

But then my coworker Griffin said, "Oh yeah, that happens with some Linux laptops. You have to hit delete twice to clear out the two spaces it inserts. Then you can enter your password. That's a known thing."

A known thing?! I didn't know! How was someone supposed to know that?

Furious, I wiped my laptop's hard disk, took it to my boss, and demanded to be given a new laptop, one that wasn't so broken that it needed some sort of secret fancy dance I wasn't even aware of just for me to use it. From then on, I worked on a user-friendly Mac. My boss grumbled. But at least I didn't feel like a helpless idiot who constantly had to beg her coworkers for help.

The next year, we held a conference for trainers who worked with our journalists and activists. That's where I met Tawanda, a digital security trainer from Zimbabwe. Shortly after introducing himself, Tawanda admitted, sheepishly, that he himself didn't regularly use the email software we'd been recommending for its security.

"Oh, honey," I told him, patting his arm. "It's not your fault. That thing is so broken."

Tawanda's face broke into a massive grin. "I like your energy!" he exclaimed. Since then, Tawanda and I have been fast friends. He and his colleagues have been willing to come right out and say it to the faces of the software developers we work with: their apps can be painfully hard to use. We don't blame ourselves when the software doesn't make sense to us anymore. And frankly? Now that they have honest feedback to listen to, the software developers are working on making their software better.

I'm going to say to you what I said to Tawanda:

It's not your fault. Technology is broken. And you have every right to feel frustrated with it.

In fact, one of the most respected experts in software design, Don Norman, has called out his fellow software designers for making people believe that they're just no good at technology—when the actual problem is that the *technology itself is no good.*

The Software Is Broken, Not You

Some things about the way software is built can make it essentially break or seem broken for most people. Have you ever looked at an app or site and said, "I can't do what I used to! They moved the button!"?

As a software designer, I owe you an apology. Software designers move buttons and features move around *constantly*. Sometimes we're doing it because the button was in a dumb place to begin with, and we're moving it to a place that makes more sense. Sometimes we're moving or changing it because the software or device has changed. For instance, when websites started to adapt for mobile devices, it might not have made sense to leave the button where it was on a computer monitor–sized webpage, because you wouldn't be able to reach it with your thumb, or it was likely you'd hit it at the wrong time. Sometimes a company is changing the look of their brand, and that changes where things are, as well as colors and designs. To be honest, though, I think there are times when designers decide they have to leave their mark on a site or app, just to prove they're doing their job.

Our reasons for moving things don't really benefit *you* as a software user. Your fingers are used to reaching to a particular spot for a button or link, and it's just not there anymore. You built up reflexes, and we broke them. Honestly? I think you're no more wrong for being angry about this kind of change than you would be if someone came in and rearranged your kitchen or desk. It's intrusive and maddening. The reorganization is usually for someone else's benefit.

And again, *it's not your fault* when someone breaks your reflexes and makes it so you have to relearn how to use your phone or app. You are not "bad" at using technology. Technology is bad at serving *you*.

Earlier I mentioned a few ideas that may run through our heads when we feel like we're bad at technology. Here's a few more. Do any of the following thoughts ring true to you?

- I kept trying and trying and the site didn't work. I gave up.
- I'm clumsy when it comes to technology. A total klutz.
- I'm technophobic.
- I'm social-media illiterate.
- I really can't do anything with my computer or phone without help.

If any of those claims have come out of your mouth or run around in your brain like a hamster on a wheel when you hit an obstacle to your digital progress, bad technology may have beaten you into a state of *learned helplessness*. Don Norman points out that this is what happens when people try to do what makes sense to them, only to have the software repeatedly react in bizarre ways and not support them in doing what they need to do.[3] Our tendency, when we can't get a technology to work, is to blame ourselves. Even if the technology is to blame! The technology has taught us to act helpless.

Then tell me: How do people who are supposed to be helping you with your technology treat you? Do they ever

- roll their eyes or sigh?
- get frustrated?
- use technical terms, but not explain what the words mean?
- grab the keyboard, mouse, or phone out of your hands and finish what you were trying to do?
- act like everything about the technology was obvious?
- act like, or even say, you were stupid, slow, or out of date, or ask something like "Why would you *do* that?!" in an accusing tone?

If they did, they weren't helping your learned helplessness, either! Some "help" they were. They were just reinforcing the message you were already getting from the bad or broken technology, just giving you one more message about yourself to set loose in your head like a hamster ready to chew up your positive-reinforcement wiring and make it into a nest of shreds.

Don't Let Them Grab the Keyboard!

If you've fallen into learned helplessness when it comes to technology, it may take some work just to get yourself to a place of confidence. Try the following:

How to Keep Calm and Log On

Scout Laws: "Control of my digital and media life should be mine"; "The struggles I have with technology are not my fault. And I'm not stupid."

The best way to learn technology skills is to get hands-on. When someone who is "helping" you tries to take the keyboard or mouse from you, tell them, "I need to build the 'muscle memory' of where things are on the keyboard and mouse. If you let me 'drive,' it's less likely you'll have to help me again next time." I hope by now you're feeling a little braver—at least brave enough to say to the person "helping" you, "Gimme back my phone! I want to do this myself!"

During World War II, women were asked to do new jobs with machinery. Some may have thought they weren't capable of doing this work. Today, we may have to overcome our sense that we're not good with digital technologies. *Source:* J. Howard Miller, Office for Emergency Management, War Production Board

The most important thing any of us can do at this moment in history is to learn more about technology and where the media we consume come from. Fighters on the frontlines of cyberwarfare—company security professionals, militaries, and even freedom fighters against censorship and surveillance—need all of us to help shore up our defenses and protect our resources. Because our own defenses and conservation efforts end up defending bigger things than we know. Our mental and digital resources are the same ones threatened by malicious hackers and disinformation-spreading bad actors.

Our communities need to come together, keep calm, conserve the truth and our attention, and not lose our heads over fake information online. All of us need to be able to maintain peace and safety in our families, work-places, and social networks. Each little thing we can do to improve our tech skills may seem small, but it can improve life for us all.

Where Else Can You Go to Improve Your Tech Skills?

The best place I can recommend is your local library!

How to Keep Calm and Carry On

It's the librarians' job to help people, and they pride themselves on doing it. They may also know of local resources in your area. Many cities also have job-training programs that include technology training.

And if you want to aim for getting a job at a tech company, there's a new kind of school on the rise that can help you reach that goal. Most of these are called something like "coding boot camps." Many of them offer scholarships or have programs where the company that eventually hires you pays for your tuition. For more information on these options, check **keepcalmlogon.com.**

2

Look for the Helpers: A Tradition in Times of Disaster

When I was a boy and I would see scary things in the news,
my mother would say to me, "Look for the helpers. You will always
find people who are helping." To this day, especially in times
of "disaster," I remember my mother's words and I am always comforted
by realizing that there are still so many helpers—so many caring
people in this world.
—Fred Rogers[1]

You may have come across this quote in recent years. It's from the children's television legend Mr. Rogers. When there is a terrorist attack, a mass shooting, or an outbreak of war, people pass these words around on social media, often with a calm, smiling, sweater-wearing photo of Mr. Rogers attached.

Some people might say it's immature for grown people to circulate a message from a kids' TV icon in response to such serious events. Some might say that as adults, our job is to put our fears aside and just soldier on. But part of Fred Rogers's point was that children look to their parents for tips on how to feel.

And we, as adults, are also affected by reports of catastrophes and violence. Stress from frightening experiences can actually change how our brains work. Our past stressful experiences may make some of us respond too quickly and strongly to frightening things (think about veterans or survivors of violence who have PTSD). Or they may even burn us out so we don't respond to frightening things at all. These reactions can keep us from managing our moods productively, can impact our social relationships, and can keep us from thinking calmly and thoroughly about what we need to do next.[2]

The news is one source of our worry, fear, and anger. And being mindful of these feelings, being able to name them, can help lower the stress we feel because of them.

Genuinely frightening things are happening in the world right now, brought to us daily via the news. Data breaches and identity theft seem to happen every other day. Climate change and government regime changes are worrying enough on their own, but combined they are even more disruptive, uprooting whole populations and causing the mass migration of refugees (like those trying to enter Europe and the United States), which then creates additional pressures and even more disruption.

But, as I mentioned before, we are not the first generations to go through upheaval. By being mindful and looking to how previous generations coped in times of trial, we can get through this frightening time, too.

Girl Guides prepare for post-air-raid emergency help in the United Kingdom during World War I. *Source:* George P. Lewis, Imperial War Museum

The History of "Look for the Helpers"

In fact, the roots of the "look for the helpers" advice come from the experience of Mr. Rogers's own mother during World War I and the 1918 flu pandemic that followed—and in the experience of her ancestors before her.

It was not common for a teenage girl to drive in 1918, but Nancy McFeely (later Nancy Rogers) insisted she wanted to help doctors and hospitals in her town. Her peers were dying in one of the worst flu outbreaks the world had ever seen, one so strong it hit teenagers and young adults hardest, instead of vulnerable populations like infants or the elderly. Meanwhile, World War I was raging. Community resources were tapped.

Nancy's father tried to discourage her by telling her that if she wanted to drive, she would need to learn how to build a car engine, in case it broke down on her. So she learned to build a car engine! And she drove loads of hazardous medical waste to incinerators, putting herself at risk of falling sick. She survived. She knit sweaters for soldiers in World War I (like the cardigans she knit for her son, which became part of his signature style).

For much of Nancy's life she continued not only to help in hospitals but also to ensure that every family in her community had what they needed to raise their children—shoes for school, medical care, and enough food.

She was not the first in her family to care for her community during disaster. Her ancestors had lived through, and eventually fled from, the droughts and crop failures that struck Scotland and Ireland. Tens of thousands in Ireland died of starvation, and hundreds of thousands more due to disease made worse by citizens' poor health. Millions of Irish fled to countries like the United States and Canada, breaking community ties and support networks. Helping those who were less fortunate was a matter of community survival, but the Rogers family believed it was also what they were called on to do as followers of Christ.[3]

Helping people who are hurt is a natural human response to a disaster. People will go out of their way, even put themselves at risk, to ensure others are safe.

Nobody knows that better than the residents of New York City. While TV shows like *Law and Order* make our city look riddled with crime, those of us who live here see it is full of helpers. When someone collapses

Strife around the world forces people out of their homes—
and requires others to lend a hand. *Source:* Ministry of Health

unexpectedly on the subway, passengers and train conductors will call for a doctor. If there is an assault, another passenger may step in and restrain the dangerous person until the police arrive. One morning, a woman pointed at me and said "Call 911!" as she held on to another woman who looked like she was about to throw herself on the tracks. I did—and a bunch of us stayed with the woman until medics arrived to help her. And that's just a daily echo of what our city saw on September 11, 2001, when everyday people put themselves at risk of being trapped in the collapsing World Trade Center to carry people in wheelchairs and others who couldn't make it down the stairs.

A Never-ending Eyeful of Crisis

Throughout history we have always helped our neighbors in times of crisis. What is relatively new—only a couple of hundred years old—is the ability to learn about crises that are happening right now in faraway places. Photographs in the news are barely 150 years old; film reels of news, about 100 years old; and live TV reporting from the field, only about 70 years. By some estimates, the increased coverage of atrocities in Vietnam made up a big part of the reason why Americans grew unhappy about that war. We were better able to see the results of the violence.

And it is new that we see *so much* of the violence. News cycles are tuned to keep frightening things coming to us 24/7. Our social media feeds are full of our friends repeating these atrocities over and over, wringing their hands about why this happened, offering their thoughts and prayers to the victims—but ultimately re-spreading news of the traumatic event.

So how has humanity dealt with the fact that we can now be aware of much more violence and disaster than our ancestors could? Unfortunately, we haven't dealt with it particularly well. We end up believing the world is a much more dangerous place than it actually is.

Feeling Scared

Most Americans have probably heard this line from someone in their lives: "The world is just so much more dangerous now than when we were growing up." If you watch TV news, that certainly seems to be true—and for local news in particular: every night it's full of stabbings, shootings, police chases, and robberies. Movies, crime shows, and other fictional TV series pile on with even more violence. And then in world news, politicians aren't helping your mood by making big, world-ending threats at each other.

But is this *really* true? Is "the world" or "our society" more dangerous than it was? The truth might surprise you.

In the United States, violent crime has gone down significantly since the 1990s—48 percent by the FBI's numbers, 74 percent according to a Bureau of Justice Statistics report. Burglary and theft have also gone down by roughly half.[4] There was a small uptick in violent crime from 2014 to 2016, but it was less than 7 percent each year. (One larger exception is hate crimes. The FBI says they are up by about 17 percent since 2016— and that's just by its own estimation, which some hate-crime monitoring groups think is low due to underreporting.)[5]

But Americans still report that they think all violent crime is going up year by year—even though violent crime is dropping, in the long term. Interestingly, in the early 1990s, Americans were aware that crime was dropping. But as of 2001, more of us started responding that we thought there was more violent crime this year than the year before.

So—aside from 9/11, obviously—what happened in 2001 to change how frightened Americans were by the news?

There were tremendous increases in the viewership of 24/7 cable news networks following the 2000 US election. CNN saw a 249 percent increase in viewers, MSNBC was up 359 percent, and Fox News had a 440 percent rise in viewers—a trend that continued in the years that followed.[6]

Channels that broadcast news all day, seven days a week, haven't always existed. CNN was really the first, getting its start in 1980 and really taking off with its coverage of the Gulf War in 1991.

The 24/7 news cycle changed how big an earful of bad news we got. Prior to CNN, the news only came to most of us twice a day—in the morning paper, and in the evening broadcast. When CNN started providing news all day long, they suddenly had to find a way to keep viewers watching that long—and other channels had to keep up with their news cycle. This is why we have a particular shape of news story, where anchors spend a lot of time saying "we don't have all the facts yet, but this event is developing, *stay tuned*" or rehash the few facts that have already become clear. There's nothing new to report on—but the urgent need to keep viewers watching means using these tricks to make sure we don't change channels, because we feel like there *is* still more to watch.

You may have heard the phrase "if it bleeds, it leads" when it comes to the news. This refers to the fact that violent news gets more attention—and therefore more viewers or readers, and therefore more advertisers. Thus, news producers tend to put violent news first.

Profit is one factor that shapes what we do and don't see in the media. Not to say that politicians or companies pay journalists to make news about them in a particular way—that is not so common in the United States, where professional standards mean that journalists could lose their jobs for taking bribes. But in a more general way, profit determines what *kinds* of stories show up in news and entertainment media.

Murders or child abuse attract a lot more outraged attention than, say, how the school board votes on funding, or a local politician who tells a company it doesn't have to pay taxes if it opens an office in your town. So even if journalists have plenty they *could* be reporting on when it comes to local or state representatives doing (or not doing) their jobs, you're still going to get an eyeful of violence. I'll go into this further in later chapters.

And the internet has only made that worse. When Facebook changed its algorithm in early 2018 to keep from burying news deep in people's feeds, the company defined news as "politics, crime, or tragedy." Not sports, not business, not "timely reports which could help people improve their health, their schools, and their communities" but politics, which seems to imply the horserace and posturing of politicians in elections, crime, and tragedy. Without thinking too hard about it, or taking the advice of news editors who usually provide viewers a range of news, Facebook single-handedly continued the decades-old "if it bleeds, it leads" problem.

Facebook accelerated our new problem: because we all act as the media now on social sites, bad news spreads through conversations with our friends, our work email, or apps we use to distract ourselves.

Mean World Syndrome

The result? We have a case of "mean world syndrome."

George Gerbner, a journalist and professor of communications, coined the phrase "mean world syndrome" based on his studies of the effects of mass media. He found that people who watched more TV also tended to see the world as more dangerous than those who watched less. And he saw this happening in the 1970s, *before* the rise of 24/7 news or the internet, so it didn't even account for the intense dose of worrying reports that we get today.

"Mean world syndrome" was part of Gerbner's larger "cultivation theory" of the media: the idea that what we see repeatedly in the media shapes our view of the world around us. Obviously media aren't the only things that shape our sense of the world. But media make up a bigger part of our understanding when it comes to seeing things outside our own daily lives, unfamiliar things or people far away from us.

News and fictional shows that emphasize crime and violence nudge us to see the world around us as violent, even if it isn't. Even if your own community seems perfectly safe to you, you may be developing an idea that in the wider world, things are really, really dangerous. Or maybe you *have* gotten the idea that your community is dangerous, or certain neighborhoods are, and you've avoided those areas or changed how much you go out.

And that idea can be dangerous! How we view the world shapes how we treat others around us, what we buy, and how we vote. All of which, in turn, shape the world. If we don't understand what we're seeing, we may be shaping the world in ways that harm others—for example, calling for police to be "tougher on crime," which may end up putting innocent people in jail or increasing the number of fatal shootings by police officers. We can even harm ourselves by voting or acting against our own interests. Then there's the issue of big, frightening proclamations from political figures—which just make that problem worse.

It is reasonable to feel worried about some things in the news. But when should we trust the news to bring us an accurate view of the world? And why should we trust it?

In part IV of this book, I'll discuss how some of our ancestors came to an agreement among themselves about when to trust news: first in writing and books, then newspapers, and then in broadcast media such as radio and TV. Unfortunately, as the rules for making accurate news evolved, so did other pressures on the news—and those pressures made the news the constant stream of downers, attention-getters, and horrors we have to live through today. I'll talk about these in chapter 19, on the profit motive.

Mindful Sharing of Stressful Events

If we're being mindful, we should acknowledge that we're scared. It is hard to process anything else if your mind and body are pumped full of *cortisol*—the hormone we produce in response to stress.

One of the things that often gets forgotten about Mr. Rogers's "find the helpers" advice is the follow-up: when children see scary things in the news, you should *ask them what they believe is happening*. The same goes for you as an adult.

Source: Work Projects Administration
Poster Collection—Library of Congress

When something in the news frightens you, it is important to get your brain straight on what is an immediate threat to your personal safety, and what is not. If you can consciously check in with yourself about stories that seem scary, you can encourage your analytical mind to take over and keep from developing a "mean" worldview in your head.

Much of the time, we act like we're directly affected by events in the news—mass shootings and lone-wolf terrorist attacks are key examples—when we are not. When events like these happen, they may claim a large number of lives. But the deaths are generally contained in one area, in one town. That town grieves and tries to come to grips with what happened. There may be policy steps we want to take to ensure something like this doesn't happen again, but panicking or wringing our hands won't sign that policy into law.

But what happens next makes the situation worse. News outlets deliver an ongoing stream of updates about the fatalities and the city's response, showing emergency response vehicles racing around town, sometimes even footage of the event itself. They dig up the background of the shooter, hypothesize about his motives, and broadcast entire press conferences and memorials dedicated to what he did, often with a backdrop of sad or scary music.

And the rest of us—everyday people—go even further. We wring our hands on social media and share pictures or icons on our profiles to show our solidarity with those who are affected.

It turns out that when we use social media to share violent acts committed by *individual people*—like fistfights, mass shootings, terrorist attacks, and even suicide—we may make things even worse.

Concrete, scientific evidence shows that devoting extensive coverage to these events leads others to be copycats who commit more acts of violence. Those of us far away, hungrily consuming more news about the event, may be encouraging the next disturbed person to think about how much everyone will *care* about them and pay attention to them if they kill a lot of people or themselves.[7]

This is why New Zealand prime minister Jacinda Ardern refused to speak the name of a gunman who in 2019 massacred fifty people, including children, at a mosque. Ardern asked other citizens of her country to do the same: "I implore you: speak the names of those who were lost, rather than the name of the man who took them," she said. "He may have sought notoriety, but we in New Zealand will give him nothing, not even his name."[8] In refusing to give the attacker publicity, Ardern and her fellow citizens followed the advice of researchers who recommend this as a way to lower the number of mass shootings.

How to Keep Calm and Log On

Scout Laws: "Understanding what technologies actually do to my brain can help me break patterns that aren't helping me live my best life"; "If I work to understand where my own opinion comes from, I will be better prepared to protect myself from people who want to manipulate me."

Know when not to overshare, but also know when to speak out. *Source:* Work Projects Administration Poster Collection—Library of Congress

When an upsetting event shows up in your news feed, ask yourself:

- What do I *want* to happen when I share this?
- What *unintended consequences* might happen because I share this?
- Is there a *need* for me to share this?

If there's even a remote possibility that your reasoning is "I want people to know that I care" or "I want people to know I am a good (Christian, Muslim, Jewish, Buddhist, leftist, or conservative) member of some community I belong to," think twice about that. Slow your roll. Weigh your desire to improve how you look to others against possible unintended consequences.

As an educator, I hate to say it—but our desires to use an event as a "teachable moment" about guns or political situations may also arise from selfish motives:

- Are you usually the person who shares short, smart quotes or political images on social media when an event happens? What do you get out of that?
- Are you certain that the things you share are going to have the impact you desire in your community? Question yourself, once again, about your reasons for sharing.

There are times when sharing about scary things doesn't pose the same kind of problem as sharing a mass shooting or a terrorist attack. In fact, it may be helpful:

- If you and your community are directly affected by a violent event—if you know or worry that people you know were hurt by an event—it's totally reasonable to ask and share information about what's going on! I don't mean to say that *everyone* should stop posting about terrorist events or mass shootings—only those of us who are not directly affected.
- Natural disasters like tsunamis or hurricanes are not the same category of scary events as mass shootings, and sharing information about people far away and showing how much we care doesn't necessarily cause the same kinds of problems. Hurricanes aren't staying up all night watching updates about their progress on CNN—they're not going to flood worse or knock down more homes for the attention. And if we share the right information—about ways to donate, not just pictures of devastation and suffering—we can actually help those affected.
- When it comes to larger upheavals, like protests, wars, disease outbreaks, or famine, it's good to understand the *backstory* of why these things happen. Understanding our world and why it is the way it is can help us make better decisions about our lives and communities. But again, we may have other reasons for sharing about the *suffering* they cause. If you find yourself sharing stories of suffering or outrage, again, ask yourself: What do I get out of sharing this?

Finally, when sharing information about any frightening event, it's worth considering what you want to happen, and what will actually happen:

- How full of the scary news are your friends and family's minds already? Are they seeing it everywhere?
- Is what you're about to share a new perspective on the issue?

We are the news now, and we're every bit as capable of spreading "mean world syndrome" as traditional news outlets. So we should be mindful of what kind of world we are shaping for the people around us. We should consider that we might actually be spreading violence—or, as we'll talk about later, misinformation that may benefit someone who does not share our interests.

Attention-Getters

The ways media get our attention are part of how they upset us or obsess us. Thinking about how it is that they get our attention can help us change our response to them.

Music is often one of the subtlest ways media can shape how we feel about what we are seeing. Next time you watch a political video on social media, or a news clip, your favorite show—or when you're "on hold" waiting for someone to pick up the phone!—listen for music playing in the background. That music is there to shape your view of what you're watching.

To test the impact of music on you, there's always "Yakety Sax"—the ridiculous song from the old TV comedy show *Benny Hill.* Try the following to experiment with how music makes you feel:

- First, find a news clip that you expect may be using techniques to worry or frighten you.
- Bring "Yakety Sax" up on YouTube and leave it playing in another tab or window in your browser.
- Mute the news clip and watch it with "Yakety Sax" as its new soundtrack.
- Check: Does your feeling about the video change when the soundtrack changes?

Music isn't the only technique used to get your attention or shape how you feel. Surprising, disgusting, or cute images, animation, film cuts and camera angles, sound, and writing techniques are all used to bring a media audience in and keep their attention, both online and in traditional media. (Think about those "one weird trick" ads and others of that ilk—they are sometimes displayed in what's known as a "chumbox," a banner or sidebar on a website or app that presents sensational ads.)

Again, this doesn't mean we are powerless or brainwashed by these techniques: they are just part of the picture. And if we can be mindful of them, we can be better prepared to observe the media that wash around us, and keep calm when they might want us to freak out.

How to Keep Calm and Carry On

Scout Laws: "Understanding what technologies actually do to my brain can help me break patterns that aren't helping me live my best life"; "Mentally preparing for life online can help me keep calm and understand what's really going on."

Pay attention to your body as you scroll through your social media or watch TV. First of all, you want to notice: ARE you calm? What emotion or sensation are you feeling as you encounter this particular form of media? Fill out the chart below while asking yourself these questions:

- Are you tense? Clenched? Arms crossed protectively? Breathing quickly? Or do you feel kind of low or sad? How's your heart rate?
- Name the feeling you're having. Is it anger? Worry? Fear? Excitement? Are you depressed?
- Again, just observe the feeling. You don't have to act on it.

  What thoughts come to you along with this physical sensation?

- Focus on the content of the thoughts. If you're worried about a terrorist attack or mass shooting, ask yourself, "Is it true I should really be afraid of the thing they're telling me to be scared of? Does the danger really affect me, right here, right now? How would I know?"
- Then do it again. "No, really—is that going to happen to me right now?"
- Then ask yourself about the feeling: "Is worrying, or getting furious, or feeling gleeful about someone else getting what's coming to them (or any other overwhelming emotion), going to protect me? Is it going to solve the problem?"

Take a second look at whatever medium you're looking at. Is it making an appeal to your fear? Or to some other emotion? Use the "Media Techniques Checklist" and worksheet in the section below to keep track of the tricks or special effects the media may be using to sway your emotions.

So: you've identified that you are upset or fearful, and there are elements of what you're looking at that are making you feel this way, and you've sat with that feeling for a moment. NOW it's time to figure out whether there's something you can do about it.

Ask once: "Is there really anything I can do about this?" If there is (like volunteering, calling your congressperson, protesting, or donating), get ready to do what you can do.

If not, **put the thought aside.** All it's doing is freaking you out. Here are some techniques:

- This is a great time to listen to the advice from Mr. Rogers's mom: look for the helpers. Focusing on people helping in these situations can reassure us that even if we can't do something, someone is.

- Better yet, distract yourself. Switch to something more light-hearted: comedy, fiction, music, cat videos—whatever will get you out of the feeling.

- At the very least, don't watch the whole video. Fast-forward past parts that may be gory or otherwise upsetting. This is a technique used by moderators at social media companies who have to review a lot of "flagged" content.

- Get exercise. Step away from your device and elevate your heart rate to reset your brain chemistry.

- The writer Anne Lamott has a great visualization for dismissing an anxious or frightened thought: think of it as a mouse in your head that won't stop squeaking.[9] Envision putting that mouse in a jar, screwing the lid on tight, and putting the jar where you can't see it.

- Avoid the 24/7 news cycle. Set yourself one or two daily checkpoints for the news if you find yourself constantly checking for updates. Don't schedule them in the hour before bedtime, or before other important things you want to be present for (such as an important meeting at work, or spending quality time with your kid).

- If you're a naturally anxious person, it's OK to stop watching or reading the news for a while! Seriously. It'll still be there when you get back.

Media Techniques Checklist

To stay mindful of the techniques media are using to get our attention, it can be useful to pay close attention to detail. Try the following exercise to keep an eye on what might be stressing you out.

Pick something (or several things) from media you've interacted with in the past week—say a couple of videos or alerts posted to your timeline, a show that reports on current events, some ads around the edges of a site you're looking at. In those media, see if you can find the attention-getting and emotion-moving techniques that I describe in the following checklist. Use the Media Techniques Worksheet (right after that) to keep track.

Then, think through your reactions using the guidelines from the "Keep Calm" box. Record how not only how you felt, but also what you did in response, in the My Reactions Worksheet at the end.

Animation

- Does it **move or flash** so you're more likely to look at it?

Images

- Do the **images not make sense** together, so you look at them longer and try to figure them out?
- Are the images **disgusting or frightening**?
- Are there **cute animals or babies**?

Film Techniques

- What about **cuts** between different camera angles? Are they fast? Do they leave anything out?
- Is the **image changed**—is it darkened, turned black-and-white, or made brighter?
- Does the **camera angle** make a person on screen look tall and power-ful, or short and vulnerable? Which people do we see up close, so we might trust them more? Or are they turned away from us, so we find them mysterious or suspicious?

Music

- What is the **mood** of the music? Is it dramatic, sad, energizing, uplifting?
- What happens to your feelings about what you are watching when you **mute it** and turn on a totally different kind of music as a soundtrack? (Recommendations: in addition to "Yakety Sax," try rap, classical, video game music, or heavy metal, most of which can be found on a streaming music or video service.)

Sound

- **Surprise sound.** Websites will sometimes automatically play a video or sound when you load a page, drawing your attention away from whatever you might have been looking at.
- **Volume.** Ever notice how ads are louder than everything else on TV or the radio? That's deliberate, to get attention.

Writing

- Look at the **shape of the letters** and the fonts used. Are they no-nonsense? Silly? Scary? Beautiful?
- **Clickbait headlines.** News and websites will often use attention-grabbing headlines to make you want to click and find out what they're saying. Some examples: anything with a question mark, and most things with numbered "best of" lists; phrases like "Then this happened," "This one weird trick," "Here's why," "You won't believe," "Shocking," and anything that implies there's something you don't know but really should.

Media Techniques Worksheet

What I watched	Animation	Images	Film techniques	Music and sound	Writing

My Reactions Worksheet

Media event	What was my physical reaction?	Name this feeling	What did I do in response?	What could I have done better?

Attention, Attention . . .

Many of the techniques in the media that frighten or stress you out may also distract you and keep your attention glued to social media, long after you'd really rather put down your device. In chapter 3 I'll talk more about the ways those mental processes work, and provide some tools for coping with them.

3

Conserving a Valuable Resource: Our Attention

We're scattered.

With the rise of mobile devices, many of us increasingly feel like our attention is being pulled in a dozen different directions. Our phones beep and blink, letting us know about new messages, email from the boss, likes on our photos, and updates on our games. Our computers, too, pop up flags and windows with alerts. Ads make noise, use motion, and play emotional music to grab our attention. Everything's always *right there*, in our hands, on our desks and walls. Some of us sleep with our phones by our beds (guilty!). They're there with us in important meetings, conversations with our friends, and even at important life events like weddings.

Do we just put down our mobiles for good? Am I going to recommend that we just leave social media? I don't think everyone necessarily needs to do that, though everyone should have the right to make that decision.

I've successfully reclaimed my attention, and I want to share with you the techniques that helped me do it. I decided to call this book *Keep Calm and **Log On***, not *Keep Calm and Log Off*, because I think there are some parts of the digital media landscape we can save—parts we can mindfully choose to get what *we* want out of our time online.

In this chapter, we'll work to identify what's capturing our attention. I'll discuss how the chemical dopamine is generated in our brain when we interact with our devices and social media, and I'll offer some techniques we can use to break the cycle of addiction that chemical contributes to. I'll talk about how apps and sites wreck our attention by interrupting us or continuing to give us stuff to look at when we want to STOP. Then I'll pose some questions about sites and apps to help you decide whether you want to keep using them, and how you want to use them, once you've broken your chemical addiction to them.

Hard times require better use of resources. In World War II,
this meant rubber. Today, we need to keep our attention resources
focused and out of the hands of those who want to manipulate us.
Source: Work Projects Administration Poster Collection—
Library of Congress

I'm not talking about quitting cold turkey. Rather, what I am talking about is *harm reduction*: taking small steps to make things better. It's an effective strategy developed by drug rehab programs—and yes, websites and apps can be addictive. We can break our cycles of addiction by being mindful of certain aspects of sites and apps—even ones as simple as how they refresh their content or recommend a friend. Sites and apps aren't all created equal when it comes to how hard they work to make you feel like staying online forever. Once you start seeing these addictive qualities in some apps or sites you use, you might decide you want to leave them and use others. Or you might decide to just use the same apps or sites in a different, more mindful way by turning those characteristics off.

If you can see your way to a bigger change from there, great! If not, you still have more time to pay attention to things you love—and to breathe, for a change.

How Can I Put It Down?

What's the simplest thing you can do to stop being distracted by your device?

Put the darn thing *down* and walk away from it.

One study showed that we are likely to be more distracted when our phones are even *near* us, even when they're not doing anything. Just knowing that there *could* be something going on is enough to disrupt our attention. So putting your device out of sight can stop you from checking what's going on online.

But we all know that's not easy.

Those of us who have been online for a good twenty years or more have gone from turning on the internet periodically—like I used to in high school, when we had dial-up internet, and my sisters and I had to monopolize the whole house's phone line to get online—to being online any time we were sitting at a computer, to never being *off* the internet. That evolution happened as more and more people got Wi-Fi and laptops. (Uh-oh, suddenly you're able to take your computer off your desk and to the café ... and to work ... and to the living room. Bye-bye, conversations with your sweetie or kids. And to bed with you. So much for sleep.) And then smart phones. (*Always* in your pocket. Always. Even on dates. Even at weddings and funerals. Even in the bathroom. So much for time to reflect. So much for privacy.)

"oh no oh no oh no oh no please don't make me put down my phone I have no idea what I will do with myself"

How to Keep Calm and Carry On

Scout Laws: "Even the little changes I make to my life online can make me safer and happier"; "Control of my digital and media life should be mine."

Well, that's a good mindful start: you've identified that you're feeling some kind of way about not having your device to fill your time.

• Check in with your physical response: Which parts of your body do you notice? What would you call this feeling? Is it a good feeling or a bad one? If you pick up your phone and use it for a while, how do you feel?

Next steps:

• Make a list of offline things you've wanted to do, like spending face-to-face time with your family or friends, picking up a new hobby, or trying a new class. You could even find people with similar interests online, and then go meet them in person.

• Make a list of people you'll miss most if you are off social media for a while. Then make time to call, video chat, or even text chat with them instead. Better yet, set up actual face-to-face time to hang out with people, if you can. (No, I am not great at these either; weirdly, I find it harder to call and interrupt people than it is to set a lunch date. But if you practice, it gets easier.)

As with addiction, there are a couple of ways to approach stopping a habit. Quitting cold turkey is one of them, but that can be pretty rough.

In Catherine Price's fantastic book *How to Break Up with Your Phone* (which I highly recommend), she shares author Charles Duhigg's definition of "habit": a deliberate choice we make and then continue to make regularly, without giving it much thought. Every habit, Duhigg says, is a loop consisting of three parts:

1. **Cue** (also called a trigger): a situation or an emotion that "tells your brain to go into autopilot mode and let a behavior unfold."
2. **Response:** the automatic behavior (that is, the habit).
3. **Reward:** "something that your brain likes that helps it remember 'the habit loop' in the future."[1]

Cutting out the *cue* or trigger at the start shuts down your digital habit before you even respond to it. Our digital cues often begin with the physical devices themselves. So let's explore some basic ways to cut out cues.

You Might Be Asking ...

"OK, how do I break the cue?"

How to Keep Calm and Carry On

Here are a few of the most low-tech ways to stop triggering or cueing a digital habit—these techniques don't require a new app, or anything like that. I've divided them up based on the Keep Calm Scout Laws from this book's introduction:

If Something Digital Is Not Doing Work for Me Right Now, I Can Turn It Off

- Try turning your phone or notifications off, and leaving your phone out of the room when you go to bed, eat dinner, study, or do something else you know you need to focus on.

- Go back to the list of things you want to do, or people you want to spend time with. When you're ready to do that activity or see those people, if possible, leave your devices behind.

- Bonus idea: I'm a fan of a tweet by @carrickdb on Twitter, who suggested that one way to cut off your social media addiction is by dropping your phone into the unreachable gap between your bed and the wall.

But "putting it down" or "turning it off" doesn't have to mean your entire device:

- Remove social media, chat, and other apps that are taking up too much of your time from the device you need to focus on. Don't worry; as long as you have your password and email account information handy, you should still be able to access social media on another device—for example, on a computer that isn't as easy to take to bed with you.

- Or split up your accounts. Have one social media account where you're only following or connected with a couple of accounts, for when you want to stay focused. Have another you can access at times when you are OK with taking in whatever information comes down the stream. Maybe you want to have one account where you follow the news, or entertainment content, or only your closest friends, and another one that's more general.

Mentally Preparing for Life Online Can Help Me to Keep Calm and Understand What's Really Going On

Being mindful of the time you are spending with your device is another way to make you aware that you might want to be doing something else:

- Consider using a timer—preferably one that's not on your phone! Set a kitchen egg timer or other alarm for, say, ten minutes at the beginning of your session, to help keep track of how long you've been on social media.

- Track what you are doing to begin to get a sense of where your attention goes. There are apps that can help you do this, but you can also just take notes on paper.

- Catherine Price recommends distinguishing between different kinds of apps, those that serve as "tools," "junk food apps," "slot machine apps," "clutter," and "utilities." Use these categories to start identifying which apps you really need, and which you can delete immediately.

- Here's a tip from the journalist Matt Taibbi: "Before clicking on any article, I imagine the title of the news outlet emblazoned on a cigarette box or candy wrapper (as in, 'I'm going to run outside for an MSN-BC')."[2] By equating his compulsive news reading with addictive habits, he reminds himself that he'd rather be doing better things for his health.

Try out a couple of these ideas, and check **keepcalmlogon.com** for more tips, including changes you can make to specific sites or apps. After taking steps like these for a little while you may find that you feel better about your online time and how you use it—and you may not even notice how much you've changed.

How Do I Stop Compulsively Poking at My Device?

I never thought I would miss a simple link so badly.

In the early days of the internet, a link saying "More" or "Next" at the bottom of a long page was pretty common. Internet speed was so limited that if you had a site with a ton of content, the site would only load a dozen or so results at a time, just so it wouldn't slow down so much that you'd get frustrated, give up, and go elsewhere. Shopping sites with lots of products or search results still do this, because they handle so many results.

I remember when Twitter stopped using its "More" link. One day I scrolled to the bottom of my feed, and suddenly ... there were just more tweets. Twitter had started loading older things people had posted, and I didn't even have to ask.

In my brain, a very familiar chemical floodgate opened. I was reminded of Puyo Puyo, a game that nearly torpedoed my college career. Puyo Puyo was sort of like Dr. Mario or Bejeweled—a pretty standard color-matching game—with one tiny, super-addictive difference: When you lost a game, *another game started right away without asking you.* You barely even noticed that you could maybe stop playing and, like ... eat dinner, or something. It just *kept going.* Which felt like the right thing to do, to get you over the bad feeling of losing.

This kind of automatic loading is addictive—and the people who build the software, and the people who sell the advertising that pays them, know it.

The Slot Machine Effect

Tristan Harris, a former Google employee, has come out against design choices that make software more addictive. He compares these buttons and page refreshes to slot machines—which, in the United States, are often regulated by law, because we know it's possible for people to develop gambling addictions.

And it's not like software companies are wholly unaware they're choosing to make software addictive. Some of their CEOs try to protect their own children from being affected. Steve Jobs and Bill Gates both

You could hit "more" and end up with a cute cat picture …
or something worse. Why depend on luck? Spend your attention
wisely. Go looking for cat pictures mindfully. I found this great
one in the Wikimedia Commons! *Source:* Chambers, National
Savings Committee

limited the amount of time their children spent with screens—a decision the American Academy of Pediatrics supports: it recommends that children under age two not spend time with screens, and children ages two to five not spend more than an hour a day with screens, so that they can engage in the kind of creative, hands-on play they need to grow.[3] A group of psychologists and researchers has urged the American Psychological Association to speak out about the ways tech companies engineer technology to be addictive.[4]

The Rewards

Just as stressful things in alarming media events may make our bodies release cortisol, things we enjoy or find exciting make our brains release *dopamine*. When our brains learn that we get a dopamine reward from doing something, we're likely to want to do it again.

Like slot machines, refresh and load buttons in apps give us a dopamine hit in a way that could be called an "intermittent variable reward"—the ones Price and Duhigg were talking about when they described how we develop habits.[5] "Intermittent," meaning the rewards show up sometimes. "Variable," meaning the size of the reward changes, and sometimes there might not be any reward at all.

On social media, rewards vary widely when you refresh. Are you going to get a dozen new "likes" on your posts from your friends? A thousand re-posts as your funny video goes viral? A picture of a cute kitten? Maybe some boring piece of news from a family member? Or some hateful comment? Harris points out that when the reward varies the most, we are most susceptible to addiction. Our brains may give us a dopamine hit even when we don't get the reward we expected. Meaning we'll keep clicking, swiping, and reloading no matter what we get. And when we do that, we give social media the sweet, sweet traffic they can sell to advertisers.

Which Buttons?

Behind the scenes, product managers and user researchers like me are asked to find out which buttons and other techniques keep the most people stuck to the website. Sites and apps change their design over the years,

Allied forces in World War II developed the character of the Squanderbug to remind citizens to conserve resources. Today, we need to conserve our attention to fight malevolent forces in the cyber war.
Source: Phillip Boydell, National Savings Committee

piece by piece, to make it less likely that you'll go somewhere else. For example, on some sites, when you mouse over a link, you see previews of pages and images. On others, you have to click through to see those—and this means spending less time on the site where you started. Which means that site had to tell their advertisers that people were spending less time on their site, which meant they earned less money. Previews keep you on the site where you started.

Web and app developers watch how many people are leaving a website, and what appears to have made them leave. They also look for which parts of a website are more likely to make people stay. Some sites give you the opportunity to look at this data for yourself. For example, on my YouTube series, *The Media Show*, I can look at how many people have gone from one to another of my videos. Then I can adjust the keywords on my videos, or the links from one to another, to make sure viewers spend more time with my videos instead of going somewhere else. I can look at the data again, see if it worked, and then make some adjustments—lather, rinse, repeat. In fact, this is one of the reasons I shortened the intro to my show—people got bored during it and clicked to some other channel.

Retweets on Twitter changed so that you wouldn't need to do as much work. Actually, "retweeting" was something Twitter users started doing on their own, to give someone else credit for saying something. In the beginning, you would have to select what someone else had written, paste it into the window to post, and actually write "RT" and their @name next to it to give them credit, before you hit send. Four steps. When Twitter added the retweet button, it eliminated three of those steps. And that meant more users were likely to retweet something without thinking twice about it. I actually think this made Twitter a lot less meaningful: suddenly everyone was just clicking and sending along things other people had said, instead of writing new things themselves.

You Might Be Asking ...

"So what are the 'reward buttons' social media use to keep me stuck to them? And how can I avoid them?"

How to Keep Calm and Carry On

Scout Law: "Understanding what technologies actually do to my brain can help me break patterns that aren't helping me live my best life"; "Even the little changes I make to my life online can make me safer and happier."

Take a look at the sites and apps you use most. Which of the following techniques or actions does each one offer or impose? Award each one a point and tally the score for each site or app:

- Re-post and "like" or "favorite" buttons?
- Automatically load additional posts when you scroll to the bottom of the screen?
- Autoplay the next video in a list or start the next level of a game after you've finished one without giving you the option to stop?
- Offer links to "related content"?
- Notify you immediately when a new message comes in?
- Use blinking, sounds, or other intrusive notifications?
- Display notification badges or icons to let you know there's something new?
- Show whether someone has read your message?
- "Push" content to your device or email account that you haven't asked for, such as new posts or ads?
- Recommend people to add to your network who are not actually on the site to begin with (looking at you, LinkedIn!)?
- Encourage you to mention or contact people you know?
- *Not give you the option to turn these things off?* (Some apps are better about this than others).

Games can be some of the worst offenders. In fact, many of the techniques developers use to keep you hooked on their social media site or app are often referred to as "gamification" techniques.

Once you've scored the sites and apps you go to most often, compare scores:

- Do some sites and apps you spend time on score lower on this keep-me-addicted scale? Which ones score higher? Consider limiting your access to those high-scorers by removing them from a device, blocking access in your browser, or using a timer.
- If you took the earlier advice from Catherine Price and categorized sites and apps as "tools," "junk food apps," and so on, compare scores within those categories. Do some app categories score higher than others?
- Find substitutes. Are there other ways you could communicate with friends, find new photos or news, or play games that use fewer of these addictive techniques?

To Break the Slot Machine, Find Friction

Christina Xu gave a talk about "friction" in online shopping experiences in China that blew my mind. Xu pointed out how much they differed from American or European shopping experiences. While Amazon makes it easy for you to find the color and style of shoes you want, put them in your cart, and even pay with a single click to buy them, Xu reports that the Chinese experience is often far more complicated. She was trying to buy a tote bag she liked from a Chinese website, and found that to do so, she had to—gasp!—*actually chat with a human being.*

Rather than going to a commerce site to see her options, she had to ask for a particular style in a chat channel. The person on the other end sent her a few pictures of bags similar to the one she was looking for, and she identified the bag she had seen previously. Then they had to settle on a price—Xu suggested one, and the seller came back with a counteroffer. Finally, they talked about which method would be OK to pay with, since Xu was making her purchase from the United States. And all of this was pretty standard, Xu said, for a Chinese site. Similarly, ride-share drivers in China expect people who contact them through an app to eventually call them and nail down the exact place they want to be picked up.[6]

This is unimaginable to most American and European internet users. It sounds like so much *work*! But Xu pointed out that Chinese customers liked the fact that they got to talk with someone when they were making a purchase. Americans and Europeans, she said, were likely to view all those steps of asking for pictures and setting prices as *friction*. We're not used to being slowed down by anything, especially not when we're buying something.

And friction is exactly what American and European software designers work to avoid. Why? Because when websites and apps slow down the people who use them, those sites and apps lose money. Customers expecting a quicker experience might go elsewhere. Impulse shoppers might rethink buying their fifteenth meme T-shirt.

The same goes for social media, actually. The easier it is for someone to just keep going with their slot-machine-like feed, the more likely they are to spend hours there. And that means the site can show them more ads— making more money in the process.

App and site makers have an incentive to change their software in ways that get people to stay. In fact, some of the time, their jobs or bonuses depend on it—they may have targets to meet for "user retention." If friction looks like it's getting in the way of user retention, they'll do what they must to smooth out the process.

But maybe those of us who are using a particular site or app *want* friction! We may want to put down our devices to call our parents, spend time with our kids, hang out with our pets (without recording them, for once), or fix that thing in the house. We may want to spend more time with a hobby or passion project instead of mindlessly poking at some new site. Heck, who among us hasn't had some time on a website when we just said, "Come ON, I really want to talk to a human being!"?

How to Keep Calm and Carry On

Scout Laws: "If something digital is not doing work for me right now, I can turn it off"; "If I didn't ask for something my device is giving me, I should make it go away"; "Mentally preparing for life online can help me keep calm and understand what's really going on."

Here's the good news. Friction isn't entirely under software makers' control. If you want to stop spending time online, you can put more obstacles in your own path to slow you down. Friction can work *for* you, too.

- Again, delete offending apps from your devices.

- Don't store your user name and password in your browser or the app on your phone. Make yourself go through the process of signing in every time you try to access your social media or shopping site.

- Same goes for your credit card information—if you are an impulse buyer, don't save your credit card info on sites where you shop. (It turns out this is a good security tip, too.)

- Add other security measures. I use two-factor authentication and a physical hardware key that plugs into my laptop. These both make my logins more secure *and* slow me down when I'm trying to log into my social media accounts—and that makes it more likely that I'll stop if I should be doing something else. See upcoming chapters on your "security garden" for more information on two-factor authentication and hardware keys.

- If you want to really make things hard for yourself, pick a slower internet connection. See **keepcalmlogon.com** for tips on how to do this. Added bonus: this could lower your data bill.

- Some people even use a dumb-phone strategy: they downgrade to a phone that can only make calls and texts, and keep that on them instead of a smartphone. Extreme, but if you're looking to free up larger portions of your attention, this could be a way to quit.

If these all feel like too-technical solutions to you, there are some simpler solutions recommended by Catherine Price in *How to Break Up with Your Phone* (which, again, I highly recommend!).

- The first one is a mindfulness recommendation: Before you pick up your device, check in with yourself. Make a note of what you are picking up the phone to do. Write it down or just think to yourself: "OK. All I'm going to do right now is see if my boss has mailed me back, then I'm going to put this down again." Just checking in can make it easier to get back on track.
- Write yourself a reminder that you want to spend less time on the phone. Take a photo of it and use it as the lock screen on your device. You can get cute with this—photograph it with your kid, your dog, or whoever or whatever you want to spend more time with.

There are also productivity apps that can make it harder to access the things you want to stop yourself from using. See **keepcalmlogon.com** for more info.

How Do I Keep from Getting Interrupted?

While the frictionless slot-machine groove makes sure that we are stuck to sites and apps longer than we want to be, sometimes technology developers use the opposite tactic—interrupting what we want to do—to keep us doing what a site, app, or advertiser wants us to. This is one of the most insidious and annoying tactics in a software developer's toolkit. Some of us in web design and security have even started to call it "evil."

Have you ever meant to leave a news article or shopping site, only to suddenly see the entire page covered with a window saying something that boils down to "NOOO! PLEEEASE! DON'T LEAVE US!" These days, it's pretty common. Oftentimes, the site will ask you to sign up for a mailing list. To you, the result of signing up for that mailing list might mean finding out about cool new stuff, or getting discounts. But it also means the site has a more reliable way of finding you again—and new information about you that its owners and advertisers can use to track your preferences and spending habits and nudge you to come back some other time.

"How do they even know I'm trying to leave?! Are they in my BRAIN?!"

Don't worry—the site is not reading your mind, just your hand movement (or lack of it). A small piece of code on the page is probably looking for the moment you move your cursor to the edge (particularly the top) of the screen, which is a pretty reliable indicator you're about to use the back button, enter a new address, or otherwise leave the page. Sometimes pages will pop up a "don't leave us" sign after you've been inactive for a certain amount of time, too.

The thing is, you *want* to leave. You have a goal in mind: going somewhere else! The makers of the page don't agree with you: they want you to stay, so they can demonstrate to advertisers that they have more user retention, serve you more ads, and make more money. This is basically a power struggle. But it's your right to go where you want to online, and it's totally legitimate just to close the offending window and leave.

Ads in general are trying to distract you away from the content of the post, article, game, or video you came to the page for. Both the site/app and the ad benefit from these: the site or app gets money for displaying the ad, and the advertisers whose ads actually get clicked on get potential customers to buy their stuff.

The same goes for when an app pushes a notification to you about a special deal, or a site sends you an email about new content, which triggers your device to pop up a notification. Notifications generally disrupt and distract us from what we want to be doing—a big reason why just having your device near you can be distracting, even if you're not using it right now.

But again: you're not the one who benefits from this distraction. You have your own goal, whether it's shopping, reading an article or post, finishing a level of a game—or *being offline for a change*—and talking with people in real life.

Fortunately, there are some well-established tools for getting rid of online distractions.

Here are some tips for getting rid of online distractions, tied to the Keep Calm Scout Laws:

Understanding What Technologies Actually Do to My Brain Can Help Me Break Patterns That Aren't Helping Me Live My Best Life

Here's an unexpected way to make your brain less startled and pressured by triggers from your device:

- Depending on your device's accessibility settings (for those who have trouble seeing what's on the screen), you may be able to put your device in "grayscale" or "black and white" mode. This has the subtle effect of making it harder to see color-based notifications like the badges on apps that alert you to new content (ever noticed how often they're red?), and can lower your level of distraction. See **keepcalmlogon.com** for where to look for this information.

I Talk to Different People in My Life in Different Ways. It Should Be Up to Me to Decide Who I Want to Talk to, How, and When

- Get to know the notification settings for your device, and for individual apps. See **keepcalmlogon.com** for more information.

- It's possible to make it so just the most important people in your life can get through to you fast. If you're worried about emergency messages, or important work messages, some apps give you the option to send notifications only from a list of people you specify.

- Or, figure out another channel to move emergency messages to. Deliberately pick one in advance and work with the other person so they know which channel to use. Have backup channels. Be clear with other people that you have done this, so they don't frantically try to contact you in the channels you don't use.

If I Didn't Ask for Something My Device Is Giving Me, I Should Make It Go Away

- Ad-blocking plugins for your browser can do you a range of favors. They can prevent malicious ads from installing things on your machine, and they can also keep you focused. For recommendations of reliable ad blockers, see **keepcalmlogon.com**.

- Ad blocking in games can be more expensive, if not impossible. Usually, game developers are willing to trade the income they make from serving you ads for the income they make when you buy the game, or sometimes buy things in the game. To make game ads go away, you may need to get the pay version instead of the free version.

- Use this as a moment of friction: Do you care enough about the game to pay and make the ads go away? Do you really want to play the game at all? This is a moment to go back to the list of things you want to do and people you want to talk to ...

How Do I Cope with Pressure to Be "Always On" for Work?

It's only fair to note it's not just social media that keep us anxiously checking our devices. Our jobs are also major culprits in keeping us ready to jump at any new alert.

Lowering work pressure is harder to do than lowering social media pressure: it's tied up in making a living. So, some strategies for lowering out-of-work-hours pressure may involve getting your office or company to change its expectations. Others are actions you can take on your own.

You May Be Asking . . .

"My job NEVER ENDS. How do I get them to leave me alone in my off hours?!"

How to Keep Calm and Carry On

• When you go on vacation or are otherwise out of the office for a while, set up an autoreply or out-of-office message. Include the contact information for an alternate person, someone else to reach out to if the matter can't wait until you get back. Email programs have this function, and so do some other communication tools. See **keepcalm-logon.com** for recommendations.

Source: Work Projects Administration Poster Collection—Library of Congress

- Can someone else be on call for you when you are out? Set up those relationships.

- If you're responsible for sending out regular reminders, schedule those emails to be sent while you are away.

- Establish "work-free" areas of your house, like the living room or dining room, and don't bring your devices in those rooms.

If you're a manager, you're in the BEST position to help everyone else in your workplace disconnect:

- Write up and announce policies that people aren't expected to be responsive when they should be spending time with their families or are on vacation—or even that they *should not* be responsive in the evenings or on weekends.

- If you see people responding in their off hours, gently remind them, in public if need be, that such overtime is not a requirement of the job. Setting the rules is one thing to do; socializing them is another job.

- Establish a policy for email-free (or meeting-free) days. Some workplaces have done this to help employees cope with always-on stress. This means setting the expectation that Wednesdays or Fridays, say, are the day nobody schedules any meetings or sends or expects responses to any email, leaving everyone time to just go heads-down and get work done.

- Help employees manage their use of notifications. This is important because it's not just the actual time spent sending emails or working on slide decks that stresses people out, but also the *awareness* that those emails and slide deck requests are piling up.[7]

- Include a "best defaults" section in onboarding material or a nudge to employees. This may not only help employees keep calm (and log off!) in their downtime, but it can also reduce noise pollution in the office, too. (On a video call with a new colleague, I realized he was bombarded with loud notification noises—every time someone sent *any* message in our work chat, he was getting an earful. The noise was practically nonstop. Suddenly I had a picture of why he might not be participating in work chat. There's a phenomenon called *alert blindness*, which in this case I think became alert *deafness*: when there are just so many alerts that you start to tune them out, because processing them all would be overwhelming.)

Some places have gone even further toward making it easier for workers to manage their work-life balance. In France, for instance, workers in companies with fifty or more employees won the right to negotiate to disconnect from work communications when they're not at work.[8]

From Your Own Brain to the Wider World

In the past two chapters I have talked about things that media and technology do to *you, as an individual*. It's important to get a handle on these for your own sanity, but also for the good of your community: to support your friends and family, and make good decisions for the life of your community, you will need to manage your own attention and stress.

But media and technology also have an impact on *how we communicate with each other* by changing who we talk to, what we're aware of about how others are talking back to us, and how we feel about our conversations.

One of the most frightening, worrisome things happening at this moment in history is that people far from us, who do not share our interests, are turning our attention and communication with each other into weapons—weapons to influence how we vote, how we think, and our peaceful coexistence with our neighbors. This is happening worldwide.

But not to worry: there are strategies to keep them from disrupting our lives. I'll go over those in the next chapter, as well as in part III, where I talk about what is happening to our trust.

4

Conversation Breakdown: How the Internet Meddles in Our Relationships

I don't know exactly when it was, but at some point in the last decade, social media just started to feel *awful* to me.

People around me took to making proclamations about everything—who to vote for, the right way to raise your kids, even whether or not it was OK to talk politics in social media. Other people showed up just to harass each other. Nobody seemed to be talking TO each other; everyone was just talking AT each other. It felt like one giant roar of a crowd, screaming, all the time. I used to be really excited about going online when I was younger. Now the internet felt … hectic and stressful.

What was it about online conversation that made for a long slow decline into ugliness? I started making a list of things that had changed since I first went online in the early 1990s—what we could share online, who we could talk to, what we knew about the people we were talking to, how many people we could reach, and so on.

I quickly figured out that a lot of what was bothering me had been caused by the demands on my attention. But there were also things about online conversation that had *always* been kind of crummy. Things like not knowing how the person on the other end was feeling, whether they had stepped away from the keyboard, or whether they were joking.

As I asked myself these questions, I was reminded that "social media" were not the only ways to stay in touch with my friends and family. There were other kinds of digital communication, like email and direct messages, which encouraged different kinds of conversations.

I switched to simpler chats and calls. Quickly I started to feel happier, and much less lonely and stressed out. It became clear that Facebook and Twitter were using up my "social" time with all kinds of things I wasn't actually interested in—promoted posts and ads, things other people had "liked," people ranting, and the ever-depressing news.

I want to share my questions with you so that you, too, can ask which kinds of conversations you want to have in your online life and which ones you don't: what you want to keep, and what you want to get rid of. If you find there are particular questions that are important to you, each section will have suggestions for changing that particular part of your digital life, without necessarily sacrificing other parts. Once again, this process starts with becoming mindful of how media, digital and otherwise, are making you feel.

This chapter returns to the Keep Calm Scout Law that says: "I talk to different people in my life in different ways. It should be up to me to decide who I want to talk to, how, and when."

Questions I recommend asking include:

· Can you tell how people are feeling from their posts?

· Are you focusing on broadcasting? Is this crowding out direct conversations with people you love?

· Does the online space you're using let you distinguish between groups of people you know?

· Do you find that you're just re-posting things from other people a lot?

· Are you anxious about missing out?

· Are people in your online spaces spending a big chunk of their time fighting with each other? (Is that exciting to you?)

· Does the app or site you're using have clear, enforced guidelines for civil participation?

In this chapter, I'll explore the impacts that communicating via software have on the basics of how we talk to each other: the emotionlessness of online writing, the confusion of online comment threads, and some people's desire to harass others online.

I'll talk about the impact of communicating to *a lot of people* at once. To understand this, it's useful to consider what we've learned from older media like TV and radio. Through this historical lens, we can get a glimpse of how the act of broadcasting—of speaking to more people than the human brain is historically equipped to cope with—changes the messages we put out to others, whether on TV, in a newspaper, or online. I'll present some skills that can help us step back and be mindful of when broadcast is something we want, and when, to fulfill our craving for human contact, we may need to just speak one-on-one or in small groups.

Why Is This Conversation Stressing Me Out?!

Some aspects of digital communication have always disrupted our conversations with each other: namely, the challenges of making it clear whom you're talking to and understanding how the other person in the conversation feels.[1]

Face to face, we make sense of conversation using cues so subtle most of us don't notice them until someone breaks the rules. We make eye contact with our conversation partners and turn toward them when we are speaking. We interrupt to correct misunderstandings. And we move our hands, make faces, or nod to show other people that we do or don't get what they're saying.

But on the internet? Unless you're on a video call, all of this is stripped away. (Though even video calls have their problems. I once had a boss who thought a remote coworker was being rude to her because every time they did a video call, he didn't appear to be looking her in the eye—but it just had to do with where his camera was positioned. And a slow connection can make the most patient of us anxious when it seems as if the person we're talking to is not responding!)

If you've ever freaked out because someone didn't email or text you back, you're experiencing this kind of disruption. Your usual expectations about a face-to-face conversation tell you, for instance, that a long pause is meaningful. So, online, you might worry that a long pause in a chat or email response means the person is furious with you, or be annoyed because the person seems rude.

In fact, this is why some apps give you a " ... " or "so-and-so is typing" message, rather than just letting you sit there and wonder. It's why other apps may show you whether someone has read your message. Basically, the software developers wanted to give you feedback about what was going on with the person on the other end of the conversation. Of course, that doesn't always work; there's always the opportunity to freak out when you can see someone *has* read your message but hasn't yet replied.

What we're experiencing when we stress out about people not responding is the violation of our expectations from face-to-face conversations. That's upsetting! When this happens, it's worth keeping in mind that it's not you or the people you're talking to, it's the software. You can calm this stress down before it starts.

"They haven't responded yet! They clearly hate me/think I'm an idiot/are snubbing me/are just rude/don't love me at all/are having an affair!!!!1 😭😭😭😵😠😡💀 "

How to Keep Calm and Carry On

We've all had those feelings. But please, take a deep breath.

Ask yourself: Are you really sure you know the reason for that long pause? If not, give your unresponsive friend the benefit of the doubt. Is it possible that they

- lost connection because their internet has gone down or they moved out of range?
- went to look up something you were talking about?
- stepped away to go to the bathroom?
- went to answer the door?
- got distracted by their family or coworkers?
- spilled something and need to clean it up?
- are ordering you some flowers because you sound upset?

Check in with yourself: Is this gap in conversation really about the scary thing you think it is? No, really—are you sure?

Observe your reaction. Where is it coming from? Do you have persistent worries about being abandoned that come from some earlier point in your life? Feelings that you are inadequate or inferior?

Avoid misunderstandings by making it explicitly clear who or what you're responding to by writing it out ("Mom, did you mean ..." or "When Kevin said ...").

Be patient when you or others get confused!

How Do They Feel? How Do You Know?

All of that confusion and frustration can come from just talking online—and that's even *before* we start talking about other feelings.

Look again at some comment threads or text messages from your contacts. Can you tell how the writer felt about the topics or the messages they were responding to? How do you know? In most comments, all we have to go on is words. We can't hear their tone of voice, see the look on their faces to know if they're frowning, smiling, or rolling their eyes, hear if they're sucking their teeth, or see if they're crossing their arms. We usually end up imagining all of that. Often, we can't help being wrong.

Blessedly, emoji, stickers, and animated gifs can pick up the slack! If people give you a hard time for using these in personal messages, you can remind them that written words do a terrible job of communicating the look on someone's face. Emoji and gifs do at least a little bit better. But it's not the exact same thing—you're still not seeing the commenter's own face. And there's always the possibility they won't pick emoji that show their honest feelings.

Even with pictures, the lack of emotion in online messages makes them terrible at communicating irony, sarcasm, or jokes. We mostly use tone of voice and facial expression to communicate those in person. A *lot* of online fights start when someone writes something sarcastic or ironic, and someone else doesn't notice and takes what the first person was saying seriously.

For example, people routinely mistake articles and videos from the humor website *The Onion* for evidence of things that actually happened—particularly when they are copied from the source and pasted somewhere else. They share them with their friends, outraged at "reports" that the US government was considering passing the Americans with No Abilities Act, guaranteeing work for people with no skills, or that immigration agents threw a pregnant woman over the American border wall.[2] Out of context, it can be really hard to tell these are dark humor.

Why Is Everyone So Angry and Mean Online?

Why do people act like jerks online? Why do some people even seem to make a game out of being awful to each other? What is it about the internet that brings out the worst in people?

You've probably experienced this. Someone on your social media goes on long rants that burn bridges with friends. Or you're just trying to find your way around a new online game and someone swoops in just to mess with you, spewing a string of expletives. Or if you're really unlucky, a huge crowd of people shows up to mock you for something you said in public.

Believe it or not, people have been wondering why the internet gets people unreasonably angry since its very beginning, when it was still a bunch of scientists, on computers with no graphics, connected over phone lines.

So if recent changes to the internet didn't create trolls, what did?

In general, communication can suffer from our sense of *depersonalization* online: a feeling that we're not really ourselves, or that the interaction we're having isn't "real." The lack of *interpersonal cues*—the eye contact, gesture, tone of voice, and facial expressions I mentioned above—contributes to this feeling of disconnection from the people we're talking to online.[3]

And this can lead to emotions spiraling out of control. Researchers who have studied *flame wars*—long arguments online where people end up attacking each other personally—say depersonalization fuels the flames. In person, our awareness of how the other person is feeling or reacting to us, our own fear of retaliation, or cues about the status of the people we're talking with keep us from lashing out at each other.

If we lash out in person, we know it's possible someone might get physically violent with us. Online, that threat feels far away. It's almost as if the screen of our device is a shield that keep us safe. But while we're shielded from the results of our actions online, we are still able to hurt and agitate others with our words. And sometimes this does escalate to real-world, physical violence. If it does, see chapter 7 ("They Already Know Everything") and chapter 8 ("Safer Relationships, Online") for guidance.

Do I Really Want to Talk to *Everyone*? How Broadcasting Is Different

In the past twenty or so years, there has been a revolution in who we, as individuals, get to talk to. Before that, only a small, select group of people could reach thousands of people beyond their own communities—usually through "broadcast" media. The word "broadcast" is itself a metaphor:

rather than casting our ideas out like a single fishing line, broadcasting allows us to spread a wider net to catch more people's attention. Radio and TV are traditionally known as "broadcast" media. But you could say that the ability to broadcast has been around since the birth of the printing press.

Before the printing press, *nobody in human history had related to or communicated with so many people.* Scholars who study human social groups have estimated that throughout history, large communities averaged somewhere between 150 and 290 people. This is related to how many people a group can feed, and how many people our brains are able to keep track of.[4] Most communities didn't even have thousands of people in them, just hundreds.

In addition, it was also impossible to reach huge audiences before the printing press came along simply because it took a lot of time and effort for books and scrolls to be copied by hand and then transported to other places. (I'll talk more in chapter 15 about how this transformed the world when I talk about why we trust writing.) The printing press made it possible to spread the same information to a tremendous number of people in less time.

Radio and television caused the next giant leap in audience size: suddenly, someone spreading information could reach millions rather than just hundreds or thousands—and people could watch or listen; they didn't even need to know how to *read* to get the information.

Now, with digital media, *any* of us can reach far beyond our groups of friends and the boundaries of our communities. Our parents' generations may have needed to convince a TV station or newspaper to pay attention to their talents or ideas. But our own videos and posts have a chance to reach people on the other side of the world. Now we can do both: we can watch broadcasts from media like TV, radio, and newspapers, *and* we can make broadcast media ourselves.

Never before could the number of human "connections" made by one person come close to singer Katy Perry's alleged 107.8 million Twitter followers (fans she had already reached via radio and TV), or even close to my paltry 1,200. Those are broadcast numbers, not meaningful human connection numbers. The only reason we have numbers of that size is because they're profitable for media companies and advertisers, who pay social media sites to sell their goods and services alongside our conversations.

But digital media don't have to be used to broadcast. They can be used to reach a smaller group. This is a choice any of us can make. Some people keep their accounts private and set limits on who can see the things they post, effectively turning their social media into small-group media. But the pressure is on to "go viral" or "be an influencer"—so a lot of us end up using social media as broadcast media anyway.

Changes that many social media sites have made over time have pushed us all to treat digital media as broadcast media. It has taken a while for these sites to support us in treating individuals or groups of people as different from each other, if they've made that possible at all. And the incentive is there to speak as broadly as possible. Speaking to a huge number of people requires new and different kinds of communication strategies. Let's talk about what those look like.

"But I'm so proud of how many followers I have!"

Scout Law: "I talk to different people in my life in different ways. It should be up to me to deicde who I want to talk to, how, and when."

If we individually feel we need broadcast-size numbers of people listening to us, we might ask ourselves why. Is it so we can survive financially? OK, sure, it's a living. But not all of us are making a living on our followers and connections. (Be honest.)

Think about the words social media sites use for people in our networks, for a moment. Followers: Doesn't that imply power? Religious figures and celebrities have followers.

Connections: Does that imply love, friendship, guaranteed support, or understanding? Not really. It's the vaguest of all possible terms for someone you have met or want to stay in contact with. Is "connections" how *you* describe people in your life, or is it the social media site's term for those people?

Why do we feel like we need to keep that many "connections?" Why do we feel like we need more? Does it really improve our lives to have more?

How to Keep Calm and Carry On

- Be mindful of what's driving you to start up that stream, or post that hot take, just like you did with your attention and fear in previous chapters. Name the feeling that's driving you to stream or live-post something.

- Can you give a name to what you want people's response to be? Name that response, observe it, sit with it.

- Now let's do some checking on the site itself. Does the site give you a way to privately communicate with one other person? With a small group of people?

- What do you do differently in those smaller communications? Write yourself some notes.

- Finally, compare the options the site gives you with what you want out of the site. Are you more likely to get that response when you post publicly to a large group of people? To a smaller group? Or are you more likely to get the response you want if you reach out to just one person?

Who's in the Audience?

Would Your Followers Get Mad?

Broadcasting makes a lot of changes to how we communicate, especially when we're suddenly speaking to more people who are different from each other. This often means changing the message we put out there, to avoid upsetting some people. And that can keep us from saying things we really need to say.

When people craft messages for a large audience—as they do in the advertising and PR industries—the tone they use in those messages is different than it would be for a small group. A person communicating to a large group of people will try to make their message easier for everyone to understand. They may work to avoid offending sub-groups in the larger audience. If they're broadcasting in mass media, they'll also work to avoid offending advertisers.

In television and radio, the need to be sensitive to the presence of children, elders, and potentially offended groups led to what are often called *standards of decency*. It's one reason many countries set rules that tell broadcasters when they can and cannot air sexual or violent content, or use obscenities. In the United States, the Federal Communications Commission grants broadcast licenses. When the FCC fines broadcasters for nudity or cussing, they usually do so because of complaints from the public.[5] So to some extent, offended members of the community drive FCC censorship.

The "wardrobe malfunction" incident at the 2004 Super Bowl (during which the singer Janet Jackson's breast was briefly exposed by Justin Timberlake) triggered 540,000 complaints to the FCC. The Parents' Television Council, a nonprofit watchdog agency, led the charge, demanding that TV be made safe for children. The FCC seized that moment to crack down on numerous other broadcasters, including fining the Fox network for running an episode of the animated series *Family Guy* that showed baby Stewie's naked butt.[6]

But knowing that angry letters from the public may be coming, broadcasters often self-censor even before the FCC comes down on them. Viacom and Clear Channel blacklisted Janet Jackson's songs without being threatened. That's when the radio personality Howard Stern, who had been fined plenty of times for indecency over the years, decided to flee from the terrestrial airwaves, later signing a deal to move his show to satellite radio. And the self-censorship effects went even further: after the wardrobe malfunction incident, ABC insisted it would air the movie *Saving Private Ryan* but cut its graphic war scene and expletives, even though the movie had previously been broadcast in full with no complaint from either the FCC or the PTC.[7]

How to Keep Calm and Carry On

Time to mindfully check in about the impact of "broadcasting" on social media:

- When you post things fully publicly, what do you share?
- What do you hold back?
- How do you change your messages, knowing the range of people who might see them?
- If you do hold back—or get your best angle, with filters and heavy editing—what are you missing out on sharing, intimately, with your best friends and closest family members?

Who Are You "Singing" To?

Self-censorship based on "decency" limits the range of things that can be said in public. And there are parallels when we broadcast over social media.

My friend Steph explains that the difference between broadcasting and talking one-on-one is like the difference between singing on stage and singing a lullaby. You change how you sing, particularly how loud you sing. You wouldn't do one in place of the other—you'd frustrate the audience by being hard to hear, or you'd wake the baby.

Source: Work Projects Administration Poster Collection—Library of Congress

This type of "using the wrong style at the wrong time" is obvious when people you know mix up their communication styles on social media. Most of us have probably cringed when someone revealed something too private in public, or treated a friendly conversation as a place to advertise. That cringe comes from our sense that different kinds of conversations have their place. Those who post something we find cringeworthy have not matched their way of speaking to our sense of who they're speaking to. We may have called someone out for this, or heaven forbid, been called out ourselves.

Human beings have always had different ways of speaking to their peers, leaders, elders, or children. The tone of voice and the things that we say to these people just aren't the same! And when someone uses the tone of voice with an elder that they would with a child, that elder might take offense. There might be consequences for the speaker.

If you've done the delicate dance of posting to Facebook—when you know your grandma, your drinking buddies, the kids you babysit, and possibly your next employer can all read what you post—you have a gut feeling for how to alter a message for broadcast. What you're doing to walk that fine line is like what broadcast TV did for years: producing content for the widest possible audience.

Social media are really unusual in human history when it comes to social groups—they're more like your city hall or national political conversation than they are like your club, church, nuclear family, or group of friends. They're huge forums where everyone comes together, not small places where people with common interests have conversations.

Human societies have long had separate public and private spaces. (Here I use "public" to include the 150 to 290 person groups I mentioned earlier. When I say small or private groups, I mean *small*—less than a dozen people.) Sometimes "privacy" has been the difference between families and everyone else. Sometimes private spaces have been gendered, with women and men hanging out separately, or queer folks finding their own protective spaces to speak honestly with each other. Or they've been conversations only with friends of our own age.

Small-group conversations don't have the same *purpose* in our lives as broadcasting information, or even reading the news or watching TV. They're for soothing hurts, recognizing personal successes, assuaging doubts.

The huge forums of social media are often uncomfortable because we haven't all agreed on what their purpose is. Scholars have called the lumping-together of everyone we know "context collapse," meaning that the usual separate contexts we do things in (attend religious services, flirt with strangers, care for kids) are suddenly all mixed together. Awkwardly.

It's important for us all to ask: Are technologies allowing us to speak to different groups of people we know separately, and speak to them in different ways?

One problem with broadcasting on social media is that the careful choices we usually make when speaking publicly can trample all over our need for private spaces with specific purposes. I'll give you some examples of how this could play out.

We may go one of a couple ways when we broadcast and are at risk of offending people. The first way is the cringeworthy route. We all know people who just go the no-filters route and say whatever's on their mind, no matter where they are or who's around. In some cases, we might admire such people for saying what's on EVERYONE'S mind—but we don't always want to *be* them, because sometimes their mouths get them into trouble.

Or we may take the self-censoring route—the one that TV and radio have traditionally had to take—in broadcasting to a mass audience. And that's where this gets problematic. Because social media put us out in public, we may not speak up when we're struggling, worried that our next job or a college recruiter might see and limit our options in life. We may suppress new aspects of our lives we are exploring, like our sexuality or spirituality, which could benefit from talking to supportive others, because we are worried about the response from our church or family. Self-censorship hurts our capacity to grow and heal.

"What steps can I take to stop broadcasting and get back to real, relationship-building communication?"

How to Keep Calm and Carry On

It's time to do some thinking about which sites we actually want to be on. First, be mindful:

- What do you do differently in one-to-one or small-group communications than you do when you're "broadcasting?" Write yourself some notes.
- Are there conversations you want to start having? Or stop having?

    Then, let's go back to these questions about social media sites you're on, and whether they support the kinds of interactions you might rather be having:

- Does the site give you a way to privately communicate with one other person? With a small group of people?
- Is that communication the main focus of the site, or a side benefit?

    Once you've given thought to which sites support which behaviors, you may want to talk to your friends and family . . .

"But everyone I know is on [social media site X]! I can't convince them to leave!"

How to Keep Calm and Carry On

Scout Law: "I talk to different people in my life in different ways. It should be up to me to decide who I want to talk to, how, and when."

You might be surprised. More and more people are interested in changing their relationship to social media. And the more we speak up and say so, the more other people will be empowered to come forward.

    In my group of high school buddies, two of us decided a few years back that we were tired of how Facebook was handling things. We asked to move our group to a smaller group chat app. It was hard at first—one friend said she felt like we were abandoning her. But as a group, we managed to agree on what we wanted from our conversations online, and found an app that supported those conversations better.

    Here are some tips on moving to smaller group conversations:

- Think about the people in your life you want to talk to most. Make a list. (No, don't show it around. Don't be a jerk.)

- Decide whether you and small groups of your friends or family are willing to move to a new app where you just talk to your own group.
- With each group, talk about what characteristics are the most important in an app:
  ○ Is it important that you be able to save your conversations? To download and move them somewhere else if you need to?
  ○ To have multiple smaller conversations? Or one big one?
  ○ Do you want to avoid a feed that shoves more content down your throat all the time? To avoid ads? Do you want to be on a site that doesn't make use of your data to make a profit?
- If people don't want to move, you can still make use of private groups on your existing social media.[8] Email, text messages, WhatsApp, and other chat channels support these kind of private groups. Even video and voice conference calls do!
  ○ Try a strategy I have used: mute just about everyone in your feed. This way, the algorithm-generated, drink-from-the-firehose stream isn't there to fuel your addiction and stress. Instead, use the site for direct messages and groups. This way you can keep your connections and get what *you* want out of it, instead of what the company wants.

What If Your Followers Get Bored?

While adjusting the message to not *offend* a wide range of people is one effect of broadcasting, we may also do things to *keep the attention* of as many people as possible. And that can also keep us from getting what we need out of our online lives.

We may be making or sharing content to go more viral. A simple example is a change to the We Rate Dogs Twitter account. Matt Nelson, the creator of the account, gradually shifted from assigning dogs funny breed names to sharing heartwarming cute dog pictures. His audience responded more to the heartwarming cuteness, so he capitalized on that by doing more of it. It becomes a cycle: you do more of what gets a response, you get more of a response, repeat.

Other effects of the pressure of audience attention are more worrisome. Two YouTube celebrities in quick succession pushed the boundaries of acceptable behavior, one by posting video of a man in Japan who had recently committed suicide, another by hiring two people for $5 on a temp job site to carry a sign reading "Death to all Jews." Some people in violent videos on the website WorldStarHipHop can be seen chanting the name of the site—suggesting they knew the fight they were recording would earn them attention. Again, the if-it-bleeds-it-leads trend gets more people watching these videos, whether watchers are curious, are looking for entertainment, or wind up sharing the post with a comment that's meant to show off how concerned or outraged they are.

Ultimately it's in social media sites' interest to encourage everyone to broadcast. Viral videos and posts draw in people who may not have spent as much time on their sites before—and that gives the sites more opportunities to show paid ads next to popular content. But is this what we want in our social lives?

How Do We Stop Bad Behavior?

Online, we're rarely held to account for what we say or post. Think of all the names we have for people who make a sport out of harassing others: griefers, who target new, vulnerable players in online games and kill their characters; trolls, who deliberately make upsetting statements on social media to confuse or infuriate people; and bullies of all kinds, who use online spaces to make life miserable for the rest of us. Because they often aren't physically near the people they're upsetting, they face few consequences: sites that stop bad behavior are few and hard to find, and any punishment these offenders might suffer is delayed.

You may be wondering: Why, if sites and apps want people to continue to enjoy using their services—why on earth don't they get rid of bad actors? Couldn't they hire moderators?

You might be surprised to learn that the lack of moderators in a lot of online spaces is intentional. Many of the founders of social media companies—and many other builders of the internet, from its early days onward—believe in "free speech" as a good thing, with very few qualifications. They have taken the stance that any moderation at all would squelch free speech. Twitter in particular has trotted this line out for some time—even as their site has harbored Nazis inciting people to violence, not to mention tens of thousands of bot accounts known to be filling their channels with political and commercial spam.

If you ask people at social media companies about why they don't help keep the peace in online discussions, you might hear this answer: *that doesn't scale.* If a site had to pay enough moderators to respond to every complaint, websites today—social media in particular—would be a lot less profitable. If they had solved the problem of hate speech and other problematic behavior earlier, they would have grown a lot more slowly.[9]

Social media companies that grew without having planned for the cost of community managers or moderators must now add moderation after the fact—and that affects their bottom line. "Scaling up" moderation means paying salaries and health benefits. And that starts to drive down how much money investors make on a company's stock.

Mark Zuckerberg and other Facebook representatives have said they want to use less-expensive artificial intelligence to find problematic content, whether in the form of spam, fake news, or porn. They argue that AI can make it easier for fewer paid employees to get rid of offensive content. But the fact is, there are some kinds of speech that AI does a poor job of identifying. Sarcasm and jokes are big ones. The meaning intended by the person posting may be the opposite of what the message means at face value. When Facebook started working harder to respond to complaints about deceptive garbage content, the company "still relied on human moderators to identify hate speech because automated programs have a hard time understanding context and culture."[10]

Is it upsetting to you that social media companies avoid moderating damaging activity because it's not profitable? It is to me. Why should a bunch of guys in Silicon Valley be getting richer while we struggle to make productive use of the spaces they built? If we want to see damaging activity disappear (or at least dissipate), we're going to have to speak up and ask for better-moderated spaces.

We have evidence from newspaper comment sections and other forums that online discussions (particularly anonymous ones) stay the most civil when there are rules for participating, and when those rules are enforced if someone violates them. It's best if we have a range of sites available, from those that want us to provide our real names to those that let us stay anonymous. Each site should be building its policies to support the kind of conversations users want to have there, whether they be fully public or more intimate.

See **keepcalmlogon.com** to learn about some groups that are pushing social media sites to do better.

"But the person making me angry is WRONG! I can't sleep! I have to call them out!"

How to Keep Calm and Carry On

Here are a couple of mantras for you to repeat when faced with people trying to cause trouble online:

In some of the online spaces I spend time in, we use "Someone is WRONG ON THE INTERNET!" as shorthand for situations where we should really just chill out. We recognize that when you start feeling upset about how *wrong* someone is, and follow that feeling, writing huge long responses or campaigning to shut someone down, it's time to step away from the internet for a while. Get up, go putter around the kitchen, go for a walk, leave your phone and computer in another room.

My friend Abby has another phrase she uses to remind people to keep calm online: "The internet is pretendy funtime games." Meaning, sometimes it's best to lean in to the feeling of depersonalization. A lot of what happens online *isn't* real: it's just a lot of people we don't know, talking. Or people we do know, talking like nothing matters. Or people pretending to be and do things they're not. And it's not worth getting upset about.

But How Do I Cut Down Without Missing Out?

One of the side effects of broadcasting is what the internet has come to call FOMO: Fear of Missing Out. If you're *not* reached by a show or viral post, you may find that one day all of your friends are talking about a funny new meme, or music video, or series. Your friends *and* your coworkers, *and* your family—and your church or knitting group or your local sports league or yoga class and jeez even that one guy who misses out on everything—and *how* are you the *very last person on Earth* to learn about this hilarious, amazing thing?!

Is it really worth taking the bait when someone's
causing trouble online? *Source:* US National Archives
and Records Administration

Being part of an in-group that shares jokes, references, and knowledge makes us feel like we belong. TV shows have always thrived on this. If everyone around the water cooler at work is talking about last night's episode of a show, and you haven't watched, you might feel left out. You might even make sure you watch the show the next week. TV shows have actually aimed to be the subject of "water-cooler conversation" as a way to up their ratings. And now social media thrive on our FOMO, too.

But more and more people are discovering that when it comes to events in their lives, they'd rather tell people about them in person than broadcast the events over social media. In a recent *New York Times* opinion piece, KJ Dell'Antonia lamented that she "lost out on moments of seeing friends' faces light up at joyful news" by sharing on social media rather than in person.[11] In her recent book *Reclaiming Conversation*, Sherry Turkle, a psychologist who has studied online behavior for decades, confirms that empathy is better built in person.

You May Be Asking . . .

"But I don't want to miss out! How do I get over my FOMO if I cut down on social media?"

How to Keep Calm and Carry On

My favorite take on FOMO comes from a comic by Randall Munroe. He gently points out how unlikely it is that "everyone" really knows all of the things "everyone knows about." And more importantly, he suggests a different way of thinking about it: It's not that you're missing out. It's that you just haven't found out about the fun thing *yet*—and now you get to have that fun for the first time.

(Note that Munroe only includes the US birth rate—counting the international birth rate, there's *way* more than 10,000 grown people learning about things every day, not to mention people who are just now getting their first computer or phone! So many new people to show that cute cat video to.)

Randall Munroe, *XKCD. Source:* http://xkcd.com/1053

There's no way we could possibly have time to absorb all of it—there's just so much out there. If you really have *good* friends, they should be excited to share their cool treasures with you whenever you're ready, not be rude to you because you're not "with it" yet.

So go find the cool things "everyone already knows about." You're one of today's lucky 10,000.

II

STAYING SECURE

5

Planning Your Digital Security "Victory Garden"

Whether or not you believe it swayed the 2016 US election, there is no doubt that nations and political parties have been trying to influence the life and opinions of citizens by digital means. We've seen Russia do it to the US and UK; political parties in Mexico and Brazil have flooded social media to change the course of elections, too. There is no doubt that North Korean hackers have been breaking into systems in hospitals, entertainment companies, and shipping companies, not just military targets. These break-ins can affect our ability to conduct our daily lives.

In digital warfare, there are few protections for innocent bystanders. There is no Geneva Convention. Really, there are no clear-cut distinctions between civilians and targets, criminals and soldiers. Cyber criminals who encrypt disks for ransom one day turn around and sell their hacking services to a government the next day. Foreign agents and political factions can turn social media against us.

We are all on the battlefront. Bullets are flying all around us.

In the face of such huge, violent forces at work, it is easy to feel like there is nothing we can do. But like my grandmother and her generation, who lived through both world wars, we are not helpless. In fact, we have stronger tools at our command to fight for ourselves than she did in her day. And like her generation, the things we can do can start at home.

Victory gardens, a term coined by George Washington Carver, were an idea made popular during the world wars. To make sure there was enough food produced to feed troops on the front as well as people at home, Americans, Brits, and other Allies were encouraged to grow their own vegetables in their yards, even turning golf courses and tiny parks over to growing potatoes, cabbage, and corn. Children were taught that their

Victory gardens were one way Allied communities
kept themselves healthy when they were under attack.
Source: Peter Fraser, National Archives

saving and sharing of food would fight famine in Allied countries. Gardening may seem like an insignificant contribution to a war. But it was a real way that citizens fought to maintain their livelihoods in wartime.

And just like victory gardens, there are small, everyday, and yet really important actions we can take with our own digital devices to protect ourselves and our communities.

All of us have resources that are vital to preserve in order to protect our communities. As I discussed in chapter 3, we all have *attention* that we can give or withhold when it comes to things online—a resource we can use to better understand the issues facing our communities, which we can waste on "guilty pleasures," or which can be captured by groups that want to sow confusion and hatred.

In this chapter, we're going to talk about another resource we can cultivate to protect our communities: our own *security*. When security professionals make security plans, they research a company's *assets*. All of us have digital assets too. We have our phones, our computers, and our home Wi-Fi networks. We have files we care about, including our financial and medical records. We protect these assets with passwords, which we also need to keep safe.

You may have heard your friends and family say (or you've said yourself!), "I don't need to care about my security or privacy. I'm not an important person. Why would anyone come after me?"

Don't sell yourself short! As I said in the Keep Calm Scout Laws, your digital life and digital assets are important to *you*. If someone spread your medical or financial records around online, it would be important to *you*—it might wreck your life. And remember that in the eyes of a criminal, your device can be a stepping stone to someone else, including your family members, your boss, or your whole company—and to their devices.

Your digital devices support you the way my grandmother's garden fed her family during the war. Your devices help you do your work, look for jobs, manage your finances, shop for supplies, and care for your kids. It's important that you take care of their security! Let's talk about how to do that.

Fencing Your Digital Garden: Understanding Your "Attack Surface"

Everyone's garden faces slightly different pests. Some people have problems with gophers eating the roots of their vegetables. Others have nearby deer that decimate their flowers, or birds that eat their berries. Different bugs and fungus thrive in different climates and eat different plants.

All of these can be stopped with the right defense—some with fences, others with pesticide, some just by planting companion plants or enriching the soil. What you do to protect your garden depends on what's trying to get at it. You make decisions based on what's around you and what you're trying to guard: bird netting on tree branches clearly won't keep out gophers attacking the roots.

Like your backyard garden, your digital garden has specific things in it you want to protect. When security professionals start figuring out how to defend a company, they start by looking at the company's "attack surface," meaning everything they want to guard and all of the protections they have in place. They also try to figure out who might try to damage or steal from the company, and in what ways.

In this chapter, we'll work on making it clear what the "surface" of your digital garden is, so you can start thinking about how to protect it.

You may be thinking, "It just seems like they know everything already anyway—my government, other governments, companies, criminals. I'm sure anybody can do anything. It seems pointless to try to stop them." I hear this from a lot of people.

But it's not true that *any*one can do *any*thing. Just like gophers and bugs, different digital "pests" have different strengths, weaknesses, and tools at their command. And just like with deer, fencing your garden so it's harder for them to get in makes your digital resources less of an easy target. Those pests will go chew up someone else's garden instead. Even a couple of simple barriers can make a difference for your digital assets.

In this section I'm not going to go over the specifics of who can do what. Because frankly, it really is frightening to focus on what governments are doing to each other, and what criminals or terrorists have accomplished.

Later, though, we'll run through an exercise on how to apply things you're reading in the news to the things you'll learn in this chapter—so you can understand which parts of your "garden" you might need to beef up at a particular time, like changing your password or installing updates.

Let's focus on what you CAN do to help defend our digital world. Your role in that defense is not as small as it may seem. Again, as I said in the Scout Laws, even little changes can make you safer. When everything is connected, the smallest holes in the fence—from the cell phone you use everywhere to the computers you use at your job—can be exploited to get from garden to garden. Getting a good view of all of your digital property can help you understand how best to fence and protect your assets, and by extension, those of your community.

What Do I Want to Protect?

Here's an exercise that most companies do when they have digital assets they want to protect. The Electronic Frontier Foundation, which defends digital rights online, has tailored it toward everyday folks.

Understand Your Security Needs

Scout Law: "My digital life may feel unimportant in the big picture, but it's important to me"; "Even the little changes I make to my life online can make me safer and happier."

The Electronic Frontier Foundation suggests thinking through these five questions to protect your digital security:

1. What do I want to protect?
2. Who do I want to protect it from?
3. How bad are the consequences if I fail?
4. How likely is it that I will need to protect it?
5. How much trouble am I willing to go through to try to prevent potential consequences?

I've used questions 1, 2, 4, and 5 to head the columns in the Digital Assets Worksheet you'll find in this chapter. As for question 3, I'll give that one special focus later on.

As you read through the upcoming sections about the digital assets you need to protect, you can begin to fill in the columns in the Digital Assets Worksheet. (If you don't know whether an asset will need protection, you can come back to this when you read chapter 7, "They Already Know Everything.") This exercise will help you determine the size and edges of your digital security garden. You can wait to fill out the column for question 5, "How much trouble am I willing to go through to try to prevent potential consequences?" until the next chapter, where you will find some strategies and tools to protect your digital assets.

Question 3 ("How bad are the consequences if I fail?") is so important that it deserves more thought. I'll go into detail about it at the end of this chapter, where there's a worksheet to help you assess risks.

Digital Assets Worksheet

What do I want to protect?	Who do I want to protect it from?	How likely is it that I'll need to protect it?	How much trouble am I willing to go through?

Valuable Digital Devices

Steps you take to protect non-digital valuables (like your money or jewelry) from theft also protect digital valuables (like your laptop and phone). But given that criminals who steal your devices could also get access to information stored on them, it is worth giving extra thought to how you physically protect your devices.

What do you do to keep digital valuables safe in your home or workplace? Or when you travel? What devices do you own or use for work? Write these answers under the "What do I want to protect?" column of the worksheet. Include mobiles, desktop and laptop computers, tablets, digital assistants (such as Amazon Echo or Google Home), TV and radio devices that are connected to the internet, and the boxes that bring the internet to your house. Also include *internet of things* devices, like lights you control with your phone, or security cameras.

If your laptop or phone were stolen, how would you make it harder for thieves to get at the stuff on them? Screen locks or a remote wipe tool may be the key. Write these answers under the "How much trouble am I willing to go through to try to prevent potential consequences?" column of the worksheet.

Next: Add Networks

You may not think of it this way, but the *networks* you use to connect to the internet at home and at work are also digital valuables. They need to be digitally "fenced" as well, because someone who gets access to your network might be able to get access to any device connected to it—and that's where trouble starts. If you connect your computer to your router (or the wall) directly with a wire, without using Wi-Fi, you have less to worry about. But do you use Wi-Fi at home? In public places? At work?

Go back to the Digital Assets Worksheet. In the first column, about what you want to protect, also write down places *where* you use each device. Now think for a second: How much bigger is your "garden" than you originally estimated?

Here are steps to take to "fence in" your devices on your own network, and on public networks:

Your Own Home Network

Note: This topic requires a little more technical work. See the book's companion website, **keepcalmlogon.com**, for instructions.

Always password-protect your home Wi-Fi network to keep people from snooping. The rules from the upcoming password section of this chapter apply to creating this password as well.

Public Wi-Fi

When you hear "public Wi-Fi," think "public toilet." There are gonna be germs. But when you gotta go, you gotta go.

It is easy for a stranger to watch the traffic on public Wi-Fi, and possibly snatch some of your valuable information out of the air. One hacker I know used to watch Wi-Fi for image requests—when a browser asked a website to show pictures. He then delivered a picture of his face to the person's browser instead of the image it was supposed to show, as a joke.

Here are some precautions to take when using public Wi-Fi:

- When you can, use a network that is password protected.

- Most importantly, put a protective barrier up around your traffic. You can do this by using a virtual private network, or VPN. A VPN protects your communication between your computer and the servers it contacts when it gets your email or goes to a website. Check the companion website, **keepcalmlogon.com,** for some recommendations of VPNs.

Protecting Your Digital Information

Now we're going to get down to the nitty gritty—not just the physical security of your devices and networks, but the stuff that's on them.

You might think of your digital stuff in terms of what someone could steal, or what someone could know about you. "I don't really care what people know about me" is a claim I often hear when talking to people about their security. When it comes to your bank account or other financial information, what someone could steal is definitely a huge concern.

Security professionals think of digital risks more broadly. When they look at what needs to be protected, they ask, can someone with bad intentions

- learn things that should be private? (confidentiality)
- hurt you by putting in false information? (integrity)
- keep you from getting to things you need? (availability)

You can answer these questions to help secure your own digital information assets. As you read through the following sections, use the My Digital Information Risk Worksheet at the end of this chapter to list your digital information assets in that category. (Just list that you have them—you don't have to write down details like your social security number (SSN) or credit card numbers!) Then write out what could happen if someone messed with the confidentiality, integrity, or availability of each one. I'll talk about a couple of scenarios for each that you might not have thought of.

When it comes to "how bad could it be," you will definitely have a range of answers. Probably it's not a problem if someone shared what you share on social media—after all, you already chose to make it public. But then, it might be a problem if you try to keep your work and social life separate. Don't feel like you have to make a catastrophe out of each category. Just be honest with yourself.

Personally Identifying Information
What it is: your name, your government ID number (for example, SSN or passport), birth date, license number, or street address.

Financial Info
What it is: credit card numbers, bank account numbers, and so on.

You're probably pretty aware that these categories should be protected as strongly as you can. So some of what I'll say here may seem like a no-brainer.

But it's worth making sure that everyone in your family knows what you know about keeping financial information safe. I have seen young adults proudly posting pictures of their first credit or debit cards online.

There's pretty much no reason to ever take a picture of a card, and you shouldn't ever share it if you do.

Credit card or bank account numbers should *never* be posted online when you're not certain you're on the part of a site used for a financial transaction—for example, do not type them into a box labeled "message" or "comments." And before you enter your credit card number, make sure the website address is the one you expect to be using; check the beginning, high-lighted part of the address to ensure it's TheSiteYouThinkYou'reGoingTo. com. Make sure the address starts with *https://*, **NOT** *http://*—the "s" stands for "secure." Also, never send credit card or bank account numbers via email.

Generally, I would advise only getting to your financial pages through the address, app, or bookmark that you know takes you right to the right website. Even if your bank sends you an email—don't click links in it. That way, you can be sure you're not falling for a trick email. Go to the messages section of your bank's page, from a bookmark, address, or app you trust, to see if it really was sending you a message.

Practically nobody should ever be asking for a government ID (like your SSN) or passport number—particularly not the whole thing. Sadly, a lot of websites and services ask for them anyway. If the site asking for your ID number isn't financial, medical, or (in some rare cases) related to education, don't provide that number. And feel free to bother your doctor or school about how they choose to identify you. Ask, "Isn't there another way you could be keeping track of my information? Government ID numbers are supposed to be private!"

Pictures of your license, ID, or passport should not be sent via email, which could potentially be intercepted. But many institutions still ask for these documents in this way. When they do, be sure to delete the pictures from your device, your email account, and any photo-sharing service you may use (such as Google Photos or the Photos app on your iPhone). Ask the recipient to delete them promptly, too. You don't want those pictures sticking around, waiting for some snoop to find them.

Today, holding on to our social security numbers and other IDs means not storing or sending them in insecure ways— and asking organizations we work with to do the same.
Source: US National Archives and Records Administration

"Wait—did you say not to use my real name online?!"

How to Keep Calm and Carry On

Scout Law: "Control of my digital and media life should be *mine*."

Your name, like your ID numbers, street address, and birthday, is in fact part of your personally identifying information. Before you even sign up for an online service, think hard about whether you want to use your real name to identify yourself. Look into the site's policies and answer these questions:

- Does this site require me to use my real name?
- Will my real name be disclosed to other people using the service or elsewhere on the internet?
- What would the service itself use my name for?

   Unfortunately, once you've signed up, it's really hard to take your name back. Choose wisely.

   In chapter 13, about online trust, I discuss some reasons for choosing anonymity online. There are many reasons why someone might decide to make their identity either public or private. Everyone must make their own choices about which reasons are most important to them.

Your Personal Medical Info
What it is: all the details about your health—about doctor or hospital visits, lab tests, prescriptions, or family medical history—gathered and stored in digital medical records or health care websites.

Here's the good news about medical services: they tend to be subject to strong rules about protecting your privacy—such as Health Insurance Portability and Accountability (HIPAA) laws in the United States. Here's the bad news: this means a lot of them have been slow to get online (and unfortunately, the systems *in their offices* are often quite old and insecure). But when they are online, they're usually looking out for you. Again, watch the address of the website to be sure it starts with *https://*. If your doctor's website doesn't start with that prefix, it's worth complaining to them or to the Better Business Bureau that they're not protecting your information.

Medical information may not seem like it's that important to protect. But think about confidentiality, integrity, and availability. What if you couldn't get to your prescriptions because someone got your password to the website where you order them, and locked you out of your account? What if someone, let's say a potential employer, found out about a medical condition you didn't want to disclose? If there's one set of websites where you want to use stronger, unique passwords, multifactor authentication, and other security features (we'll talk about these later), medical websites might be it.

Geolocation
What it is: where you physically are, and where you go.

Do any websites, apps, devices (like the wearable that tracks your activity when you exercise), or other services know your physical location? People increasingly treat this as a totally normal feature of their digital lives. But anything relating to your body and whereabouts can open up big risks—even to your physical safety.

This was driven home to me when a friend called me from New York's Central Park in the middle of the night. She was trying to get away from a boyfriend who was increasingly abusive to her—and he kept finding her even when she thought she'd ditched him. She was frantic. How did he keep finding her?

I asked her if the location services tracker on her phone was turned on. It was. Once she turned it off, she was able to put enough space between her and her abuser to get to safety.

Information about where you are—checking in on an app or posting a picture with your location tagged—could also let a criminal know when you're not home.

I don't ever turn on my location tracker unless I need it to do work for me—like giving me driving or walking directions. When I've finished using it, I turn it off. Because a lot of the time, if my location tracker isn't doing work for me, it's doing work for someone else: mostly advertisers who want to connect my buying profile to locations in my area. If I was organizing a protest, it could be doing work for people who disagreed with me, or the police. And all the time it's doing that work, it's also draining my battery by checking in with GPS.

So that's my recommendation: Is your location tracker doing work that is important to you right now? If not, turn it off. If it is, consider this: Does the use you get from it outweigh the risk of having it on? If it doesn't, leave it off.

Biometrics
What it is: fingerprints, voiceprints, face ID, and other biological authentication techniques.

Fingerprints, face unlock, and voice recognition require careful and judicious use: they're things about you that you can't change. Using them for online services could have serious consequences down the line. For more advice about biometrics like voice and fingerprints, see the "Passwords" section.

Shopping
What it is: a necessity and/or an obsessive habit.

Shopping both online and in person leaves behind trails of our personal information. Stores and their websites don't always treat that information equally. Financial information is more carefully guarded than other types of personal information gleaned from our shopping habits.

In the store, rewards cards let a retailer know what we buy, so it can create a profile of us, market to us, and sometimes sell those profiles to other stores. Online, shopping sites are among those that save your activity using cookies that track what you looked at, the area where you live, connections to your social media sites, and more.

The question of whether you want companies to have this information is more likely a personal, ethical choice than a security one. Do you want companies to profit from knowing details about your buying habits? It's worth knowing that marketers put people's information into categories like "Caught in a Pickle" (people who owe more money than they will be able to repay), "Oldies but Goodies" (senior citizens who are known to gamble), or "Astrology Success" (people who have responded to a direct mail solicitation offering supernatural solutions to their problems).

There is the security question, however, of where your credit card information is stored. Never, ever store it in your browser if your browser offers to store it for you—that's just one more place you'd have to digitally "fence in." Browser security is historically patchy and hard to manage, due to the fact that your browser is the main connection between you and the wilds of the internet.

Personally, I almost never allow online shopping sites to save my credit card information, either. There have just been too many breaches in which customer information is stolen. It's annoying to have to enter my credit card information every time I make a purchase, but I think it's worth it when weighed against damage to my credit or finances. It also slows me down when I feel like making impulse buys!

Email

What it is: your connection to work, and the key to recovering most of your other accounts.

You may be starting to feel like email is way less important in your life than social media. But email is often the key we use to unlock other accounts, retrieve passwords, and receive important financial, work, or family documents. For that reason, your email account deserves stronger security. See later sections in this chapter for advice on protecting your email with unique passwords, multifactor authentication, or other harder-to-use security features.

Watch Your Spelling!

On the internet, a simple spelling error can be the difference between security and embarrassing, costly mistakes. Part of fencing your digital security garden involves not visiting fake websites (which sometimes live at misspelled addresses) and not making typos in your own or someone else's email address.

Misspelling a web address can walk you right into a trap. Criminals sometimes buy misspelled popular addresses and wait there to steal from you or install malware on your device.

Misspelled email addresses are another way people sometimes send things outside their security "fence" by accident. I have two email addresses where I now receive a frightening range of real email (not spam!) that is meant for other people. I get offers of job interviews, pleas for college professors to extend a paper deadline, pictures of car accidents meant for insurance adjusters, notifications saying I'd been signed up for Facebook, news that someone has cancer, and more. All because someone mistook my address for someone else's.

When a woman in Florida signed up my email address to shop at Target online, I drew the line. She had basically handed me her credit card! Because I had access to the email address she had used to sign up (after all, it was mine!), it would have taken me no effort to log into her account, change her password to lock her out, change her shipping address to mine, and order thousands of dollars of merchandise using the credit card she had on file.

So I looked her up, called her on the phone, and explained the consequences of her mistake. It turns out her email address was one letter different from mine—and she'd left that one letter out when signing up on Target's website. She agreed to be more careful when signing up in the future, and I agreed to close that Target account so she could start a new one with her correct address. She got lucky. Not everyone who misspells an email address ends up sending their information to someone willing to call them up and fix the problem.

How to Keep Calm and Carry On

Scout Law: "Security happens because of my behavior, not someone else's, and not because of a gadget or app."

Check and double-check the email addresses you are mailing to. If email does not seem to be getting through to someone, look closely to see if there's a typo in the address you sent your message to.

One more step—you may need to delete the bad address from your address book, and re-add the correct address.

When you make a mistake in an email or website address, you risk your message falling into the wrong hands. *Source:* Hans Schleger, Her Majesty's Stationery Office

Social Networking and Games
What they are: unexpected ways to leak your private information.

These might not seem like as big a deal, particularly social networking. So much of the information we share on social media seems innocuous—sharing old memories with our families and friends, pictures of our pets, check-ins from our favorite hangout spots. (I'm including games here because, for a lot of us, games are also social.)

Have you ever commented on a social media post like this? Did it occur to you that it could be used to harvest the answers to security questions for your accounts?

But look a little more closely at the information in the sharing habits I just mentioned. What could someone get out of it? Sharing old memories with families and friends could give out the names of your schools or family members, or reveal childhood addresses, which are often answers to security questions. Same thing goes for pet names—those are security questions too! Not to mention how many of us use family and pet names, birthdays, and the like for our passwords ... a bad idea I'll talk about in the later section on passwords. And selfies and check-ins from your favorite hangouts can reveal information about your habits—which could clue someone in to when there's nobody at your house.

It's worth being mindful of what you share on social media or in gaming apps, and how a criminal, or someone you know who wants to harm you, could use it to get at more valuable information about you and your accounts. Social media and gaming apps are also huge users of trackers: they want to know what you do so they can sell that information to advertisers. (Remember, if you're not paying for it, *you* are the product.) So these sites put out a lot of information that could be combined with other things you share, to dig up other information you *don't* want to share. Use caution with your social media accounts.

Messaging Apps

What they are: ways to communicate digitally without being as public as you would be on social media.

Messaging apps have the advantage of not being public by default. You're sending messages to friends or family members outside of the public view. This means they're better "fenced" than social media, where you are often broadcasting information to anyone who happens by.

As with shopping sites, however, it's worth knowing more about the information your messaging app knows about you and your networks. They tend to know which people you know. They may also share information with marketers. Check the permissions you give those apps to understand more about what these apps share about you. If you don't want to share the information it asks for, consider uninstalling it and using a messaging app that asks for fewer permissions.

I've Figured Out What I Need to Protect, So What's Next?

Now that you've got a clearer picture of what you might need to protect, let's think about how bad the consequences might be if devices or accounts in your digital garden are left unprotected. Fill out the My Digital Information Risks Worksheet below. You probably want to include the information of any family members you're responsible for.

You may decide that your social media and games don't really need much protection. Or that it's time to upgrade the security on your email. Put a star by each digital asset that you think needs more protection. As you go through the next chapter, look for advice you could apply to help keep those parts of your digital garden secure.

My Digital Information Risks Worksheet

My personally identifying information includes:	What could happen if someone	How bad would it be?
	shared this?	
	changed this?	
	kept me from this?	

My financial information includes:	What could happen if someone	How bad would it be?
	shared this?	
	changed this?	
	kept me from this?	

My medical information includes:	What could happen if someone	How bad would it be?
	shared this?	
	changed this?	
	kept me from this?	

Places I go (geolocation) include:	What could happen if someone	How bad would it be?
	shared this?	
	changed this?	
	kept me from this?	

Business and shopping web- sites I go to include:	**What could happen if someone**	**How bad would it be?**
	shared this?	
	changed this?	
	kept me from this?	

The social media I use include:	**What could happen if someone**	**How bad would it be?**
	shared this?	
	changed this?	
	kept me from this?	

My school-related websites include:	**What could happen if someone**	**How bad would it be?**
	shared this?	
	changed this?	
	kept me from this?	

The games I play include:	**What could happen if someone**	**How bad would it be?**
	shared this?	
	changed this?	
	kept me from this?	

Messaging apps or sites I use include:	What could happen if someone	How bad would it be?
	shared this?	
	changed this?	
	kept me from this?	

Other websites and apps that use my information include:	What could happen if someone	How bad would it be?
	shared this?	
	changed this?	
	kept me from this?	

6

Growing Your Digital Security "Victory Garden"

Now that you've taken some time to identify what you need to protect, and thought through the consequences of not protecting it, let's talk through column 5 of the Digital Assets Worksheet in the previous chapter.

Start with the Soil, Not the Bug Spray!

Scout Law: "Security happens because of my behavior, not someone else's, and not because of a gadget or app."

What's the number one (and most simple) thing you can do to protect your digital security? If you said "Use an antivirus program," you picked the answer most people do—and you're dead wrong. Digital security experts have a very different answer:

Install updates.

In fact, some security experts think that antivirus software is pretty much useless. Installing new software patches when they become available is way more important to making sure your system is secure.

"Install updates?!" you may be thinking to yourself. "But every time I do that, it makes things break on my machine. And what's wrong with antivirus? Why would they make antivirus software if it doesn't do anything?"

I'm going to let you in on a little secret most computer people won't tell you: All technology is broken.

Software, hardware, laptops, phones, your modem—all of it ships to market broken. All anyone can do about it is make fixes as they are discovered. (You may have guessed this, or even muttered it under your breath while some clever person was "helping" you fix your machine, smugly insisting that *you* were the reason it wasn't working.)

Technology is born broken because it is highly *complex*. Think of it like a city full of cars, buildings, and people: it has a ton of moving pieces. Those parts were built by different people and weren't necessarily built to work together. (At times it's a marvel that they do!) Not every problem can be anticipated. Sometimes the security holes are there because two pieces of technology don't work together the way the developers expected.

Even when software or hardware is built by one company—or even one person!—problems are sometimes there in your app or device the first day they're released. These holes in the software are known as *zero days*, because they're in the software from day zero. The good news is that security companies are constantly on the lookout for these, and the makers of software offer bounties to security professionals who can find them. (These security folks, by the way, also think of themselves as "hackers"—ethical "white hat" hackers, like the good-guy cowboys wearing white hats in old western movies.)

So fixing these security holes is less a matter of sending in another piece of software to look around for intruders—which is what the antivirus software does. It's more a matter of making repairs to the structure of the software itself, so that other problems can't get in.

How does this apply to your digital security "victory garden"? You start with the soil, not spraying the plants. If you have poor-quality soil—your plants are yellow or brown with leaves falling off—no amount of pesticide will fix it, because the problem isn't bugs! Antivirus software is like bug spray: it takes care of intruders. To ensure your digital security garden is healthy enough to repel intruders from the inside out, you need to update your "soil."

Or think of the difference between antivirus and installing updates as the difference between installing a security camera in your house and fixing your doors and windows. The camera can get a view of people coming through, but it doesn't solve the problem of your broken lock or your wide-open window.

So when your device recommends an update, install it!

It may be tempting to leave everything up to your antivirus—or just let loose with the pesticide spray in your garden. But often, that's the wrong solution to the problem. *Source:* US National Archives and Records Administration

But How Do I Know the Update Is Real?

Scout Law: "If I didn't ask for something my device is giving me, I should make it go away."

It's good to be a little bit suspicious about this. Some malware pretends to be a system update, so you feel pressured to install it.

A rule of thumb I use any time software asks me to take action is to ask myself, "Did I just 'ask' this device, webpage, app, or program to do something?" If I didn't start up, open, or otherwise take action on my device, I'm suspicious that someone is trying to trick me. Here's what I do:

- First I check the name of the app or program that is asking me to take action; if it's not one I recognize, I close the alert.
- I also close the alert asking me to take action if I didn't somehow "ask" that app or program to do something.
- Then I go look for the app that was supposedly asking me to install updates, and see whether it asks me again when I start it up.
- If it does, I'm pretty confident this is just a regular update to something on my device. I figure it's safe to install the software.

So where do you look for whether an update to your system software— Mac, Windows, iPhone, Android, whatever—is real? On your phone, look through the "settings" app for something called "updates." You should be able to install from there. On your computer, get to know where new updates are announced on your machine. Check the companion website for this book, **keepcalmlogon.com,** for pointers.

You May Be Saying . . .

"But if I update, all of my stuff is gonna break."

Scout Law: "The struggles I have with technology are not my fault. And I'm not stupid."

You're not alone. You know who else has this problem? Rocket scientists. And a whole bunch of artists and musicians.

Many of us have one or two old apps or pieces of software that we love and cling to, even if they're no longer up to date. At some point, those apps run way too slow, or act weird, or won't even open on our machines, because they're not being updated for our latest system software. But we want that software to keep working.

Artists and musicians tend to have a lot of these poor old abandoned apps, sometimes because they can't afford to upgrade, sometimes because they have a custom setup that can't be brought up to date. My friend Joshua, who has produced music for Chaka Khan and They Might Be Giants, built his own music mixing software on the last Mac Classic system—which was discontinued in 2001! That software is old enough to go to college. But there's nothing like his homemade software anywhere, and his act, Radio Wonderland, wouldn't work without it. He can't upgrade the machine it runs on, because the software won't work on modern systems.

NASA has an even more interesting problem. When they send probes or craft into space, it becomes hard or even impossible to update their systems. Their systems back on Earth still have to communicate with the stuff in space in the same way.

So in the past few years, when security holes like Meltdown, Spectre, and Heartbleed have turned up—problems that make computers insecure at the level of chips or protocols, which are much harder to fix than applications or websites—people like NASA scientists and Joshua have had to make hard decisions about security.

And as for the rest of us, it's not always a matter of the app not being able to run. Sometimes it's just crazy annoying when an app updates and looks totally different. Why did they move the login? Where did that button go? Did they completely get rid of that feature you used every day, or did they just hide it?

Companies just figure that even though they make the changes to the screen you're looking at, you'll eventually learn how to use it the new way. And you will. It just takes a little time and practice.

How to Keep Calm and Carry On

When you get prompted to install new software, check out the notes about what the installation will do. The good news is, software developers are getting better at letting you know what they've changed in a software update. If there's a security update included, they will usually say so front and center. And it's likely that kind of update will not change anything about the buttons, windows, or other parts of the software you can see. If the update is just adding new features, fixing minor bugs, or making a change to the way the software looks, they'll mention that too. But if there's a security update, it is important that you install it quickly.

"My device is too full to install the update!"

Don't feel embarrassed! Too many family pictures, too many pet videos on your drive—we've all had this problem. It may not seem like installing an update is important enough to take time to make more room. But with security updates, I promise you, it is.

Not updating could make your device a target for attacks you may have heard about on the news—like the "ransomware" which held computers at schools and hospitals hostage until they paid a lot of money. Attacks like this could keep you from accessing important files. Defend your family from attacks like these! Clear out a couple of hours in your schedule to make room for updates.

How to Keep Calm and Carry On

Scout Law: "Even the little changes I make to my life online can make me safer and happier."

There are a couple of strategies for making more room on your drive for a security update:

- **Move your files to a thumb drive or other external drive.** These are getting more spacious and cheaper every day. My dad fit over a hundred years' worth of family photos onto one thumb drive! If there are too many files on your phone, but your computer still has a lot of space, you can also try moving the files to your computer.

- **Move your files to an online service.** This isn't an option for everyone, but see **keepcalmlogon.com** for instructions on how to do this.

- **Then don't delay—install those updates!**

"My device is too old—the update says I need a newer device to install. I can't afford a new device."

Don't be ashamed. This is another situation where it probably feels like Silicon Valley doesn't feel your pain, and just wants you to buy a new device. Frankly, you're right about that. People who work in the tech industry usually have newer devices. Their employers make sure they do, so they can be sure they're developing for them. This means they don't ever know how hard it is for the rest of us to navigate the internet with machines that may be years old.

Ideally, it would be more secure if you were running a newer, up-to-date machine. The recent security holes found at the level of computer chips mean that many machines have leaky memory—and updates might not even be possible on older machines.

How to Keep Calm and Carry On

First of all, **make sure you know how much a new device really costs.** You might be surprised by some of the prices on basic computers these days! Many do most of the simple things higher-end machines do, like word processing, photo organization and editing, and internet access.

But if you genuinely can't upgrade to a newer machine, please take the UPDATE! UPDATE! UPDATE! drumbeat with a grain of salt. Some people just need to use older machines, and some people really don't have the funds for a new machine in their budget.

If you can't afford a new device, there are still ways to reduce the harm to the "soil" of your digital security garden:

"Air-gap" your older, unpatched devices. This means never connecting these devices to the network, either by Wi-Fi or with a cable. Be aware: you won't be able to use the internet on them. I've got one air-gapped laptop that has old video editing software I need to produce my show. When I need to post videos from this computer, I use a thumb drive and transfer them to another updated machine. Use a new laptop or phone as your internet-connected device while keeping your older machine offline.

This definitely isn't a perfect security solution—malware can still travel from one device to another on a thumb drive, or via Bluetooth or other local methods of connecting—but it's better than nothing if using an old machine is absolutely necessary. Keeping your older machines off the network reduces the number of "open doors and windows" which bad actors who may be scanning networks at all times (even at night, when your machines are on but you're not using them) can find on your device.

Passwords: Grow 'Em Big, Store 'Em Well

Scout Laws: "My digital life may feel unimportant in the big picture, but it's important to me"; "Security happens because of my behavior, not someone else's, and not because of a gadget or app."

I'm just gonna come out and say it: passwords are a pain in the butt. If you're nodding along, you're not alone. Security experts even complain that they wish they could make passwords go away.

Passwords are the weak spot in most systems—mostly because they rely on the human brain, which generally can't remember multiple passwords, or passwords that are strong enough. We end up using passwords that are easy to remember, and reusing the same passwords over and over.

It's worth noting that like gardening experts, security experts are not in 100 percent agreement about the best ways to cultivate and store strong passwords. Their advice depends on your "fence," and on the "pests" you're worried about. Security experts ask:

- Are we most worried about someone *guessing* passwords, or *stealing* passwords?
- Who can get hands-on access to your devices, and the stuff around them (like the sticky note you wrote your password on)?

Depending on the answers, expert advice is a little bit different. Some don't think you should write your passwords down. Others don't think it's useful to have people memorize long phrases. But all of the following tips could be good advice, depending on your situation.

The Simplest Strong Password Trick: Forget Your Password

If you **change your password every time you log in** you can use crazy-strong passwords that would be really hard for attackers to guess.

Use this trick when

- a website makes it easy to reset your password, *and*
- you are 100 percent sure you will have access to the email account, phone, or app where the reset will be sent when you try to log in again.

    Don't use it if you're not sure you can always get to the reset email or text.

    This is NOT a good strategy if, for example, you spend a lot of time in a building where you don't have good cell phone reception. Or if your company makes you call IT support every time you want to reset your password.

But **if you have your backup set up, there's nothing wrong with clicking "Forgot my password" every time you log in.** It's a little slower, but it can actually be safer, because you're confirming you're you with something else you that identifies you (your phone or email address).

How to do it:

- When the system asks you to enter a new password, put in a huge long string of random garbage you don't even have to remember. Just mash the keyboard.

- Get ready to copy and paste, though—you have to be able to enter the password twice to confirm it.

- The next time you go to log in, click "Forgot my password" again, start the process over, and have the reset sent to your email or phone.

- Enter a *new* long string of garbage as your password.

Cultivating Bigger, Better Passwords

To grow good passwords for your digital security victory garden, think about growing prize-winning vegetables for the state fair: each one has to be **big**, and it has to be **unique**.

The challenge is, to make the kind of passwords that are really strong, **they shouldn't be ones you can memorize**. Because, like I said, the human brain can't memorize passwords that are long and random enough to be strong.

Unique Passwords

When I say a password has to be unique, I mean you're not using that password for any other system you use. Passwords have to be **unique** because reusing passwords is a key way that attackers figure out what our passwords are.

Did you know there are actually lists floating around out there of the most common passwords, and previously used passwords? In a "dictionary attack," hackers try one of these lists of passwords or words on a login, one by one, until they get in. Seems stupidly simple, right? And probably pretty slow? But they have software that goes through the list faster than you could by hand, and it works.

The security researcher Lorrie Cranor—who is also an expert quilter—
made fabric with some of the most common passwords on it.
If your password shows up on her dress or the quilt in this picture,
it's time to change it! *Source:* Photo courtesy of Lorrie Cranor

Big, Strong Passwords

By now we've all had a login system ask us to make passwords that are
strong—we're told our passwords must include capital and lowercase
letters, numbers, and special characters. That *does* make it harder for
attackers to guess your password.

The challenge, again, is the human brain. We all use tricks to make
our passwords more memorable to us. Unfortunately, those tricks also

make them easier for attackers' software to guess. We think we're being random, but our brains need patterns to be non-random in order to memorize them. Do you put exclamation points at the end of your passwords? Replace letters with numbers, L1k3 th15? Those are common, memorable, but also guessable patterns.

Patterns of speech actually played a part in the Allied defeat of the Nazis in World War II. If you've seen the movie *The Imitation Game*, you may remember this. Cracking the Nazi Enigma code was going to take Alan Turing, his team, and their machines millions upon millions of guesses—until the women translating the messages pointed out that messages often ended "Heil Hitler." Knowing how that was turned into code, they found that guessing at the rest of the messages was easier.

Guessable phrases can lose a battle—so it's important to come up with passwords that are harder to guess. How do we do that?

Tips for Growing Big, Strong, Unique Passwords

Don't use short, common passwords. Names, important dates, and individual words that appear in dictionaries are easy to guess. (Yep, any dictionary.) They're the ones people can remember, so they're the ones people use. Criminals take advantage of this by using the password lists I mentioned earlier.

The current best advice is to actually use a **random** string of letters, numbers, and special characters for your password. It should be at least eight characters, ideally longer. Length and randomness make passwords harder to guess.

So what do we mean by "random?" Not "that's so random!" We're not talking about a password made up of something your friend said while they were drunk. "Random" here means *mathematically* random.

How do you come up with a mathematically random password? Often, the best way to do this is to use software or math tricks for the purpose. We recommend some on the companion website for this book, **keepcalmlogon.com**. Among the software that can do this are password managers. So this leads into another recommendation:

Use random *phrases* instead of words. Not every system will let you do this. But if a website doesn't limit how many characters you can enter for a password, using a pass*phrase* instead of a pass*word* can also be helpful in making it hard for a bad actor to guess. See **keepcalmlogon.com** for more details on how to generate random phrases.

Don't reuse your passwords across multiple sites. I know. I'm sorry. This is the hardest advice. But reusing your passwords across sites is just asking for someone—even just your kid, spouse, or coworker—to try breaking into different sites you access. This is where storing your passwords becomes important. Read on to find out how.

Storing Your Passwords

Now it's time to learn how to can, jar, preserve, or freeze your passwords—like food from your garden—so you can keep more of them. The best passwords are ones you can't memorize. You're going to need a way to store them. Check out **keepcalmlogon.com** to take a test to figure out which storage technique is best for you, and get recommendations on the best tools for storing your passwords. But first, a couple of don'ts:

Don't Send Your Password to Anyone

We've all done it at some point: emailed or texted a password to someone—particularly at work, where people often have to get access to each other's documents to get their work done.

But remember, when you send email or other messages, they go outside your own digital "fence." Frankly, you don't really know where they go. Your coworker could forward your password to someone else; your friend could screenshot and save it; an attacker could get access to your email provider and go looking for passwords. To keep your passwords safe, keep them inside a strong fence.

If you need to share passwords, many password managers have team solutions. See **keepcalmlogon.com** for recommendations.

Don't Leave Your Passwords Lying Around

Particularly in offices! You may have the idea that hackers use their coding expertise to get passwords. But you'd be amazed how many times digital break-ins rely on a note someone stuck to a monitor. A password book might make sense for those who only use their computers at home. But in cases where there are more people around, it makes sense to keep any written-down passwords under lock and key. If you write a password on paper, it should eventually be shredded (which is how you should dispose of any valuable document).

Stronger than Passwords: "Companion Planting" with Multiple Factors

Scout Law: "Even the little changes I make to my life online can make me safer and happier."

Expert gardeners know that some plants grow bigger and stronger when paired with other plants—like the "three sisters" technique that sustained Native American communities for generations. Plant corn, beans, and

The Iroquois artist Ernest Smith illustrated the Three Sisters—corn, beans, and squash—for the Work Projects Administration-funded Indian Arts Project. The shared agricultural knowledge of companion planting sustained Native American communities. *Source:* Ernest Smith, from the Collections of the Rochester Museum & Science Center, Rochester, NY

squash together and you get a cornstalk pole for beans to climb on, nitrogen added to the soil by the beans' roots, and a weed-blocker in the shady leaves of the squash.

Similarly, your security is stronger when you set it up so you need multiple factors to access an account. These "factors" are things you can prove—something only you know, something you have in your possession, or something about your identity (something you are). You're demonstrating that you have more than one of those, so the system can be extra sure that it's you trying to get in.

Your bank or email account may have already recommended multifactor authentication to you. One example is when, after using your password (something you know), your account sends you an email or text message or calls your phone (something in your possession). When you tell an account to "trust a device" you're logging in from, like your home computer, your account also uses the unique ID of that device as a way of confirming that you are logging in from a machine that you control.

Voice recognition and fingerprint logins can also be used as part of multifactor authentication—they prove that you are who you say you are, because it's hard to fake the nuances of your voice or your fingerprint. These can be pretty strong ways of confirming that you are you.

But stories have been circulating of tricksters who have found their way around fingerprint and voiceprint. With some current technologies, someone can record your voice and use it to impersonate you. Airport security has been known to compel people to unlock their phones with their fingerprint. And there are stories of kids taking their sleeping parents' fingers and using them to get on their phones and buy things! So it's still a good idea to back up voiceprint or fingerprint with another factor.

And let's not get started with face recognition as a way to log in. It is way too easy for someone to hold your device up to your face to get in. Face recognition also needs to be backed up with another form of security.

Multifactor authentication is stronger than passwords alone. So whenever you're given the ability to have your account call or text you, set up that option! I've included some additional kinds of multifactor authentication, like hardware keys and authentication apps, on the companion website.

Recognizing Dangerous Software

We've talked about protecting your "soil" with system updates, identifying the edges of your digital garden so you know what to protect, and passwords and multifactor authentication. But malware (malicious software) can also get on your devices by tricking you and pretending to be nonthreatening software—the same way some insects mimic poisonous insects to avoid being seen or eaten. When you say yes to this software, it may not matter that you have an antivirus program—it may install anyway.

Here are some tips to help you recognize malware "pests" and make sure you're not welcoming them into your digital security garden.

Did You Ask For It?

The first Scout Law for pretty much any surprise alert on your device is: if you didn't ask for it, tell it no and make it go away.

The second Scout Law is: if you didn't ask for it, **tell it no and make it go away**. Yes, if your *device itself* wants you to install a software update, you should install it. If your antivirus finds malware, you should wipe it out. And if your laptop or phone lets you know you are running out of memory, you will want to free up some space so your machine doesn't run painfully slow. But to be safe, you need to know that what you're installing is real.

You may be saying "How do I know which alert is actually from my antivirus? And how do I keep from missing the real updates my device wants me to install?" Totally fair questions. See **keepcalmlogon.com** for more information.

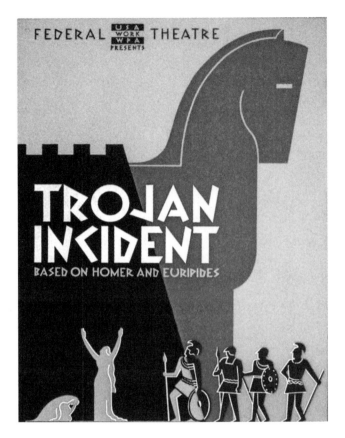

One kind of malicious software—the Trojan Horse—takes its name from the large wooden "gift" Greek soldiers hid in to conquer the city of Troy. *Source:* Burroughs, Work Projects Administration Poster Collection—Library of Congress

You May Be Saying . . .

"But I'm worried I'll break it!"

The good news is that every day, devices are being made harder to mess up by accident. So be brave!

How to Keep Calm and Carry On

- Get to know the digital gardener's best tool: **Undo**. For the vast majority of the changes you make to your phone or computer, there's an

Undo function. Or you can turn off the button you just clicked to "on." When you're really about to make a change that you can't undo, your device will usually warn you.

- The worst you'll do is change something you needed to work a particular way. If you **only change one thing at a time**, and then check to see what that change affected, it will be easier to undo and go back to the way it worked before.

"All of this keeps changing. It's so hard to keep up with protecting my stuff."

No kidding! Security experts have to race to keep up with new pests and holes in their fences. And it's not always easy to understand what you should do in response to the news.

The good news is, security advice is reported in the news more thoroughly than it used to be—and in ways that are more understandable to everyday folks. You can use security websites and news as a sort of farmer's almanac to prompt you to take steps to update your security.

How to Keep Calm and Carry On

Keep an eye on security reports in the news. We've also recommended some user-friendly security sites on **keepcalmlogon.com**. When reading, ask yourself the following, to figure out which "garden" section you may need to update:

- Is this a report about a **data breach, password theft, or leak of personal information**? Then it's a good time to change your password for the affected site, and any other sites or software where you use the same password (but please, please, don't use the same password across websites!) Depending on whether credit card information was involved, you may also want to take action on your credit rating, bank, or credit card website.

- Is this a report about a **vulnerability in an operating system or other software**? It's time to take care of your "soil"—make sure to open the update centers on your devices and install any updates!

- Is this report about an attack on **email accounts**? Definitely update your email password. Adding multifactor authentication is a good idea if you didn't already add it. You may also want to change passwords on accounts that use your email to reset.

- Is this a report about a new kind of **malware**? Time to run your antivirus or malware blocker. Listen closely to the report, and see whether they're also recommending that you change passwords or install updates.

- Is this report about some kind of **physical or social attack**, like people tricking you to give them information, or a fake credit-card device stealing your details at a bank or restaurant? Again, follow the details. For anything related to financial information, you may want to check your bank, card account, or credit report. Keep an eye out for shady-looking devices.
- And remember that basic rule: if it doesn't look right, and you didn't ask for it, tell it no!

But Who Are the Pests?

Now that you've got your victory garden laid out, you have better knowledge of how to keep out people you don't want mucking around in there. I explained earlier that I wasn't going to launch right into who could get at which parts of your garden, because frankly, that can be overwhelming. But in the next chapter I will explain a little bit about who knows what about you. I'll refer back to this chapter to explain which parts of your defense protect you against which bad actors or prying eyes.

7

"They Already Know Everything ... and There's Nothing I Can Do"

When I talk to people about online privacy, I often hear: "I figure they already know everything. And there's nothing I can really do about it. Besides, I'm not that important a person, so it doesn't matter what they know."

Hold up. Step back a second. Again, as I said in the Scout Laws, you *are* an important person, in your life and to your family. Your digital life and your information are *yours*, and that matters! If your social security number, bank information, or passwords fall into the hands of an identity thief, it may not bring down the government, but it is going to make your life hell for quite some time. And speaking of revolutions: In the United States, our forefathers fought for the right to be protected against unreasonable searches of our stuff by the authorities. Let's not give that right up easily in this revolution.

This chapter will clarify who's the "they" paying attention to your information. There's more than one "they," and each group has different abilities to learn things about you and have an impact on your life. By understanding more clearly who can do what—and why they *want* to do what they do—you should gain a little peace of mind, and some strategies for protecting what's important to you.

following page

In hard times, we're all a little more susceptible to offers that look like they could solve our financial problems. During World War II, the UK government cautioned citizens to watch out for such offers, and the same holds today. *Source:* Abram Games, Her Majesty's Stationery Office

The Problem: Identity Thieves

The tools: credit freezes; your digital security victory garden.

The techniques: don't leave crucial information in your online accounts; don't reveal too much on social media; take steps with financial institutions; change passwords; watch out for questionable email; don't open attachments.

"Identity thieves" come from all different walks of life. Take the case of the beauty queen from Hawaii who was sentenced for stealing identities and going on a shopping spree.[1]

Some people blame the internet for this kind of crime—and that leads them to log off and avoid the internet as much as possible. But the fact is that *people you meet face to face* are often the culprits. Some retail and restaurant workers have been caught stealing credit card numbers, copying them from your card when you make a purchase and then using them for their own purposes.

Vulnerable populations are particularly at risk from identity thieves. Elderly people are often tricked into turning over account information, in part because many of them may not be checking up on their accounts online or have not set up fraud alerts. Children in foster care have been hit hard: some unscrupulous relatives and foster parents have stolen their social security numbers to create new credit card and bank accounts or take out loans in their names. These kids grow up to discover their credit is shot before they even have a chance to build it.

Identity thieves *intentionally* steal your data. This sets them apart from legitimate companies that set cookies and trackers in your browser in order to passively make money off your online traffic. I'll talk about those in a minute.

The main way to protect against identity thieves is to guard your most critical information carefully. If you set up your digital security victory garden based on tips in the previous chapters, you're already on your way to protecting yourself from identity thieves. This may include being vigilant about things that seem totally harmless and unrelated to your financial information—remember that example about social media posts asking people to share the names of their pets, their first-grade teachers, and the street they lived on growing up?

When a credit card or other data breach happens, check news reports to see if you may be among those affected. There are some websites that keep track of major breaches and the email addresses associated with accounts that have been leaked; see **keepcalmlogon.com** for links.

Credit bureaus can help ensure that no new loans or accounts are set up in your name without your knowledge. And you don't necessarily have to pay their fees for a "credit lock." These companies are obligated to let you put a freeze on your account for free.

If your company or school requires you to send sensitive information like pictures of drivers' licenses, birth certificates, or social security numbers in regular email, speak up and let whoever oversees your IT department know they need to find a safer way to do this. Regular unencrypted email is not safe enough for these kinds of documents. If criminals get access to an email account at your company or school, they could conceivably have access to a massive treasure trove of information that is crucial to customers' livelihoods. If they get access to the sender's email account (which is only as secure as the password used by the account owner—in other words, not likely to be so secure), they have access to those documents. Secure document transfer tools are available (see **keepcalmlogon.com** for more information), and they cut down this risk. Recommend that your company or school start using them.

If there's no way around it, and sensitive documents need to be sent via email, completely delete the documents involved from your email accounts after sending them. Ask the receiver to do the same. This may involve a couple of additional steps like emptying the trash, or checking both your webmail and your desktop mail. But wherever possible, explain to the receiver they are putting everyone at risk by asking you to send important documents via email. It is only through raising awareness that we will begin to make our communities safer.

The Problem: Trolls

The tools: security and privacy settings on your accounts; "report account" options on social media.

The techniques: change passwords; clean up online information about yourself; document abuse.

When used online, the term "troll" has long meant someone who causes trouble for others for fun or to get a rise out of people. Basically, while your idea of online fun might be playing a game or watching cute cat videos, trolls' idea of fun may be getting a rise out of you in the comments on a video, killing your character repeatedly in a game in unfair ways, taking down your website, spreading misinformation, or giving people your phone number to make prank calls or otherwise harass you. Trolls have a huge toolkit at their disposal to make life unbearable for others online.

The most vivid representation I've ever seen of the trolls' toolkit was when I worked at Second Life, the online virtual world that launched back in 2003. Behind the scenes, where only employees got to go, an island that had some shocking stuff on it rose out of the sea. This was the Second Life equivalent of the closet in a principal's office where they kept the stuff confiscated from kids who caused trouble—think spray paint, slingshots, brass knuckles, or what have you. When you got closer, you could see the things that trolls had been using to make Second Life awful for everyone else: things like robots so large that they caused the app to freeze for anyone in the area, or a device that would spew tiny transparent . . . rather adult . . . images until the software couldn't handle drawing all those images and crashed. Like many troubled teenagers, the trolls were out to offend people and commit acts of vandalism. The Second Life governance team kept their confiscated toys in order to get a better sense of how they worked, and protect against them in the future.

The too-many-floating-images invasion was an easy-to-see example of what is known as a denial of service (DoS) attack: using the sheer volume of information sent to a computer as a way to take it down so people can't use it. This is a common tool used by both trolls and political protesters. So is breaking into websites to deface them.

Another popular tool in the troll toolkit is "doxxing," an old hacker term that is shorthand for publicly posting identifying documents about a person online. In a less frightening but more annoying example of the floating particles attack, doxxers could DoS *you* with one kind of mass mailing or another—be it signing up your email account for as many lists as they can, or delivering dozens of pizzas to your door.

Doxxers who publicly post someone's home address, job or work information, specifics about family members, birth name, or sexual preference may then threaten the victim with violence, or exposure of additional information—or make it possible for others to do so.

With most trolls, your best protection is to maintain your digital security garden, with an emphasis on choosing better passwords and keeping an eye on where your documents are going. But if trolls escalate, and their harassment moves into the real world, it may be time to take additional steps to protect yourself and your loved ones.

How to Keep Calm and Carry On

Take a look at the perimeters of your online "garden." Are there any sites where you used to spend time but don't anymore? You might want to take down any old pages associated with you, so that they can't be hacked or defaced.

You might want to set up an alert to let you know where and when your name is being used online. This can give you an early warning of abuse, including fake profiles in your name. Look for information about you that was not created by you, in particular. If you find pages and do not know how to take them down, take screenshots; these can be useful later when trying to make a case against people who are harassing you. Take screenshots of what is said and the date it was said, and of the profiles of whoever is posting it, if possible. Also be sure to capture the URL (web address) of the page.

The Problem: Physical Threats

The tools: WHOIS privacy (also known as "domain privacy"); restraining orders in some cases.

The techniques: clear online information about yourself off of aggregator sites; take steps with financial institutions as needed; change passwords; document and report abuse by taking screenshots across multiple sites and submitting them to the police as necessary.

If you or someone you know has been personally threatened online, you may be aware that this is not "just online," as some people who dismiss it might say. Online harassment is increasingly a problem in the "real world" in frightening ways, especially as it can escalate into physical violence (which doxxing makes possible). Gaming communities, in particular, have been ground zero for people threatening each other in these ways.

"SWATting" is another form of online harassment that doxxers use to threaten victims. Don't let the name fool you—it may sound as harmless as "swatting a fly," but it can be lethal. SWATting is when someone calls the victim's local police or other law enforcement and tells them that a violent situation, with an active shooter, is unfolding at the victim's house. Law enforcement agencies may then send an armed SWAT team to the address, ready to shoot anyone who appears likely to do violence. In late 2017, a Kansas man was killed by police officers when a 25-year-old in Los Angeles sent a SWAT team to his house over a $1.50 wager on a *Call of Duty* game. The man who was shot wasn't even involved; someone else in the argument gave the victim's address to the SWATter.[2] One 16-year-old boy in British Columbia, Canada, SWATted and harassed dozens of people including other gamers and young women, but also targeted the FBI's weapons of mass destruction unit and Disneyland. SWATting wastes law enforcement attention and resources in addition to being incredibly dangerous.[3]

I personally want to recommend that if you have a heavy gamer or regular user of 4chan or 8chan in your house, keep an eye on their moods and an ear out for what they talk about online, and don't just dismiss violent talk as "boys being boys." We need more parents, in particular, who understand the cultures of gaming (there are many game communities, and they are *not* all the same), and can talk to kids whose peer groups may make a game out of threatening others or who take violent action (while understanding that other game communities are all about puzzles or role-playing or making videos or even music). But so long as there are traumatized and unstable people out there, there will likely still be cycles of violence like these, so the rest of us must defend against them.

Again, cultivating your digital security victory garden is a good first step for ensuring that doxxers don't get your personal information to begin with.

You will want to be sure that you keep track of where your physical street address or phone number appears online (and maybe your work address and phone number). There are many sites out there that post this information as a "service," but unfortunately one service they provide is letting doxxers know where to find you (and possibly even send a SWAT team to your door). Do a search for your street address. Any sites that have posted it should have a mechanism for you to request that they take it down.

If you know you own a domain name (website address), take the step of signing up for identity protection with the company you pay for the domain. WHOIS information for a domain often points to your work or your home street address, and it takes extra steps (and often a small fee) to ensure it is hidden from public view.

In the extreme, you may also want to contact your local police department to warn them about SWATting, and explain what you're going through if you have been doxxed. If possible, a restraining order might be a good idea (though this isn't possible if you don't know who is targeting you).

See **keepcalmlogon.com** for information on how to set up an alert, clear your information from public sites, take yourself off email lists, or talk to the police, as well as links to resources for those who are under attack. You don't have to let online harassment silence you. But know that you also have a right to step away from the internet for a while, if it might put you at ease.

The Problem: Creepy Ads, Social Media Tracking, and Online Retailers

The tools: ad blockers and private browsing; tracker obfuscation tools.

By now most of us have seen it happen: You search the web for, say, some shoes you like. You find them, but you don't buy them. You head back to your email. Suddenly, there are the shoes again! And they're there on social media the next time you log in! HOW DID YOU FIND ME, STALKER SHOES?!

This is the work of "cookies" and other ad trackers. Many people aren't too bothered by stuff like this. After all, it means we have more chances to get things we like. But if ads are following you around all over the net, it's not just that data about your shopping and surfing preferences are being sent around to all kinds of sites you're never being told about—your online experience is also more stressful, more distracting, and even more prone to viruses and other malware.

A small percentage of the time, ads get through that are actually designed to deliver malware to your machine. Some of them get you to click through to scams saying you've won, or can win, some cool device for free. Others, even more rarely, deliver malware without you even clicking on them. Google and other advertising providers do review ads to ensure they are safe. But every once in a while, they miss a malicious ad.

You should understand, though, that ad trackers are generally not the same problem as identity thieves or doxxers, and vice versa. Knowing about the sites you've been looking at, in this case, *doesn't* apply to super-sensitive information like social security numbers or pictures of licenses. Sites should not use or store such information in the part of your browser that keeps track of your online surfing or shopping for the purpose of sending you ads—it's a legal and security liability for them if they do! Generally, advertisers are looking for your shopping information, and not your super-important documents.

The exception may be your zip code, and possibly your street address—information that is very valuable to advertisers, as it helps them know who in which neighborhoods is buying what. But this doesn't mean, for instance, that doxxers can get at your address if you provide it to a shopping site like Amazon. Shopping sites should be protecting your mailing information and not showing it publicly. Doxxers mostly work off information that is publicly posted.

Anyone looking at the traffic on your network can get a sense of where you are, or what websites you're requesting to look at, just from the addresses. *Source:* Abram Games, Her Majesty's Stationery Office

The Problem: Your Boss, Your Company, Your School

The tools: VPNs (but *not* your corporate intranet), web proxies (to defend against net nanny software, though it may not protect you if the proxy is unencrypted).

The techniques: try *https://* and alternate domain names (such as m. twitter.com).

Sometimes it's hard to get online at work or at school. These spaces sometimes set up net nanny or other blocking software that prevents you from getting to certain sites. There may be various reasons: some may be for security (bad news: a lot of sites with adult content or nonsubscription media streaming sites are hotbeds of malware); some may be to keep you focused on your work; and some may just be outright censorship (there, I said it).

The funny thing is, though, like Dr. Ian Malcolm says in *Jurassic Park*: life finds a way. Clever girls and boys (and grown-ups) will always find some way to get around a blocked internet. At one point I was doing research about how students at two high schools played video games. Interviewing a bunch of boys at a private high school, I learned that their school blocked YouTube, Yahoo!, and a number of other sites they might use for fun or things that weren't schoolwork. But the students had taught themselves a way around the school's net nanny software. They figured out that if they changed the address for the site just slightly—directing their browser to https://website.name rather than http://website.name— the site would load just fine. The net nanny software wasn't set up to block the secure versions of the sites, so students could sail right by its defenses by manipulating the address in this way.

There are a couple of different kinds of nanny software. One lets your boss or school watch your internet use. The other keeps you from getting to the sites you want to visit. Both make use of the *addresses* of the pages you are going to, like cnn.com or foxnews.com.

Do you see what they can learn just from that? The address itself can tell the watcher what it is you're looking at.

Address monitoring alone can't tell your employer what comments you're leaving on the site or what messages you're sending through them. But your company or school may also be watching your internet use in another way. They may use keystroke loggers (aka keyloggers) on your computer, which simply capture everything you type. That way they not only capture the address—they also see what you write in email, in documents, and any other message you write on your computer. These loggers are really insidious.

It's worth asking what your company's IT department monitors, so you have a heads up on whether every single thing you write is being watched or whether it's just the addresses of sites. At some companies that maintain valuable information, you might think it would make sense to use keyloggers to see if employees are writing about important information. But as it happens, keystroke loggers often also have bad security—and they can leak that important information to criminals. If you're comfortable doing it, you might talk to your boss or the head of IT about the potential problems with keyloggers.

The really alarming thing is that starting with Windows 10, Microsoft automatically uses a keylogger on your machine. It's "to help us improve typing and writing in the future," they say. You can turn it off in settings, fortunately. Your boss isn't likely to make use of this, but a criminal could try to access it.[4]

Because the ways your company or school may be watching or blocking you, you need slightly different sets of tools to deal with them:

How to Keep Calm and Carry On

To keep them from watching what you're doing on the sites you're going to, a VPN (virtual private network) may do the trick. This is sort of like an armored tunnel you send your online communication through. Notice, though, that if your company has you log into its *own* VPN, you won't be able to use another one with it, *and* your company will be able to see what you're doing. Your company might block VPNs, however, and VPNs can't protect you from keystroke loggers.

To get to sites that are blocked, the technique used by the students I talked to may work for you, too. Try going to the *https://* version of the site instead of the http version. Or try using the mobile version, where the site's address may be spelled something like m.facebook.com. Play around for a while, comparing the addresses for sites that work on your mobile (not on the company Wi-Fi) with the ones in your desktop browser.

Another tool that may work is a web proxy. I'll put a list of recommended ones up at **keepcalmlogon.com**, along with VPN recommendations. NOTE, though: proxies and changing addresses will not protect you from prying eyes. I'll say it again: **no privacy tool is a magical invisibility cloak.**

The Problem: The Police

The tools: VPNs, burners, encrypting your device.

The techniques: turn off geolocation, leave your phone at home, back up your data, set up a check-in time with a friend, don't use software that doubles as tracking software; reinstall your operating system if you suspect your device has been tampered with.

Police forces have different capabilities for seeing your stuff than advertisers or the government do. I'm mentioning advertisers specifically because ad tracking casts a wider net and is more day-to-day than the type of tracking police forces generally use to find what they go looking for.

Certain laws are supposed to govern what police are and are not allowed to do in order to watch what you do. They are generally supposed to get a warrant before intruding on private places—like your computer or phone, your work networks, or the records of your email or internet provider. Increasingly, though, police around the world have been found to be snooping on citizens by making fake social media accounts and "friending" people they want to watch.

I'm not recommending that you commit illegal activity (or suggesting that you already do!). But the fact is that throughout history, police worldwide, even in the United States, have been called on to shut down and disrupt activity that is *not* illegal—from religious community meetings to peaceful protests to union organizing to gay bars. It's important to know your digital rights. See the companion website for more information about them.

The Problem: "The Government"

The tools: secure text messaging and chat, Tor browser, Tails operating system.

The techniques: same as for the police.

Part of the problem with thinking "the government" is after you, in any country, is that you're probably not being specific enough. Which department? At a local, state, or federal level? Why would they care about *you,* specifically? Are you involved in protests? Are you a member of a minority group that has historically been more surveilled by the police or the government in your country?

A flighty friend of mine once came to me in a panic insisting that martial law was being declared in New York City. When I calmed him down and got him to talk, it turned out he had heard a curfew had been set in some of the parks. Which is really, *really* not the same thing as martial law! In the United States, the parks department and local police, who would be enforcing the curfew, do not have the same bosses as (or work under the same rules as) the military. All departments of our huge urban police force are not in daily contact with the military. The police and the military don't get funding from the same places (though, as it turns out, they are beginning to get hand-me-down equipment from the military).

Motor vehicles licensing, federal investigations, your city government, park rangers, international intelligence, the military—these are separate departments, and they don't *necessarily* or automatically all share information with each other, at least until there is a warrant out. And they don't all share the same capabilities. It's worth doing some research to get some evidence of who does what. This might be a good moment to check with your local librarian, if you are curious. (Libraries very *definitely* do not get the same funding or have the same bosses as the military or central intelligence.)

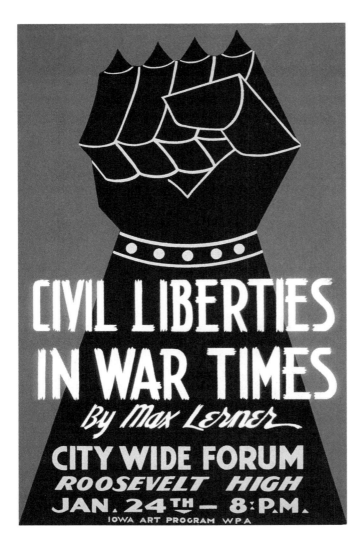

Source: Work Projects Administration Poster
Collection—Library of Congress

Your mileage may vary, depending what country you live in. In some countries, the police and military are much more tightly intertwined with each other. And mass surveillance is used against activists or minority groups in many countries. Whether it is used against a broader range of everyday citizens is another question, which differs from nation to nation.

Secure messaging and chat applications are available that can take the place of your usual chat apps if you are worried about your government. The best source of advice I know to find these tools is eff.org.

There is also Tor, which protects your online communication and browsing like a VPN while also hiding where you come from and to some extent who you are. It can't protect your identity if you're logged in and posting as yourself from your account, though. Tor is one of the strongest tools available for protecting your communications, though using it may stand out as questionable to someone looking at your network (like the IT staff at your job or school).

Finally, there are also secure operating systems that help protect your computer at a more basic level of your system. More advice on all of these options is up at **keepcalmlogon.com**.

One more time: **no privacy tool is a magical invisibility cloak.** Each of them has strengths and weaknesses that you should get to know and work around, or combine with other tools, if you have serious concerns for your privacy or safety. And again, as I said in the Scout Laws, security requires us all to change our behavior, not just download an app and expect it to solve all our security problems.

The tools you use to protect against the government are definitely not the tools you use against an abusive partner: your partner can quietly grab your phone from your bedside table while you're sleeping, but the government would more likely get a warrant and demand you comply or knock your door down if they wanted to get your phone. In the next chapter, I am going to pay special attention to keeping calm and carrying on when danger is coming from inside your own home rather than outside. It is complicated to protect yourself from someone who is so close to you. Let's take a look at how to protect your digital life in a situation like this.

To retain our personal liberty, we have to take steps to sow the seeds of privacy. *Source:* US National Archives and Records Administration

8

Safer Relationships, Online

A revolution seems like such a dramatic event that everyone must be able to see exactly when it starts, with a gunshot, say, or a bombing. Those of us living through this technological revolution know that while everything is changing fast, it didn't start overnight. There were many signs of change, coming slowly.

When a relationship changes from a loving one to an abusive one, it can happen the same way.

We've talked about groups of people who can see what we put online—our relatives, coworkers, or groups like advertisers or the police. But sometimes, it's what a single person sees that could cause us a tremendous amount of harm. Sometimes, the most dangerous person to us is one of the closest: a spouse, romantic partner, parent, sibling, or child.

The digital age has given our intimate partners a kind of power they've never had before—to keep track of us, check up on who we talk to, and maybe even control what we do. But we can take steps to protect ourselves in relationships from day one, and we can take steps when someone we know has gradually proved to be violent, emotionally abusive, or controlling. Perhaps more importantly, we can take steps at the start of any new relationship to build in safety and peace of mind.

I'm going to recommend we start by questioning one line that many people feed their partners from the beginning. It's an idea that I think is dangerous, because it starts our relationships off from a place of *mis*trust, rather than trust.

"If You Love Me, You'll Give Me Access"

So much of the time, partners pressure each other into getting total access to each other's digital accounts with this one line:

"If you love me, you'll give me access to your accounts."

Let's break that idea down for a second:

My question is "Why?" Give you access *to do what*? If you love someone, you want access to their accounts so . . . you can post to their account? That seems kinda weird. So you can know them—and by extension their best friends—*so well* that you know absolutely every single thing they think or do when you're not around? I get wanting to be so deep with someone that it's like you share the same mind, but still . . . isn't watching your partner that closely, in person or online, a little creepy?

And this, as I said when I introduced the question above, raises issues about privacy and trust.

My friend Nick points out how privacy may need more protection in online relationships than it does in person: online, how can you can actually tell when someone is going through your stuff? Nick shared a story to make this point:

> Neither of my parents would ever rummage around through the other's respective area except in exceptional circumstances. If Mom started poking through Dad's office, it would be obvious to him, just as the reverse would be true if he went through Mom's credenza. Things would be out of place and they'd know. Almost always there would be a good reason, but maybe one would forget to inform the other until after the fact.
>
> I got Mom to change her own passwords and exert her privacy rights by showing her it would not be as obvious if Dad started poking through her computer, her email, browsing history or other accounts.

But there's more at stake here, of course, than getting caught (or getting away with) snooping. Oftentimes when an intimate partner asks for access there are ulterior motives: "So I can make sure you're not cheating on me," or maybe "saying anything bad about me." That last one can cause what we call a "chilling effect": knowing that someone else is watching you can chill your willingness to speak freely.

Keeping your own private account isn't just something to do because you're afraid of abuse. Everyone needs to vent sometimes. Even those of us in happy relationships (or for that matter, happy workplaces) need a place where we can "dump out" rather than "dump in" when we're having a bad day, or need to figure out some frustrating part of a relationship.

Having your loved one see *everything* about your digital social life at all times means you don't have that private space to vent. It's healthy to make sure you have opportunities to vent to someone outside the relationship, rather than to your partner. Knowing that your partner is watching what you're saying in your private messages is more likely to hurt your relationship than to make it more loving.

Even if you feel like this person is your whole world, you still need to be able to communicate with other people. Buildings have fire escapes for a reason: it's not like we want fires to happen, but sometimes they happen unexpectedly. Relationships might even change because of the unexpected rise of a partner's mental illness, like depression, bipolar disorder, schizophrenia, or dementia. You may not expect the person you love to become abusive, but it can happen to any of us, even in relationships that look "perfect" and even to well-educated and well-off people. It's best to leave yourself a clear channel of communication with the outside world.

I've always been mystified that people justify sharing their accounts as some kind of safeguard against cheating. Having access to one account is no guarantee that your partner has been faithful to you, and it doesn't guarantee that your partner hasn't set up *another* account to conduct an affair on the side. It's really not that hard to establish another email account or social

Preventative measures and open pathways of communication can save lives. *Source:* Muller, Tenement House Department of the City of New York

media profile. But then, to find out if your partner is cheating, you'd have to set up some sort of net nanny or spy software, whether on a computer or phone.

To me, that looks like an escalation in an arms race: How far are you going to go to demonstrate to your own satisfaction that someone *is* cheating on you? If you don't find anything, will you install some more software to check further? What are you spending the bulk of your time on in the relationship: enjoying it with your partner, or trying to confirm for yourself that your partner doesn't want to be with you? What do you *want* your relationship to be about?

A person who trusts you would not ask for access to your email or phone. My friend Nathalie points out that *not* sharing passwords actually demonstrates high trust: "I trust you, so I don't need or want to read your email."

And this doesn't just apply to romantic partners. In some religious groups and other communities, the expectation is that parents should be able to see absolutely everything that their kids do online. This may seem normal to some people. In fact, there is no one choice that is normal. I know plenty of partners and families who maintain separate accounts; the kids still have great relationships with their parents, and the parents and partners are no more likely to cheat or divorce than anyone else.

"If you love me, you'd give me access to your accounts" looks like a red flag to counselors and staff at shelters for domestic violence survivors, who regularly see relationships turn violent. Controlling or monitoring the behavior of a partner or family member often goes hand-in-hand with emotional or physical abuse. Some abusers are triggered into violence by fear that their partner will abandon or cheat on them—and that trigger may come from something they see while keeping tabs on their partner's social media, email, or phone use.

"Come on, I HAVE to share accounts with my partner. We've got a household to manage, and not sharing accounts would be a nuisance."

How to Keep Calm and Carry On

Scout Law: "Control of my digital and media life should be mine."

Of course! For people who are married or well established in long-term relationships, there are good reasons to share *some* accounts. You may share bank accounts and phone plans. You may need to coordinate school and activities for the kids, and keep track of each other's schedules to plan dinner and vacations.

There are alternatives to straight-out sharing of every one of your accounts. Nathalie has an example:

> My partner and I have a shared Evernote notebook where we keep info we both need access to (emergency phone numbers, trip itineraries, passport/document numbers ... the list goes on). And I know other couples who use a shared folder (on a cloud service).

Notice these examples are not saying "If you love me, you'll give me access to *your* accounts." They're saying, "We have to work together, let's *share* accounts." So why share personal email? Or individual social media accounts?

Below, I'll help you think through some ways to be strategic about how you share accounts, and when. The key is to build good habits of account sharing from the beginning. Because when you find yourself in trouble, it's harder to take their access away.

Know Yourself First

Scout Law: "If I work to understand where my own opinions (and feelings) come from, I will be better prepared to protect myself from people who want to manipulate me."

Just like with understanding your reaction to things in the media, it helps to first understand and be mindful of your own self before you get into a relationship, whether online or off. Experts in relationship violence, including the creators of the long-standing Model Mugging self-defense program, suggest taking an inventory to see if you recognize any of the following qualities or situations in yourself—look at it as sort of a mental and emotional "family tree."[1] (Much of the inventory here comes from the

Model Mugging program. The "family tree" idea is mine, and I'll play it out in another way in chapter 9.)

If you relate to any part of these lists, it doesn't mean you can't ever get into a good relationship! Everyone deserves love. But it helps to be aware of your history and motivations, to understand whether you are getting into a relationship for the right reasons. Otherwise you could become vulnerable to people who are physically abusive, socially and emotionally controlling, or likely to take financial advantage of you (and from its earliest days the internet has certainly had plenty of people ready to take financial advantage).

When you are looking to get into a new relationship, ask yourself, am I

- lonely?
- grieving? (People who take financial advantage often move in on someone who has lost a loved one.)
- someone with low self-esteem?
- a survivor of trauma or family abuse?
- afraid of being abandoned?
- afraid of being embarrassed?
- someone who has a hard time saying no?
- depressed and/or anxious? (These emotions can lower your assertiveness and self-esteem.)
- struggling with addiction? (This makes for legal, emotional, and chemical vulnerability.)
- argumentative/always needing to be right? (This can escalate fights.)
- financially dependent or precarious, including in debt, living in an expensive area, or on government assistance?
- convinced that others can change?

These questions apply as much to divorced, widowed, and separated people, and to people in their later years, as they do to young people. Even those of us with years of experience in relationships have moments of vulnerability.

Once you've gone over the list, ask yourself: Do I consider all of these to be vulnerabilities? Do some of these things make me stronger, or *less* likely to seek out someone who might take advantage of me? They might even reflect both weakness and strength, depending on the situation.

If some of the characteristics above make you vulnerable, you can take steps to protect yourself.

Setting Boundaries

Identifying your vulnerabilities can help to set relationship boundaries for yourself, both online and off. Considering what boundaries you want to set up at what stages of a relationship—first date? couple of dates? long-term dating? moving in together? marriage?—can also help you understand when you want to be vulnerable at moments when it might feel safer to do so.

- What are you comfortable doing? At what point?
- What would you say a hard "no" to—which activities?
- How do you feel about power? About "fixing" or controlling your partner?
- How do you react to violating boundaries—is it exciting? Why?

You can think through how those questions apply at different stages of sharing your online accounts—when you're adding someone you're interested in to your friend network, or when deciding to share accounts more intimately with a romantic partner.

When you've met someone new who seems interested in you, when does it feel appropriate to add that person on social media? If people you connect to online turn out to be creepy, what would happen if you block them again?

At what stage do you think it would be appropriate to use a shared email or social media account with someone (with the caveat that you also have your own account, which you should)? Many parents I have spoken to say they found it necessary to start up shared accounts to respond to their children's schools, or they started a joint photo-sharing account to share their photos of their kids with their families. When would it be appropriate to share accounts with access to your credit card or bank, including shopping sites? You might decide that this would be appropriate when you move in together.

A list like this is your protection against going back later and saying to yourself, "I wish I hadn't done that." Reviewing this list often can keep you from making snap emotional decisions at critical times when it would be easy to quickly post something online or send a message you'll later regret.

"OK. I've set my boundaries. What do I do next?"

How to Keep Calm and Carry On

- Don't overshare info early in a relationship. For your physical safety, addresses, names of family, work or school location, and the like should be off limits on first dates.

- Be clear, up front, and honest with yourself and the person you're interested in about your boundaries, and stick to them.

- Plan neutral things to say when your boundaries are violated, like "I want to be left alone."

- Don't go out with someone, give them your contact info, or invite them into your social networks just to be polite when you feel uncomfortable. Trust your gut. Avoid giving someone your phone number, email address, or social network access out of pity; this can be misinterpreted as interest.[2]

  Already overshared, and things are starting to go bad?

- Cut problematic interactions off early, blocking the person online if an interaction online goes bad. It shouldn't be a big social deal.

- Don't worry about hurting the person's feelings. A hard "no" now is better than being stalked later.

Meeting in Person

The panics were already underway when I was a teenager, some (mumblemumble) years ago. Parents were worried that their kids would be seduced by people they met on AOL or bulletin boards, and then arrange to meet them in person. There were stories about kids who had been molested by online strangers.

But as it happens, the stranger danger was exaggerated. Not that many people were actually kidnapped or hurt by people they met online. And some of us did end up meeting people we had met online, and everything was just fine! Many of us went on to have deep, long-term, rewarding friendships and even marriages with people we met on online forums.

How to Keep Calm and Carry On

There have always been safety precautions you can take when going to meet someone you only know online—even if romance is not your goal. Here's what you do:

- Select a safe public location to meet the person, like a shopping mall or restaurant.
- Tell a good friend or family member where you're going to meet.
- Ask them to be on call in case of an emergency.
- If you and the person you're meeting are driving, drive separately.
- If you must ask the person to pick you up, don't make it at home or work.
- Have someone else there to see you off.
- Don't be absorbed in your phone or have your headphones on.
- Be aware of your surroundings: look for people around you, watching you.
- Have an emergency backup plan to get out. Just having your phone on you isn't enough.
- Make sure you have a way to get a ride, as well as pay for activities or dinner.
- Out-of-town trips and distance travel are riskier; it can be harder to get home if something goes wrong.

Sending Pictures

The first thing to know about any image you take—photos of your dog, pictures of your vacation, or more intimate pictures—is that all photos have attached data called EXIF tags that can tell when and where they were taken. So if you want to send or publish pictures but don't want them to be traced, know that there are ways to manipulate these tags to stay safer.

The amount of data in an EXIF tag is pretty breathtaking. Not only can it include information on the date and time the photo was taken, and what kind of device it was taken on, but it can also include the GPS location where it was taken—right down to the latitude and longitude coordinates, and even how far you were above sea level.

This can be a big problem if, for one reason or another, you don't want people to know where you are—your boss, people at your school or church, trolls harassing you, or an angry partner who may want to hurt you or gather evidence that you weren't where you said you would be.

When you take photos, if they are circulated around the internet, that EXIF information goes with them, and can be used in unexpected ways. Criminal cases and investigations have been built on investigators' use of EXIF tags to find criminals. And one wildlife preserve in Africa asked visitors to turn off their geolocation when taking pictures: poachers were using shots of rhinos and other

Technology has changed the nature of photography as well as the ways in which our images can be circulated, tracked, and even manipulated. *Source:* Work Projects Administration Poster Collection—Library of Congress

animals to find out where in the preserve they normally gathered, and then came to kill them.[3]

You Might Be Asking . . .

"I don't want anyone stalking me through my photos! Or killing rhinos! So how do I stop people from exploiting my photos this way?"

How to Keep Calm and Carry On

Scout Law: "If something digital is not doing work for me right now, I can turn it off."

- The first thing to do, as I recommended before, is to turn your geolocation *off* and keep it off at all times.

- Of course, also don't tag your location on social media by hand!

- Keep an eye on what's in the background of your photos, and try to avoid locations (or even furniture) that might let someone trace who or where you are.

- Don't share photos using apps that require your phone number to register—they might display your number next to your photo, which could show up if someone took a screenshot of the image. Similarly, be careful with your real name and email address.[4]

- There are additional tools that can help you take photos without EXIF data, and others that can clear the data after you've taken them. See **keepcalmlogon.com** for tools and techniques.

- Also check chapters 5 and 6 (about your Digital Security "Victory Garden") for tips on stronger passwords, secure connections, encryption, and specific apps.

There are laws that may protect you if photos of you are being circulated or misused. Depending on the situation, the person who shared your images without permission could be charged with unlawful surveillance, coercion, domestic violence, or even criminal impersonation. Many countries have laws protecting our rights to control our images as well as the rest of our personal data. You can demand that internet service providers (ISPs) take down images of you that were shared against your will. See **keepcalmlogon.com** for resources to help you if your photos are being used against you.

Signs of Abuse May Show Up in Social Media

Scout Law: "If I work to understand where my own opinions (and feelings) come from, I will be better prepared to protect myself from people who want to manipulate me."

As I said at the start of this book, we don't always know immediately who in our lives will turn out to be a danger to us. Sometimes we miss the signs because we think abuse "doesn't happen to people like us." For example, we may think we're not important enough to harass. People may believe that abusers don't prey on people who are from their cultural community, their income bracket, their level of education, or even their gender. But the fact is, intimate partner abuse happens in every community.

It's not always clear from the start that someone is going to be violent. Abusers are pretty much never abusive right out of the gate. As relationships begin, everyone's on their best behavior. And yet someone who is charming and attentive can send other signs to give us a picture of what's to come. The signs of abusiveness may be there, but in the glow of a new relationship, we might miss them.

There's a double-edged sword in the fact that digital media stick around for a while. They can be used against us, but they can also make it easier for us to go back to messages, voicemail, videos, and other things sent or posted by our partners or family members. This can help us be mindful and reflect on whether a relationship is caring and supportive, or controlling and abusive.

Sometimes we can even see warning signs before we get involved with someone, in the messages the person posts to others on social media. Look over the messages you've sent back and forth with the person you have a crush on, or your new partner, and check out their social media feed. Do any of the following descriptions fit them?

- They know a lot about you that you haven't told them yet, and act as if they know you intimately when they don't.

- They speak negatively or disrespectfully about potential partners or their bodies, or see potential partners as opponents (particularly if they are straight men talking about women).

- They rant about how unfair the world is to them.

- They have financial problems or can't hold steady employment, or do not see the need to provide for themselves.
- They say others are responsible for their feelings or actions; project strong emotions like hate and jealousy onto others; and act paranoid that others are out to get them.
- They own weapons and talk about using them for revenge or power over others (particularly against you or your friends and family, once you have gotten involved).
- Even though things are sometimes good, you find yourself in moments where there's a lot of tension with them, or you feel afraid.[5]

All of these are good indicators that someone could become abusive. If a couple of these patterns show up in the messages or social media posts of people you know, it may be time to go back to your self-assessment, to see whether you might be taken advantage of by someone with those characteristics.

Take a look back at the earlier exercises. Can you see any ways in which a person like this might exploit your vulnerabilities? How do the things this person does relate to your boundaries? If you begin to think about this now, you might catch problems before they arise.

It can be a good idea to get a second opinion—better yet, opinions from a handful of people in your network. Show the profile of the person you're interested in to a friend, family member, or counselor whose opinion you trust. What do they think? Do they foresee any problems and challenges based on their knowledge of you and your vulnerabilities? Be ready to take advice that may be hard to hear, either because of your background or because of what your heart wants right now.

Believe it or not, it can even be a good idea to talk to the person's ex (or exes). If there's really been a problem where someone has been abusive, ex-partners will likely tell you about it. Yes, there's a possibility that they will lie because they're jealous, but listen to how they're talking about their ex. Ask them why they are telling you about an issue. Trust your gut. See **keepcalmlogon.com** for more warning signs.

If you see these patterns in someone's posts and messages, it's time to take stock. The first question to ask yourself:

Do I feel better or worse about myself when I am with this person?

It all comes down to that. If you feel worse about yourself when you are with someone ... how much of your life do you want to spend feeling bad about yourself?

Thinking back to your list of vulnerabilities, ask yourself:

Am I used to the idea that this is just the way someone's friend, romantic partner, or family member is supposed *to act?*

If you take it for granted that people are going to talk down to you, that it is your job to build them up, that they're going to cheat, threaten you, or start a lot of fights—where does that come from in your life? The assumption that you don't deserve any better than constant conflict, or that you're worthless, ugly, or otherwise unlovable, has to come from somewhere in your mental and emotional "family tree" (which I'll be talking about more in chapter 10). Every person is worthy of love. The idea that love is control, or violence, also comes from somewhere. Where did that come from in your life? If you don't look into the origins of that thinking, you may continue to be vulnerable (or attracted) to people who continue to give you more of the same abuse.

Here's another question to ask yourself: Do I feel trapped or threatened by this person? The next set of questions can also help you think through this dilemma:

Patterns of Control

Scout Law: "Control of my digital and media life should be *mine*."

When you think about domestic abuse, what comes to mind? Many of us will think of a man hitting his wife, or we'll picture a husband and wife in a violent shouting match.

The truth is generally more complicated and nuanced. For one thing, domestic abuse can involve various family or household members and be psychological as well as physical: an adult child who bullies and intimidates an elderly parent, or a mother who tells her children they are worthless or punishes them by depriving them of food. Partner violence takes place between people who aren't even married yet; it happens in queer relationships as well as straight ones.

When it comes to emotional and verbal abuse, control is a huge issue. Abusive people often try to control not only what their partners and family members do and say but also what they think.

Even before the rise of digital technology, abusive people used the environments of the people they loved to control and hurt them. Technology makes this ever more possible, in ways our parents' generation might never have dreamed.

For example, at a security conference I went to a couple of years ago, a researcher presented on the kinds of wired home devices that get grouped into the "internet of things" category. He spoke about a husband who had locked his wife and kids out of their digitally controlled thermostat. In this case, he just wanted to keep the temperature a couple of degrees colder than his wife wanted to, and he was annoyed when she changed it back.

But consider what this device could do in the hands of abusive spouses or parents looking to "punish" their families for something. They could lock the temperature uncomfortably low—for example, just barely warm enough to keep the pipes from freezing, but far too cold for human comfort. Risks like these are always present in the hands of someone abusive. (And frankly, between that risk and the fact that internet of things devices are notoriously insecure, I don't recommend welcoming any of these Things into your house. I think the risk outweighs the benefit.)

Similarly, fitness wearables—supposedly innocuous devices that count how many steps we take or calories we burn in a given day—also store details about our health and well-being that we may prefer to be in control of, whether that means keeping them private or deciding who we share them with. And what those details can reveal may be surprising. For instance, at that same conference I just mentioned, a researcher reported meeting a man who had known his wife was pregnant before she did. How? He had been following her fitness tracker, and noticed her heart rate had gone through the roof.

Fertility- or menstrual-cycle tracking apps reveal even more intimate knowledge that an abusive or jealous partner might take advantage of if the person menstruating shared them, such as details about fertility or related moods.[6] An abuser could use this kind of information to make their partner financially dependent on them through pregnancy, could coerce them to end the pregnancy, or could manipulate their partner knowing a child was on the way.

Abusive people control their loved ones using less-cutting-edge devices, too. Does someone in your life:

- Accuse you of cheating when they see you talking to any other person online or on the phone, or see anyone you talk to as interfering in your relationship?
- Control your use of phone or other devices, particularly to keep you from being in touch with friends or family?
- Email, text, or message you nonstop; call you constantly at work, make you late for work, or get you fired?
- Use spyware or net nanny software to see what you're looking at online?
- Use tracking software, either on your laptop or phone, or by putting a GPS device on your car, to know where you are at all times?
- Insist on access to your personal finances; max out credit, fail to pay bills; constantly need loans and not pay them back?
- Hack your accounts; delete or manipulate messages?
- Covertly or forcibly record or photograph you having sex; use it to blackmail you?

You May Be Asking . . .

"My partner knows where I am all the time and I don't know how! How do I make this stop?"

How to Keep Calm and Carry On

Take a second to consider the situation. How is your partner going to react if your location signal suddenly goes away? I'm not necessarily saying don't remove it; just plan for what's going to happen next. Are you going to confront your partner about it, or not? Will your partner react badly? Will you need evidence for a restraining order? How will you keep yourself safe?

Once you've made plans to take action safely, open a "private" or "incognito" browser window (so that your partner will not be able to see your browser history) and take a look at **keepcalmlogon.com** for more tips for getting control of the signals you may be sending out about your location.

How to Stop Someone from Watching You

"Spyware" is a broad term for a number of apps that someone could use to watch you. Personally, I believe any app that gives someone the *ability* to watch you can be spyware, even if it's something otherwise harmless that you use in your daily life, like your smart home app or even your email.

But some apps are specifically created to help one person watch someone else. Apps that parents use to watch their kids, or bosses use to track the use of company-issued devices, fall into the "spyware" category, and it's why app stores don't stop this type of app from being sold.[7]

Spyware's effectiveness depends on it not alerting you to the fact that it's running. But there are a few telltale signs that someone may have installed spyware on your device. Is your device

- running really hot or, in the case of a laptop or desktop, making a lot of fan noise?
- draining the battery at a faster rate?
- using more data than it has in the past? (Check the settings panel on your phone to review data usage.)
- receiving cryptic text messages full of a bunch of garbage letters and numbers?
- getting static or feedback on calls?

Many of these symptoms are the same ones caused by malware, so you may not want to immediately want to jump to the conclusion that it's spyware. Either way, removing the cause of these problems is a good idea.

The most effective way to get rid of any bad software is to back up the things you need on your device, then do a factory reset or reinstall the operating system. You may want to get help with this to make sure you're not reinstalling the spyware (or malware) app again. And remember to consider whether it's safe to reinstall, or whether there's a risk the person watching you will notice.

If you are pretty sure that your partner is *not* using spyware on your device, but still seems to know what you've been looking at on the web, use online private or incognito browsing in a common browser like Chrome or Firefox; it can hide the things you have searched for from your browser history. (Spyware, however, might keep track of what you searched for even if private browsing is on.)

Here are some other specific security tips you can take if someone in your house or romantic life is being abusive or controlling:

- Don't use your browser to store passwords. This makes it too easy for someone else who has access to your device to get into your accounts. Use an encrypted, stand-alone password manager instead.
- If you have home security or "smart home" devices, learn how they work so that you understand who can get access to them and what they can learn. (And after leaving a dangerous situation, if you decide a home security device would make you feel safer, be sure to know how to lock it down so it can't be accessed by your abuser.)
- See **keepcalmlogon.com** for a list of recommended password managers, password-protected secret locker apps, domestic violence support agencies, and other digital services.

The Bottom Line

It was the creators of the Model Mugging program who inspired this Scout Law:

> *Security happens because of my behavior, not someone else's, and not because of a gadget or app.*

Just handing over safety to someone else or to some technology might seem easier, but nobody is ever going to keep you as safe as you can, yourself.[8]

The questions we have to ask ourselves about new people in our online lives have a lot to do with our own individual ability and inclination to *trust*. Trust, as it happens, has been a major casualty of the digital revolution: it has broken down our relationships with individual people, social groups, governments, and especially the things we read and the images we see. This breakdown is so crucial that I devote all of part III to exploring trust, and refer back to it in part IV, the last part of this book.

III

CONSERVING AND REBUILDING TRUST

9

The Roots of Trust

2016

During the 2016 US election, it came to light that a bunch of teenagers in the Balkans were running websites crafted to catch the attention of Americans. The teens' only goal? Make more money than they usually could as kids their age in Macedonia.[1]

They spread outrageous fake stories. One said the Pope forbade Catholics from voting for Hillary Clinton (he didn't). Another claimed that in 2013 Hillary Clinton had said she wanted to see Trump run for office, because he was "honest and [couldn't] be bought" (she never said that). The kids in Macedonia began by writing headlines supporting Hillary Clinton or Bernie Sanders, as well, but ultimately found they didn't get as much attention on Facebook.

These teenagers were only in it for self-interest. But they weren't the only ones turning our attention into weapons.

We also learned that Russian government–related groups targeted American voters on social media, reaching 126 million Facebook users and publishing more than 131,000 tweets on Twitter during the election, not to mention buying countless ads.[2] Their aim was to sway American voters, pitting more and more extreme opinions against each other, with the aim of de-stabilizing the election.

Russians were not the only ones to try this. Evidence of governments' and politicians' attempts to sway public opinion through fake social media accounts traces all the way back to 2010. Groups and factions in at least twenty-eight countries have tried this type of manipulation—including Australia, the United Kingdom, the United States, Mexico, Brazil, Germany, and India—in attempts to influence either their own citizens or those of other nations. They comment on things people post, flooding hashtags to hide criticism of government policies. They target journalists and movements, harassing them and smearing their reputations. They spread pro-government messages, making it look like there are more people who agree with them. They harness armies of automated "bots" to post more than any set of human hands could manage in a short period of time.[3]

Person-to-person communications are just as subject to spreading misinformation as news, if not more so. Just ask Rema Rajeshwari, a police chief in the Telangana region of India, where rumors of child kidnappers spread like wildfire on WhatsApp. Before it became clear that these rumors and the videos that accompanied them were faked, dozens of people across India were murdered because villagers suspected them of kidnapping children. Rajeshwari's police force managed to get a handle on the viral rumors by going around to villages face to face, talking (and even singing and performing) to locals about rumors and fake news.[4]

Humanity is facing an absolute flood of *disinformation*—bad information that some people spread intentionally. This is a global crisis.

One of the hardest things about living through this information revolution is the impact it has had on our trust. It seems like you can't trust anything you read or see online or in the media, and that ranges from the everyday to the large-scale. Messages that appear to come from our friends are actually from someone trying to steal our money or our identities. News items turn out to be faked—and sometimes even put out by malicious politicians or foreign agents.

For the past couple of years, "fake news" has been on everyone's lips. But what news is fake? Accusations fly from all sides. People attack media that have been trusted for generations. Others hint at "vast conspiracies." It's a rare person who hasn't worried about media bias on news shows, or garbage posts in social media.

This is an information revolution. That means the sources we have trusted may be toppled, like a statue of a dictator. Or, to survive, they may have to transform. Information is a weapon in the warfare we're living through. It's a target, too.

How can we trust anything anymore?

The more we hear about untrustworthy information, the more likely we are to throw up our hands in despair and reject ALL information (akin to the "learned helplessness" I talked about in chapter 1).

But we can't give up. There is too much at stake in our communities.

Here's the Keep Calm Scout Law I want you to understand in this chapter. Like our security, our attention and the rest of our digital lives:

Trust, and the information we trust, belong to us.

They are resources we build in our communities, together, for each other.

To defend our communities, it's time for us to recommit to conserving and rebuilding our trust in each other, by asking "What do we trust, and why?"

This is also the source of other Scout Laws:

- If I can understand where my own opinion comes from, I will be better prepared to protect myself from people who want to manipulate me with fake news.
- Likewise, if I understand how communities decide what information to trust, I will be better prepared to identify disinformation.
- If I understand how news, books, and other media are made, I will be better able to identify bias.

Get ready to think about these ideas in the next few chapters. First, let's take a look at what trust is, at the same deep level in our brains that we looked at stress and enjoyment. Where does trust come from? What happens in our brains when we trust people?

What Is Trust?

At a basic level, trust is the feeling we have that things and people around us will continue to behave in the ways we expect.

Think about a stray dog or cat, or a wild animal. What would you need to do to get it to trust you? You'd need to be calm and consistent.

Brains—both human and animal—process familiar sights and sounds differently than new ones. When we see something for the first time, our brains register the newness, and they slow down our processing to try and make sense of what is going on. This slowing down may barely be noticeable. Or it may be highly visible in the form of a "disgust" or "startle" reflex.

A good example of this reflex showed up in videos people took where they placed cucumbers behind their cats while they were eating. (Yes. Cucumbers and cats. I have *no* idea who came up with this.) The cats were so startled that many of them leapt straight into the air and then scooted out of there like their tails were on fire. Why? Just because the cucumber wasn't there before! It was new and unexpected ... but also shaped like a snake. As it happens, natural selection ensured cats that had an immediate "run away now" reaction to anything snake-shaped would survive to pass on their genes to future generations of kittens. That's a dramatic illustration of what a brand-new, unfamiliar sight may do to brains and reflexes.

But once we've seen a person, animal, plant, or object multiple times, our brains process those sights and sounds more quickly, filing them away into our mental patterns for "car," "bird," "policeman," or what have you. We may become so used to passing cars that when someone asks us "Did you see that Lamborghini?!" we might not even remember that a car had gone by. Our brain just didn't even register it as worth noticing. This familiarity with patterns is at the root of our trust.

What you'd do with an animal to get it to trust you is build this familiarity, which would set an *expectation*: that the next time you showed up, you would not move quickly (if you did, the animal would think you were going to chase it or hurt it). Maybe you would build an expectation that you'd bring food, which would make the animal feel good. Expectation, habit, and feelings all go into building trust.

Trust is in many ways the same for people as it is for animals. Our capacity to trust develops from the moment we are born. Neuroscientists have hypothesized that this is in part because we have "mirror neurons": cells in our brains that go off like fireworks when we see another person (or even an animal!) doing or feeling something we could also do or feel—like eating, walking, or even caring for someone else, or feeling sadness, anger, excitement. Or trust.

As infants, we develop trust in the people who take care of us, if we are well cared-for. We trust that when we are hungry, they will feed us. That they will clean us up when we are uncomfortably soiled, cuddle us when we need a hug, and make sure that we are warm and safe.

This is our first basis of trust in other people: our belief that they will be consistent. We then go on to develop trust with other people in our neighborhoods and schools. We look to our parents when we meet other people, to gauge their reactions: Are they relaxed and smiling? Is this new person also safe?

If those earliest needs are not met, though, it can have disastrous consequences for our ability not only to trust, but also to speak, care for ourselves, and function in society with other people. In *The Boy Who Was Raised as a Dog*, the psychiatrist Bruce Perry reports on the unhappy cases of some children whose needs were not met in their earliest years; as infants, they were left alone without being fed, changed, or cared for over long stretches of time. The consequences were severe. One child was unable to talk, threw feces, and flew into violent rages whenever a new person approached him. Another, having determined the only thing he could trust was his own ability to manipulate others, developed into a sociopath who ultimately murdered two teenage girls.[5]

Without trust, we're in deep trouble. Trust based on knowing the people around us builds the bonds that keep communities and societies functioning, sharing resources with each other and helping when crises arise.

Sociologists who study trust tell us it involves being able to see other people's perspectives, and based on those perspectives, predict how they'll behave.[6] Say, for example, you're at lunch, and your friend forgot her wallet at home. You might think to yourself, "She's always paid in the past. I'll cover lunch, and trust that she'll pay me back." If, over time, we have come to expect kind, thoughtful, careful behavior from other people who are familiar to us (just like infants or animals who have been treated well), we trust them. We don't always instantly trust people who are unfamiliar to us.

Disruption of Trust

Our trust seems to be badly disrupted these days, and our digital lives may seem very much to blame. But there are many indications that the disruption of trust has been building for centuries.

Scholars who study human migration around the globe have noted that as people have moved en masse, social ties have frayed. Mass migration has broken up families, and made it more likely that people do not know or create ties with their neighbors. In his book *Bowling Alone*, Robert Putnam noted a decline in American society of socializing outside of work—including participating in religious groups, social organizations outside the family, and sports teams like bowling leagues. And this was *before* the worldwide rise of the internet—the book was published in 2000.[7]

Modern society is very complex. Rather than producing our own food, making clothes, healing ourselves, teaching each child at home, researching issues that affect our lives, and making direct decisions about the rules governing our communities, most of us rely on complex systems of other people who make all these things easier for us. Media—print, broadcast, and digital—bring us images and news of people who are located far from us.

In a world like this, how do we come to trust people we don't know—people who are far away, like celebrities, politicians, journalists, the people who make products we use, scientists who make decisions about medical research, people in other countries, and people we meet online?

Sociologists suggest that in modern society, with all our ability to see people far away, and with the likelihood that the movement of people around the globe will mean we run into more strangers, our trust is based on things other than our personal familiarity with someone. It may be based on appearance. Or we may put our trust in the systems that other people are a part of, such as hospitals, schools, professions, companies, and political parties.[8]

Trust in Appearance

Trust in appearance can take a couple of forms. Branding is one. Most of us are familiar with the idea that products under a particular brand will be of the same quality, no matter where we find them. For example, McDonalds has a whole system of timers and quality control measures for

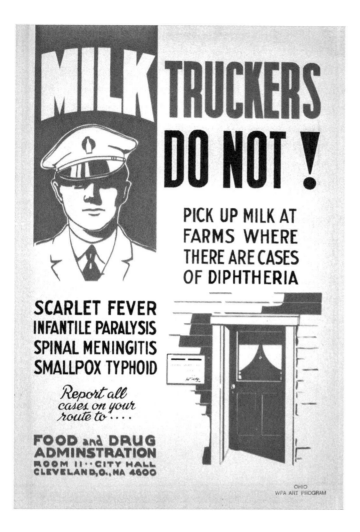

We ask people employed by systems in our society to work in a way that earns our trust—for example, that they produce and deliver our food cleanly. Our agreement on what "clean" means develops over time, and relies on other systems, like science and medicine. This poster, produced with Work Projects Administration funding during the Great Depression, educated milk truckers about their role in preventing the spread of deadly diseases. *Source:* Work Projects Administration Poster Collection—Library of Congress

their fryers to ensure their fries will have the same golden crispness wherever you buy them, whether it's Beijing or Dallas. The familiar appearance of its brand logo is there to inspire our trust. But a logo is never the whole picture of a company. The logo and product quality may be what we expect, but we may never know if behind the scenes, the company is underpaying or exploiting its workers or causing environmental problems. The corporate image a company wants us to see is usually a tightly controlled product of a public relations office.

With celebrities and politicians, we see some of their behavior in the media, and through their familiar appearances we begin to trust that they will act in a particular way (sometimes this is even called their "personal brand"). But we may forget that what we see from them is only partial—and it is probably a well-edited picture (think soundbites, manipulated photos, and makeup artists). It is not the same as the trust we develop in people around us, who we come to understand more thoroughly and whose behavior we have a more complete picture of.

Trust in Systems

Trusting systems requires us to trust the people who participate in them. We trust factory workers to build cars that don't have flaws that could cause accidents. We trust the people handling the food they make for us to do it cleanly, so we don't get sick. If we trust journalists and newspaper editors, it's because we expect them to get many perspectives on a story, and check their facts. And if we trust medical researchers, it's because we expect they have followed the rules of science to confirm that a new drug or procedure will heal, rather than harm.

Often there are particular people in our communities who are designated as *authorities*: whether they be elders, priests, lawmakers, or someone else, our social systems give them the say-so in a community. We take what they say as *authoritative*, worthy of trust, because of their knowledge, the things they have witnessed, or the work they have done.

Humans have always needed a few people to try to understand the world a little more deeply than everyone else, to keep us safe—whether

CERTAIN PEOPLE of IMPORTANCE

that person was a shaman studying the weather and plants, a religious
figure interpreting the will of an angry god, a judge trying to solve a dis-
pute without everyone killing each other, or a medical scientist looking
for the answers to diseases in our DNA. We trusted these authorities so
we could survive—so we didn't eat something poisonous, go somewhere
dangerous, get in a fight, and so forth. The people who have authority in a
community may accept, reject, or change a new way of verifying the truth
of information, but most people agree that whatever they say goes.

In our time, many of the authorities we trust are *professionals*. What does being a professional involve that builds our trust? I will talk about that in chapter 14.

Rebuilding Trust

I've discussed three forms of trust: trust we build by knowing people directly; trust we build on appearances; and trust of people based on their positions in systems. The first and last types of trust in that list are the most disrupted today. That's to be expected. Existing systems—like journalism and education—are changing. The people involved in those systems have to change the work they do. New systems arise in our digital lives all the time.

So how do we rebuild trust?

One toolkit for rebuilding our trust in information comes from a surprising source: the American Library Association.

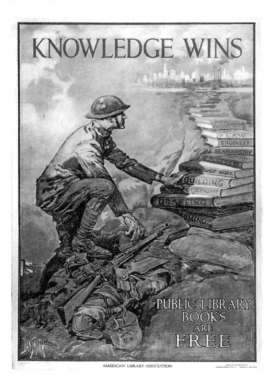

The ALA set forth the following guidelines to help us understand the systems that produce information. The guidelines point out we may trust a piece of information for one purpose, and not another. All of us *socially construct* information by sharing it, reviewing it, selecting it, and using it.

Librarians want us to understand that the search for knowledge is a path, not just a destination. *Source:* Dan Smith, American Library Association

The ALA suggests that we consider the following guidelines (which my Keep Calm Scout Laws draw on)—not only for books, but also for any information we encounter:

- Information is *made and spread by people.*
- Information may be *trusted differently* by different people, for *different purposes.*
  - As a result, different people may create *conflicting information.*
  - Information can be valuable for a number of things, including to educate people, to influence others, to find my way around the world, or as a product to sell.
  - Whether a given piece of information is valuable depends on *which needs* for information I currently have.
- Information may take *different shapes.*
  - The shape of a given piece of information doesn't necessarily tell me how truthful it is.
- *How* the information is made and spread changes the information.
  - Learning how it was made—including how it is edited, reviewed, controlled or not controlled—can help me weigh its value to me.
- All of this impacts how *authoritative* I may find the information—how willing I am to trust it.
  - One piece of information, even if it comes from someone with authority, may not be the only perspective out there. It may not be the view of most authorities.
- I won't always find the best information in my first attempts to search for what I need.
  - As a human being, my search for information never ends—so I may want to *wait to judge* a single piece of information until I understand more.[9]

When we run into conflicting information, librarians want us to know, we should come up with questions about it, and look for gaps and weaknesses.

Before we use the ALA guidelines to look at why we trust information, we each need to understand our *own* trust in individuals. To do this, we'll make use of mindfulness tools from another surprising source: an anti-propaganda effort that dates back to 1937, right before World War II. We'll use these to understand the "family trees" of our trust grown by our ancestors, and the opinions about people and institutions that we form as a result.

Then we'll look at the flipside of that trust: our bias. We'll look at how we come to trust information that may share or reinforce our biases, and how the biases of information producers may keep us from getting a full picture of the truth.

In the following chapters, I'll address one major disruption to our trust that the internet has worsened: it has become *hard to actually know who is saying something*. And how can we trust information when we don't know who or where it comes from? As it turns out, this isn't even just a problem with the internet: it's a challenge that comes with *the written word* itself. I'll tease apart the basic ways people have historically understood that a written document is from who it said it was—including signatures and dates.

Then we'll have a good basis for understanding how the internet is changing publishing, and how we know who's publishing. Online, we need to know about things like addresses, certificates, encryption, Wikipedia, and search engines and other algorithms to ensure we know who said what.

But let's start at the root of our trust's family tree.

10

Trust and Our Opinions' Family Trees

1938. Following the Great Depression, people around the world struggled. Unemployment rates were as high as one in three workers in some countries. Governments were still working to revive their economies. Banks closed.

Mass production of cars and commercial travel by airplane had only been around for about twenty-five years. Communities were still reeling as they handled the impact this had on people's ability to travel, move, and work.

Mass radio broadcasts had existed for about fifteen years. People were still figuring out how to understand the information those broadcasts brought into their homes. In October 1938, a radio play called *War of the Worlds*, adapted from a science-fiction novel by H. G. Wells, aired as if it were a news report, and terrified some Americans into thinking that aliens had actually invaded the planet and were wreaking havoc.

Real invasions and other big, frightening events did happen that year. Japan invaded China. Hitler and Mussolini gained direct control over their countries' militaries, and Germany made moves to take over Czechoslovakia. Hitler expelled from his government those who disagreed with him. The Nazi government built the death camps that were part of his Final Solution. Nazi sympathizers destroyed Jewish-owned businesses. With hundreds of thousands of people trying to flee from Germany, US president Franklin Roosevelt called the Évian Conference to address how the thirty-two nations in attendance would cope with a growing wave of refugees.

Everything was changing at that time—rapidly. The shape of cities, and even of nations; the shape of families, nearby and emigrated far away; the shape of jobs, when people could find them—who did them, and the tools they used to do them. And of course, how we got our information changed dramatically as well.

Newspapers had been around for centuries, but journalism was only beginning to be defined as a career. As journalism grew, so did a related field: public relations, or the management by companies and political figures of what people thought. Advertising was also growing, with newspapers and magazines relying on ads to pay the bills. Radio made it possible for more people to hear charismatic figures whose reach might otherwise have been limited to their local communities, and it brought to life dynamic speeches that had previously been stripped of emotion when they reached audiences in writing.

Between mass unemployment, mass migration, the development of public relations to shape people's opinions, advertising that convinced people to buy products, and radio speeches that roused people's emotions, people's trust was radically transformed. Some people worried for democracy.

It was a time of massive upheaval—not unlike today.

And it was in the middle of this time of disrupted trust that a former journalist, a teachers' college, and the head of a department store—Edward Filene, whom those in the northeast United States may know as the founder of Filene's and Filene's Basement—joined forces to help their communities conserve truth and trust at a time when the world was sliding into war.[1]

The exercises developed by their organization—the Institute for Propaganda Analysis (IPA)—are surprisingly useful to us today as we try to keep calm and mindful of what information we choose to trust. In this chapter, I'll introduce these exercises. In the next few chapters, we'll use them to reflect on how our own families and communities trusted different information and the institutions it came from.

The goal? Going back to a garden metaphor, we want to understand the "soil" of our own trust, so we are mindful of how the "seed" of information may land with us.

Democracy and Information: The Institute for Propaganda Analysis

The IPA's founders believed, as the founders of many democracies have, that the system of democracy would never survive if the voting public did not have trustworthy information, and the skills to evaluate that information. Without it, citizens could be easily led to harm their communities by people violating their trust. In the *Group Leader's Guide to Propaganda Analysis*, IPA's educational director, Violet Edwards, wrote:

> The cornerstone of democratic society, fundamental to the improvement of democracy as a way of life, is reliance upon the free play of intelligence in solving problems of human concern. This ideal is held in direct contrast with the making of decisions either by a minority or by the majority on the basis of traditional beliefs, uncritical acceptance of authority, or on blind impulse.[2]

In its time, the IPA saw the rise of fascist movements and demagogues like Father Charles Coughlin and Huey Long. The IPA's founders worried about the "uncritical acceptance of authority" these movements demanded of their followers. They were concerned that citizens were giving their trust to people whose interest was power at any cost.

The IPA's focus was propaganda. But what was propaganda, as compared to other kinds of information?

The word "propaganda" comes from the same Latin word as "propagate" (which means "to spread"). We see that same spreadable quality when something online "goes viral," or in what we today call "memes."

The IPA's founders worried that propaganda appealed to people's emotions, rather than their ability to rationally think through the facts of an issue. This concern with emotion-driven communication goes all the way back to ancient Greek philosophers. Socrates had a long argument about "oratory"—the art of speaking. He didn't much like oratory, for the same reason the IPA was worried about propaganda. Speakers who worked to get people emotional, he thought, had the same relationship to truth as candy-makers had to doctors: most people like the way sweets make them feel, but your body cannot survive on sweets alone. He also compared

Sinclair Lewis's novel *It Can't Happen Here* also played out the concern that a fascist dictator might rise to power in the United States. During the Great Depression, it was adapted and produced for theater with Work Projects Administration funding. *Source:* Richard Halls, Federal Art Project

emotional speech to makeup: cosmetics might make you look younger and healthier, but they can't actually make you healthier. Both makeup and sweets are short-term and superficial.

You could say the IPA and Socrates were both concerned with trust based on appearance—the kind of superficial trust we develop when we haven't met someone personally and haven't had the opportunity to come to trust their behavior. The IPA wanted us to better understand our trust in systems like democracy and industry, so we wouldn't trust companies or politicians for superficial reasons.

Propaganda in the late 1930s came from all sides, appearing in many kinds of media. Much of the time, this propaganda exploited our gut tendency to mistrust anyone who wasn't familiar to us. The American military made posters with ugly caricatures of Japanese and German soldiers to rally people to the effort to defeat these enemies. Nazis wrote children's books that told stories blaming Jews for the world's problems.

Other propaganda presented pictures of systems that were also far away and difficult to understand or trust. Socialists spread leaflets that blamed bosses for workers' problems and depicted a world where workers ran everything. On the radio, Father Coughlin denounced socialism and hinted at his support for dictators like Hitler and Mussolini.

Around this time, the field of public relations was on the rise, helping governments and businesses alike smooth over the rough edges of what they did and said in order to present an emotionally appealing message to everyday people—one that played easily to people's readiness to trust appearances, rather than getting them to dig deeper and understand the systems of government and business.

The IPA saw propaganda as a problem because it was "deliberately designed to influence opinions or actions of other individuals or groups," specifically to influence them to share the goals of the person spreading the propaganda.[3] The goal of the people or governments spreading propaganda was to *make people act*, unlike scientists, whose goal is "trying to discover truth and fact."

Was all propaganda bad? No, the IPA allowed: some propaganda may be spread to try to encourage people to do things that are good for them and their communities. Public health campaigns, for example, might work to get people to stop smoking or to wash their hands to keep from spreading disease.

Did the IPA think their fellow citizens were all unthinking sheep, trusting what propagandists said? Were they, as some conspiracy theorists say today, "sheeple"? Not at all, wrote IPA cofounder Clyde Miller, describing them in a way that probably describes us all:

> The intelligent citizen does not want propagandists to utilize his emotions, even to the attainment of "good" ends, without knowing what is going on. He does not want to be "used" in the attainment of ends he may later consider "bad." He does not want to be gullible. He does not want to be fooled. He does not want to be duped, even in a "good" cause. He wants to know the facts and among these is included the fact of the utilization of his emotions.[4]

None of us want to find out that our trust in information was misplaced. It's hard to even admit when that happens.

With surprising clarity, the founders of the IPA recognized that just analyzing propaganda would not be enough, because that's just half of the communications equation. In communications, there's always a message sender, and at least one message receiver.

And who is the person receiving the message? Which messages will they trust?

The IPA came up with a technique that, from our viewpoint today, shares a lot with mindfulness. The technique asked those who were analyzing propaganda to start by understanding *their own* opinions—built on their trust of the people, communities, and systems that shaped what information they received.

That technique is still relevant today, so I'm going to share it with you.

"Just My Opinion"?

"You're entitled to your opinion." In the United States, we hear that a lot. It's said to be a right given to us by our Constitution.

But where do our opinions come from? Does each of us invent them ourselves, out of thin air? Are they made up of our thoughtful, neutral analysis of the world around us?

This Depression-era poster encouraged American citizens to take free courses offered under the Work Projects Administration. *Source:* Work Projects Administration Poster Collection—Library of Congress

We'd like to think so. But we base our opinions on those we trust because we see them around us—or we don't have much to base our trust on when we're asked to form an opinion on people we don't see often. We learn our sense of who and what to trust from family members, teachers, religious leaders, and others around us.

In a list they called "The ABCs of Propaganda Analysis," members of the IPA urged readers to think about how our opinions are never wholly our own. Whether we trust the opinions of others, or whether we reject their ideas, we don't come up with our opinions in a vacuum. Here is a sample from their list, along with some of the IPA's recommendations for being mindful of how we react to and trust new information:

- "BEHOLD **your own reaction.**" First, consider how you are responding to the information. Go back to some of the earlier exercises we did, to be aware of how the internet or other media may be affecting you. Do you feel fearful? Angry? Proud? Excited? Do you trust this information? Or does it seem so nonsensical that it feels like your head might explode? Does it seem like the information wants you to take sides? Which do you feel like taking? Understanding where we stand, first, is the key to calmly and objectively thinking through new information.

- "DOUBT **that your opinions are 'your very own.'** They usually aren't," the IPA argued. "Our opinions ... have been largely determined for us by inheritance and environment." In other words, by our families and those we see around us who we have come to trust. "We are born white or black, Catholic, Protestant, Jewish, or 'pagan'; rich or poor; in the North or East, South or West; on a farm or in a city. Our beliefs and actions mirror the conditioning influences of home and neighborhood, church and school, vocation and political party, friends and associates. We resemble others with similar inheritance and environment and are bound to them by ties of common experience. We tend to respond favorably to their opinions and propagandas because they are 'our kind of people.' We tend to distrust the opinions of those who differ from us in inheritance and environment.

AMERICANOS TODOS
★
LUCHAMOS POR LA
VICTORIA

★ AMERICANS ALL ★
LET'S FIGHT FOR VICTORY

Citizens of the United States have been encouraged to have different opinions of Mexico over the years. How is this poster from World War II, encouraging collaboration between the US and Mexico, similar to or different from US politicians' opinions about Mexico today? *Source:* Office for Emergency Management, Office of War Information.

Only drastic changes in our life conditions, with new and different experiences, associations, and influences, can offset or cancel out the effect of inheritance and long years of environment."

- **"EVALUATE, therefore, with the greatest care, your own propagandas."** The IPA recommended we dig into our own family histories to understand better why we were more likely to spread some information than others. "Do we believe and act as we do because our fathers were strong Republicans or lifelong Democrats, because our fathers were members of labor unions or were employers who fought labor unions; because we are Methodists, Seventh Day Adventists, Catholics, or Jews? This is very important."[5]

So, the First Rule of Anti-Propaganda Club is: *do* talk about where your own opinions, reactions, and trust come from. (This is not the movie *Fight Club*, where the first and second rules were both "You do not talk about Fight Club.") To understand your opinions, start by exploring *why* you trust or are upset by particular information. Being mindful of your existing opinions will make you aware *when* you are reacting to people and media around you, too. And it will help you keep yourself from trusting and spreading propaganda that seems to agree with your opinion, but may be created by malicious people in the media or online.

Like our own opinions, our families' and ancestors' opinions were also shaped by their trust in the people and institutions around them. This included media and technology. For one generation back, this may have meant the early internet. For a few more generations back, that meant mostly television and radio. Further generations back just had newspapers, magazines, and books. How did those media shape *their* opinions?

To get some clarity on what you and your family have come to trust, and how it shaped your opinions, we're going to work on drawing a family tree in the next few chapters. This basic mindfulness work will help you understand the emotional reactions you have that might make you fall for propaganda and other disinformation.

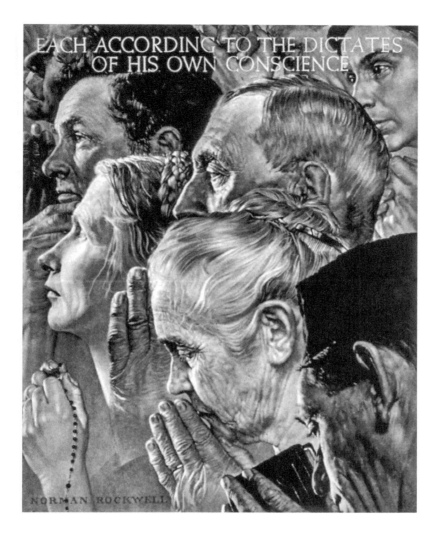

One of "four freedoms" identified by President Franklin D. Roosevelt in his 1941 State of the Union Address was Freedom of Worship—which he identified as a universal human right. The Institute for Propaganda Analysis urged us all to consider how our families' faiths shaped our opinions. *Source:* illustration by Norman Rockwell

Worksheet: Your Opinion's Family Tree

Scout Law: "If I work to understand where my own opinion comes from, I will be better prepared to protect myself from people who want to manipulate me."

Pick one thing out of your social media or digital life today that you agree with or disagree with. This could be a video, comment from a friend, news article, an image with some text, or a meme. Just find something you agree or disagree with—preferably something about politics, morals, or another controversial topic—rather than something you don't feel particularly strongly about. We're going to work with this piece of digital content for the next few chapters (though you can choose a new piece of content at some point if you feel it's a good idea).

First step: consider what this item is about. More than likely, if it's an issue people are passionate about, it will touch on a number of related topics. For example, let's say your family member has posted about an anti-abortion politician who is calling his opponents "baby killers" because they support a woman's right to obtain an abortion. Think of all the messages your family member could be trying to send with this one comment. They could be talking about their own religious beliefs, or their attitudes about women's health and their control over their bodies. They could be talking about the politician's support (or lack of support) for health care or education for these children after they are born. Or they could be talking about whether politicians have a responsibility to serve as role models and refrain from name-calling. That's a lot to fit into one message!

So think about the message you chose. Is it about

- money, work, and business issues,
- health and people's bodies,
- race and culture,
- gender roles,
- children—having them, raising them, teaching them,
- the natural world,
- political participation,
- government and the law,
- faith and spirituality, or
- learning, media, evidence, or truth?

Make a note of the issues involved—there may be more than one.

I'm going to guide you as you draw the "family tree" of your opinion on this subject. This will begin to shed light on the trust you've developed in people, religion, and other social institutions—and in your parents, grandparents, and other key people in your life. It will dig into your trust of books, newspapers, TV news, social media, and other ways information has come to you over time.

And I do mean "draw" literally! Start with a sheet of paper (a large one if you have it)—or, if you prefer, pop open a drawing program on a computer where you've got a nice big screen to work with. Just make sure you have space. This family tree is going to be a little more detailed than the one you might have drawn for an exercise in elementary school: you're going to include details about your family's work, religious institutions, schools, and other background that's not always included in family trees.

Draw a big box in the center for a trunk. Write a summary of the item you agree or disagree with here. (For my earlier example, you'd write, "Politician claims opponents are baby killers.") Under that (still in the trunk), write down what the item was about, including all the topics it touches on (in this case, children, religious beliefs, bodies and health, and politicians' responsibility for making claims).

In the lower third of the page, add roots. These will be your family.

In the top third of the page, you're going to draw branches. We'll come back to these in a minute.

You may want to write the names and information that apply to the roots and the branches on small sticky notes instead of directly on the page. This will make it easier if there's a lot of information to add, and to swap out certain information in upcoming exercises.

For the roots of your tree, add in messages you heard from your parents, grandparents, and siblings about these specific issues. If you like, include aunts, uncles, cousins, family friends, neighbors, or others who had an impact on how you think about this particular issue. Near the relevant people on the tree you're drawing, add your thoughts about the following:

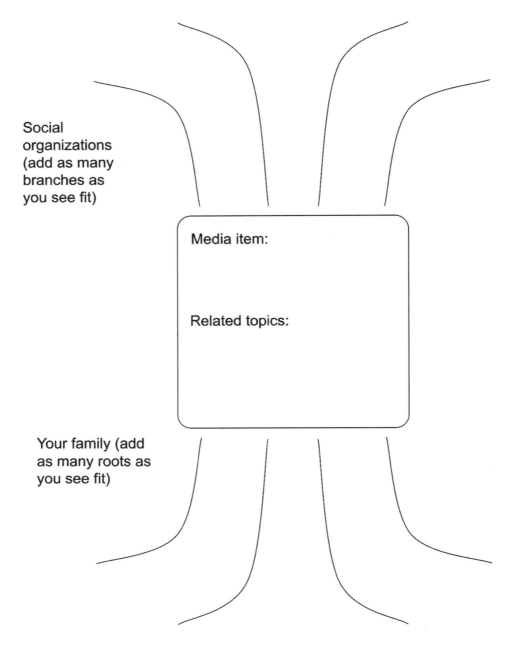

Social
organizations
(add as many
branches as
you see fit)

Media item:

Related topics:

Your family (add
as many roots as
you see fit)

Source: The author

- What messages about who to trust or how to feel about this issue did you get from people around you?

- Think of influences that were positive and negative. Whether you decided to agree with and work with those messages, or rejected them, the messages had an impact on your opinions and your trust.

- You don't have to list absolutely everyone in your family. If it feels to you like the person had an impact on how you think about this issue, include them in the tree. In some parts of my family, I think it's valuable to go a couple of generations back; in others, it doesn't seem necessary.

Now, for the branches of your tree, add in social organizations you directly interacted with, and which may have shaped your opinions on this subject: schools, religious institutions, government agencies, labor or social groups, companies and other places you worked for, and so on.

- Again, you don't need to list every single institution you ever interacted with, but think about ones that impacted your opinion on these issues.

- What messages about who to trust or how to feel about this issue did you get from these institutions?

Go back and take a pass at your roots again, and make notes next to your family members:

- What institutions or people did your family members interact with that had an influence on their trust and opinions on this subject? Again, it's much more likely they developed positive or negative reactions to things they experienced. People don't usually come up with completely new ideas and opinions out of the blue. (Even if you have one relative with a completely wackadoo theory or lifestyle, I bet you can figure out who or what in their family, school, or town they were reacting to if you dig a little bit.)

Related to those institutions, add:

- jobs your relatives have held in them (including details about leadership positions or union membership, if they seem important);
- political membership and/or organizing experience.

Have you considered how the following factors in your family might have affected your opinion? They may also have had an impact on how you feel about this issue. Add notes to your roots about your family's experience with the following, if you feel they might be related:

- disabled family members
- deaths
- domestic violence
- divorces
- interracial marriages
- gay relatives
- adoptions
- interactions with the law or social services
- relatives who lived very far away or nearby
- moves to other countries or states
- membership in a particular social class, if you feel like you can describe it

Now, as a final step, make one last note at the bottom of the page:

Did you agree or disagree with the original item you wrote down in the trunk?

Now that you've got a picture of why you trusted that a particular claim made in the media was true or false, we're going to go into what's missing: the things and people who aren't in your opinion's family tree.

11

Bias? We've All Got It

As I said in an earlier chapter, we trust the people who have become familiar to us because we have seen and heard them repeatedly. We don't trust the opinions of people who are unfamiliar as quickly; we may react with surprise, disgust, or distrust. (Again, think of your brain as a startled cat leaping straight into the air when it finds a cucumber on the floor.) When we see conflicting information, we often identify one side or the other as *biased*. It has become chic for news outlets to talk about how they go out of their way to avoid bias, using slogans like "fair and balanced" or "question more."

Unfortunately, there is no way for information produced by human beings to not be shaped by their perspectives. As humans, we each have one set of eyes and ears, a brain that remembers things in incomplete ways, and a personal history that means we have been in one particular path of places, and not in others.

What can cause bias? As the Institute for Propaganda Analysis (IPA) said, our opinions on the world around us are shaped by our "inheritance and environment." And, as the American Library Association (ALA) information guidelines point out, information may be *valued differently* by different people for *different purposes*, and different people may therefore create *conflicting information*.

That gives us a few places where we can start looking for biases:

- our own perspectives,
- our communities,
- who does and does not show up in the information we are sending out or receiving,
- and what purpose the person creating the information might have.

Let's start with our own imperfect perspectives.

Perspective at Its Simplest

Here are a couple of stories that illustrate exactly how perspective can warp what people believe about the world around them—without even bringing in questions of their family history or political biases.

A professor at my college told a story that highlighted how just standing in one place and not somewhere else can radically change what people understand about a story. This professor was a young journalist in an era (before 1973) when hijackings of flights to get to Cuba were a pretty common occurrence. News outlets reported that one hijacker was a Cuban revolutionary. But my professor knew better.

By random chance, he had run into this hijacker in an airport some weeks earlier. The kid wasn't a revolutionary. He was an American citizen, just some college student, and possibly mentally ill. Other reporters assigned to cover the hijacker had based their stories on the many other cases where hijackers had expressed allegiance to Cuba—perhaps without researching as thoroughly as they could have—and hadn't had the totally accidental experience of talking to this same guy that my professor met at an airport.

In addition to our perspective being limited by our inability to be multiple places at once, our own memories, even group memories, are fallible. In the European Journalism Centre's *Verification Handbook*, the journalist Steve Buttry encourages journalists to reflect on how their memories affect the stories they tell. He recalls reporting on a high school basketball team's championship that had happened twenty-five years before. He interviewed all twelve members of the team and the opposing coach, all of whom remembered that a five-foot-tall player on their team had repeatedly fouled a taller member of the opposing team, flustering her and tipping the game in their favor.

It wasn't until Buttry reviewed a video of the game that he was able to see how the memory had become exaggerated in the minds of the players. The five-foot player had only fouled the bigger girl once. But everyone's excitement over the win, and the retelling the story over time, had colored their memories of what had actually happened.[1]

So that's how we can get it wrong in our own heads. But our sense of trust can also be biased based on who we are and aren't familiar with. And this can be influenced by those we know in person as well as those we see in both social media and broadcast media.

Worksheet: Who's Missing from Your Family Tree?

Scout Law: "If I work to understand where my own opinion comes from, I will be better prepared to protect myself from people who want to manipulate me."

Next, it's time to think about what might be missing from our communities, and how that might lead to bias in our opinions.

Go back to the family tree you drew for the exercise in chapter 10. This time, let's think about who *isn't* there in your family tree. Start a new tree, on a separate piece of paper. In the new trunk, write in the same item from the media you used in the previous exercise. (Or, if you like, swap both "trunks" to add a new media item you've seen today.)

For each person and institution you included on your original tree, consider if there were other people in your life who

- were members of other faiths or political parties,
- came from other countries,
- were members of other ethnicities or social classes,
- were of different genders or sexual orientations,
- had different experiences with health, the law, or education from yours, or
- for whatever reason, trusted a different opinion?

Put them in the roots of the new tree if those people were family, or the branches if they were at your job, school, religious institution, or other social group.

Compare the two trees. Are there more or fewer branches and roots on the second one? How have the roots and branches on the second tree influenced your opinion—a lot, some, not at all?

Now, on your original family tree:

Change one thing.

Change one important thing about one of those people or organizations you trusted, who shaped your opinion. Let's say you had worshipped in a different way, went to a different school, had parents who worked different jobs, had a family of a different race, or family members who were disabled, or maybe didn't have certain family members. Play it out in your imagination.

For example, on the issue of a politician accusing others of killing babies, how might your opinion have been different

- if you or members of your family had held different religious beliefs, or none at all?

- if you had known (or hadn't known) someone in your family who'd had an abortion, or had died as a result of surgery or pregnancy?

- if you or one of your family members had run for office, or instead, had always expressed a mistrust of government?

Write down, or talk out with a friend, how you think your opinion might have been different in one of those scenarios.

One caveat: When you are thinking about how your life might have been different if someone around you had held an opinion or faith you strongly disagree with, try not to go to extremes. Try not to end by saying "and then I'd be an awful person," or "I'd hate my life," or something like that. The point of this exercise is to think through the reasons for other people's very different opinions. Who might you love? Why would you feel anger about issues that are different from the ones that currently anger you? If you don't know, acknowledge that. This may be time to expand your own perspective by listening to some new people to understand how they think.

Our Families, Our Filter Bubbles

In the digital revolution, we don't just take in the opinions of our families, friends, and community members in person. Their perspectives also show up in our social media, right alongside those of celebrities, news reporters, and other total strangers. All of these perspectives shape our view of the world around us—remember the "mean world syndrome" or "cultivation" of our perspectives that I talked about in chapter 2?

Not all perspectives show up equally in our feeds and on our TVs. Who we know biases us, but social (and other) media may make our bias worse by selectively showing us some opinions and not others. The author and online organizer Eli Pariser coined a phrase for this: *filter bubbles.*

In his book *The Filter Bubble: How the New Personalized Web Is Changing What We Read and How We Think*, Pariser recalls the day he realized that conservative people he knew disappeared from his Facebook feed. Was this liberal media censorship? Hardly. Because on conservatives' feeds, liberal posts disappeared at the same time. Dog-hating cat owners got more posts about cats and fewer about dogs. North Carolina–style barbecue fans suddenly didn't have Kansas City barbecue purists up in their grill about the correct ingredients for barbecue sauce; each side of the West African jollof rice wars suddenly found itself in a Facebook feed where everyone was vigorously agreeing with each other.

OK, I'm stretching this example; I'm not sure about barbecue and jollof rice. But in short: Facebook was giving its users the same things they had been "liking," clicking on, and posting. Most social media, search engines, video and music services, and other sites and apps that serve up a lot of content do this.

It was not always the case that social media made changes to the order and content of what we see. In the early days of social media, you would mostly see what your friends and favorites had posted, in the order it was posted. As people flocked to social media, it became like drinking from the firehose: less about quenching your thirst, and more about getting knocked over and disoriented by the sheer volume of it all.[2] If you wanted to read everything, it was going to take a looooong time, and meanwhile, your FOMO was likely to be sending your stress levels through the roof. You were likely to miss something in all of the noise.

So sites and apps began picking and choosing which posts they showed you, and in which order. They based these decisions on algorithmic "recipes" (I'll talk more about those in chapter 18). Sites that use algorithms may move certain posts higher on your feed if you have clicked, liked, or commented on other posts with the same words. They may also move posts higher on your page if *other* people have interacted with them. Or if you or others hide posts, they will move those posts further down everyone's feeds.[3] They may also make changes based on other factors, like where you live (if they know it) or what device you're using.

Cats, dogs, and food preferences—not the end of the world. But when it comes to politics and other social issues, seeing exactly what you want and nothing else creates a "filter bubble." As Pariser said, "This moves us very quickly toward a world in which the Internet is showing us what it thinks we want to see, but not necessarily what we need to see."[4]

The problem with filter bubbles is that we don't have conversations with our neighbors who believe things that are the polar opposite to what we believe. As a result, we end up with no common ground to agree on, and no language for talking about changes that would help our communities. And we don't even get a say in changing the algorithms for a better balance of information.

Today's version of this World War II poster might read, "Conserve your attention. Don't give control of your information firehose to those who want to manipulate you through your biases." *Source:* Kerkam, Work Projects Administration Poster Collection—Library of Congress

"How do I get out of my filter bubble?"

How to Keep Calm and Carry On

Some folks are working to ensure that we can see different sides of an issue. Here are some strategies they use:

- **Meet people and talk to them in person.** Research shows that we build empathy and can see others' perspectives better when we have conversations with them face-to-face.

- **Listen, don't debate.** Instead of getting ready to counter what someone is saying to you, prepare yourself to put what they just said in your own words. Ask questions if you don't understand something. If you're talking in person, what does their body language tell you?

- **Seek out additional perspectives.** Comparing coverage of an issue from different kinds of people is important to getting around your biases. Simple choices in how you use social media can be profound. Famously, Anil Dash decided he would only retweet Twitter posts by women for a year. The result? He says his feed was less full of "inane" or "horrible" stuff. He also saw people around him bringing up more changes they could make to solve societal problems.[5]

- **Check out news from sites in other countries.** Their governments, corporations, news organizations, and readers may have very different interests than your own, and the focus of the stories you may see may turn up perspectives you hadn't thought about.

See **keepcalmlogon.com** for links to groups doing this kind of work, and for tools that can help you burst your bubble.

The People You Don't Know *and* Don't See

Even before the beginning of social media, there were signs that our opinions and trust could be limited by who and what we see in books or TV, radio or magazines. Who shows up and who doesn't can shape what we think about the world and what we trust.

George Gerbner—the guy I mentioned in chapter 2 who came up with the term "mean world syndrome"—believed that our views of the world and who to trust are also *cultivated* in part by media we consume. He was writing before the dawn of social media, so he was specifically talking about "mass" media like TV, films, and traditional newspapers and news broadcasts.

Just as we may become convinced the world is dangerous the more we consume violent media, Gerbner found that we also come to understand other people through the media—particularly when it comes to people we don't know well.

This understanding can be shaped by how media are produced. In the news, in particular, not having commentators, reporters, or eyewitnesses from different walks of life can be problematic. For example, without reporters on staff who are from Africa, news coverage about that continent is often limited to poverty and the "exoticness" of African cultures. Without reporters from working-class backgrounds, coverage may skew against unions or socialism, and in favor of corporations. These biases can limit what's included in the news, and how the news outlet presents it—which in turn limits what we learn about our world.

This also happens in entertainment media, not just news. For example: Do you watch medical dramas or police shows? Think for a second: How many doctors do you know in real life? How many cops? Studies have found that people who watched a lot of medical dramas tended to view doctors as courageous, even if their daily jobs are as routine and boring as most of ours are.[6] (My favorite fan edit of *Law and Order* tried to make the show as realistic as possible—by showing cops doing paperwork at their desks and looking tired of it.) Our views of these jobs are shaped by what we see in the media.

The same goes for other situations. When she visited colleges for the first time, my best friend was surprised to find people having a chill evening playing pool and talking about books. Nobody was drinking or partying hard! She was the first one in her family to go to college, and all she knew about it was what she'd seen on TV.

How about celebrities on Instagram? Or do you watch reality shows—about unusual people, romance and dating, jobs you'd never have, or other people's hobbies? Do you know people like that—or do those shows introduce you to people and places you've never met or seen?

Keep in mind that "reality" TV is so heavily edited and staged that *you may not even be hearing what people actually said*—thanks to the "frankenbite" sound bite phenomenon, where TV editors stitch together monster sentences. And you're certainly not seeing these people's lives as they would be without a camera in the room. This isn't just the case in roommate-drama staples like *Big Brother*—even the most routine show about fashion or home renovation may be heavily edited. And online celebrities often tightly control what images of them appear in their public stream.

Don't believe that these edits, cuts, recreations, and stage-managing influence you? How about this. Do you find yourself relying on characters from shows to explain things in your own life: saying "he's a total Sheldon," or debating over which house in *Game of Thrones* or *Harry Potter* you and your friends "belong to"? Those are some of the clearest examples of how we use TV and movies as patterns to help us understand how people act. We do it for real people as well as fictional characters. It's worth being mindful when you find yourself using media as a model: catch yourself in the act, and think, do I really know these people are like this?

You May Be Saying . . .

"I don't **think** the media I consume have shaped my take on the world ... "

How to Keep Calm and Carry On

Well, let's take a look. Start by listing some of your favorite shows, games, and accounts you follow on social media, using the following worksheet.

Exercise: Who Is Represented? How?

Scout Law: "If I understand how news, books, and other media are made, I will be better able to identify bias."

For this exercise, we're going to count people who show up in the media we consume, to get a sense of how they might be shaping our opinions of different people and groups. Keep something to write with handy while you watch TV, play games, and surf the internet. For every person you see, jot down the following details to fill out the appropriate columns in the worksheet:

- What are their ages (roughly—"teenager" or "senior" would be fine)?
- What gender are they?
- What race are they?
- If it's mentioned, what is the job or social class, religion, first language, and/or political leaning of each person?

For each person, ask yourself:

- Are they shown behaving and talking in a way that you usually expect to see people of that age, gender, race, or social background behaving and talking?
- Or are people like them being shown in a new light?
- Take note of any instance in which people are being shown in a way that would make someone say "Those people are always like that." It's likely to be a stereotype.

Tally up the counts for age groups, gender, race, and aspects of social background:

- Which kinds of people got the highest counts—and which kind of person did you see the most?
- Then look at where there is a low or no count. Who did not show up in the media you consumed today?
- What might you be missing if you don't hear from the kinds of people who did not show up?

"Who Is Represented?" Worksheet

What I watch/read/view	Who I see	What are they like?	Who do I know like this in real life?	What's missing?

What Is the Solution?

Finally, here's one last strategy for undoing our biases.

The IPA and most media literacy organizations recommend that once we've identified that we trust a piece of information, we should slow down and be mindful of the *solution* to a problem that information is suggesting. (Mind you, this is for information that *agrees with us* as well as information that doesn't.)

Now, not every piece of media will contain a problem or a solution. In the case of cat videos and other simple, entertaining media, the problem and solution are often delightfully contained in one snippet: I am bored/frustrated/depressed; there are not enough cats in my life; hey look, a large round cat jumping into a tiny box! Problem solved.

But some entertainment thrives on problems (storylines get pretty boring if they don't!). Plot lines, as well as the dialogue and interaction between characters, shape the way problems get solved. Beset by problems? Martial arts films suggest we punch our way out. Single and lonely? *The Bachelor* and similar reality shows walk us through what eligible single people consider when they choose a mate—and viewers may end up referring to those ideas as they think about their own relationships. Finding solutions in entertainment media doesn't end with reality TV, either—who hasn't made a parallel with some screen romance or buddy comedy to think through their love life or their friendships? (When I was a teen, most of us knew which character in *The Breakfast Club* we were.)

In the news, solutions to problems can take the shape of policies that governments vote on, or they could take the shape of politicians' slogans—like "build that wall" or "no new taxes." In social media, solutions can sometimes seem more direct. Someone in your community has cancer? Donate to their crowdfunding page. Changes coming in a government policy? Share this post with everyone you know, and encourage them to sign this petition.

We go along with suggested solutions because they agree with our opinions, and because we want to help our communities. But just going along with people we usually trust, or sharing things that "just feel right" can be a serious problem: people (or governments or institutions) may be trying to manipulate us for purposes that don't actually align with our goals or values. It's worth digging deeper into a solution, figuring out what it would really accomplish.

If a solution to a problem is suggested in the media you are looking at, let's look into it a little more to see whether it's backed up by evidence of how it will work, rather than just how people feel. This is a great way to pick apart the assumptions we may be making based on the family trees of our opinions.

Exercise: What Is the Solution?

Scout Law: "If I understand how news, books, and other media are made, I will be better able to identify bias."

In this exercise, you'll take a simple solution suggested in an item from media you're looking at—social media, TV, newspaper, whatever—and try to understand what it would really accomplish, why, and how. This could be a political solution (raising the minimum wage, building a border wall) or an interpersonal solution (telling off the boss, breaking up with a lover, getting in a fistfight).

In the middle of a blank piece of paper, write out the simple solution suggested by the item you've chosen.

We're going to look into the "whys" of this solution. We're going to ask "why" about this five times—just like some toddlers you might know. But this technique is actually a business-planning tool, originally created by Sakichi Toyoda, the Japanese inventor whose son went on to found the Toyota auto company. When business people want to determine the steps to take as they attempt to solve a problem, they sometimes run through a "Five Whys" exercise to get at the root of why they think taking a particular direction is a good idea.[7]

Draw a stack of five short arrows pointing upward, from the solution to the top of the page. Then ask yourself "why?" about the solution. For example: Why would someone want to build a wall between their country and another country? In the United States, Donald Trump suggested a wall would keep immigrants out of the country.

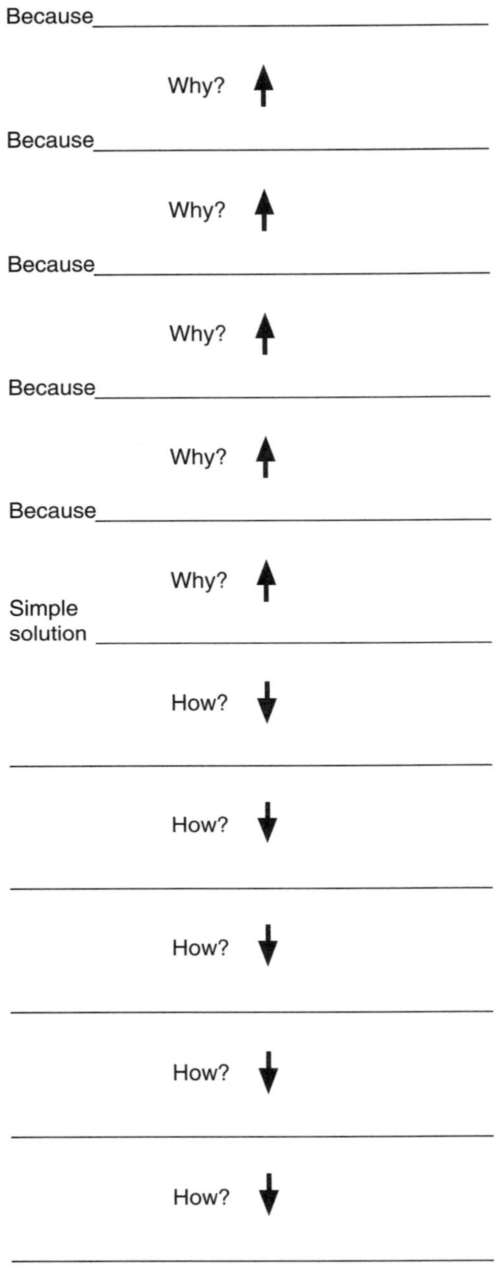

Because_____

Why? ↑

Because_____

Why? ↑

Because_____

Why? ↑

Because_____

Why? ↑

Because_____

Why? ↑

Simple
solution _____

How? ↓

_____

How? ↓

_____

How? ↓

_____

How? ↓

_____

How? ↓

_____

The "Five Whys" exercise, originally developed by Sakichi Toyoda.

Then ask "why" about the reason you just came up with. For example, why would people want to keep immigrants out of their country? Or ask, why did immigrants want to come to the country to begin with? For each answer you come up with, write it above the next arrow up. Then ask "why?" about that answer, and write it above the next arrow. After a few whys, compare it back to the solution. Does the solution really fix the deeper "whys"?

Now it's time to look into the "hows." Draw another five arrows stacked downward from the simple solution. For the "hows," start writing out what would need to happen for the solution to be put in motion. Would laws need to change? Would money need to be raised? How would that happen? Does it seem possible?

Compare the hows with the whys. Are there any conflicts? For example, if "smaller government" or "taxes are too high" is one of your whys, does the cost of funding the project conflict with that?

Reflect: Is the solution as simple as it seemed? Is it really possible? Would it really fix the issues it says it will?

You May Be Asking ...

"What do I do when I find information that makes me uncomfortable? That feels like it's going to make my brain explode?"

How to Keep Calm and Carry On

We've explored how we all hold our own opinions, and how they may be based on our family histories, their attitudes, and our responses to them. But what happens when we run into something that contradicts our opinions?

Specifically, what happens when we run into something that challenges our sense of *who we are*, which authorities we trust, or who belongs in our communities? We all encounter new information daily that conflicts with our beliefs or opinions, and either ignore it or incorporate it into our sense of the world. Human beings have a tendency to see things that agree with our already-held beliefs, and ignore things that disagree with them. This is called *confirmation bias.*

When we run into something that doesn't fit our beliefs, we may experience what is called *cognitive dissonance* ("cognitive" meaning "thinking" and "dissonance" meaning "like two notes in a song that just sound *bad* together"). This is an especially important feeling or thought to observe while you are attending to what is going through your head.

Signs you may be experiencing cognitive dissonance:

- When you are mindful about your thoughts, you would describe your feelings as "torn" or "conflicted."
- You notice yourself feeling two ways at once.
- You catch yourself thinking or feeling something that you think would get you punished, would attract unwanted attention, or would get you kicked out of your community.
- You think of people you believe in as being "good," but you observe them doing something "bad"—or vice versa (for example, if your religious leader preaches love but speaks hatefully about a group of people). This can even apply to yourself.
- You feel like you have no idea where the ideas you're hearing could take you, or what they could do to your feelings about your community, and that is frightening (for example, learning that your government inflicted violence or death on a large group of people).
- You find yourself coming up with explanations to make this conflict go away, or quickly denying what you're seeing.

Cognitive dissonance can be a useful feeling. It's a sign that your brain has noticed there's something different, something off, something that doesn't match.

Many religious people have been taught that doubting is a path to damnation, sin, or expulsion from their community. They may worry when they feel cognitive dissonance. But not all religious leaders believe this. The pastor at my friend Adriane's church tells his flock, "God is not afraid of your doubt." Other sects of Christianity, Judaism, and Islam see doubt as healthy, as it leads people to not assume they know God's will, but rather ask more questions in search of truth.

You May Be Saying . . .

"So you're saying I can't trust anything, ever? Everything is biased!"

How to Keep Calm and Carry On

Scout Law: "If I work to understand where my own opinion comes from, I will be better prepared to protect myself from people who want to manipulate me."

I'm not saying we should decide to tune out all media or information. Saying "all information is biased!" also leaves us vulnerable to falling for anything that *claims* to be fair and balanced, or claims to be "local" or seen by "eyewitnesses" who we know personally, when it actually isn't. It might also drive us to seek alternative sources of information that agree with our *own* biases, but which come from sources that aren't trustworthy.

What I'm saying is that we need to be able to *identify* our own biases, and those of the information we take in. That awareness helps us weigh different sources of information for our purposes, like deciding what to buy, who to vote for, or how to act in our communities.

It's important to get a sense of *why* and *how* information may be influenced by the purpose and point of view of the people who create or manage it, or by the companies or algorithms that might be shaping the bias behind it. Armed with tools for spotting what information producers *believe*, and what they want us to *do* based on what they show us, we are better equipped to take in the information surrounding us, no matter where it comes from.

This chapter has been devoted to sources of bias that are personal or that come from our communities and environments. But there's another major source of bias I haven't accounted for here, and that's at the level of what media companies do: profit. That's what I'll talk about in chapter 19.

Systems of Trust

In this chapter I hope you've come to understand the reasons for your own trust, and your own opinion, a little bit better. You may have a better grasp on your gut reactions, how your family's history of trust may shape your reaction to information you encounter, and how it may bias you.

I mentioned earlier that the complexity of modern life means we can't just rely on our trust of individual people who we know well. We often have to take a leap of faith and trust people because they are representatives of a system—whether that is a systemic way of confirming who you are, of producing information, or of participating in a particular kind of work, like medicine or law. What do I mean by "trusting a system"? Is this like that one friend many of us have who dismissively says, "It's the system, maaaaaaan, you can't trust the *system*," when they're frustrated with how something is going? Is there just one system? What is it?

In the next few chapters I'll be breaking down what "trusting one person" may look like when we're hearing from that person through written or recorded information—and how that kind of trust connects to the trust you develop when you see someone face to face. In part IV I'll talk about systems we have trusted for centuries: from the basic signing of a document and the written word itself, to books and the professionals and other authorities who produce them, to journalism, broadcast media, and the internet.

12

In Writing We Trust? Seals, Signatures, and Testimonies

In chapter 9, "The Roots of Trust," I talked about how our trust begins when we are infants, as we get familiar with individual people around us. As we grow into our communities, we often learn to trust information from those around us because of what they have gone through: their *experience*, and their *testimonials* about that experience.

The Priority (and Perils) of Personal Experience

Our trust in people's testimonials may be based on their age ("respecting your elders"), or on experiences not everyone has had (being a parent, living through a disaster, or fighting in a war, for example). We often extend our trust of other people's firsthand experience to recorded versions of their experience, such as their posts on social media, audio interviews in which they tell their experience, or videos they make or appear in. With videos and audio recordings in particular, we can see and/or hear for ourselves the people who are involved, right? We call firsthand testimonials different names in different situations: "personal interviews" or "eyewitness" accounts in the news; "testimony" in law or religion; "oral histories" in history.

People have extended trust to others based on their testimonials for as long as humans have had language. Changes in communications technology have made our trust more and more complicated over the centuries, as it has become possible to record testimonials. Every time a new technology appears, we have to renegotiate what we trust about the accounts of firsthand experiences we receive through that technology. It happened when handwritten documents gave way to machine-printed pamphlets and books. It happened when audio recordings became available, and people's spoken testimonials could be spread via the airwaves. It happened with the invention of photography, film, and video. And now, with the internet bringing all these technologies together in one place, we are yet again rethinking how and why we trust recording technologies.

What does it look like when people have to negotiate these changes? Let me start by explaining what people had to figure out just to trust the system of *writing*—the written word itself! First I'll go to back 1066 AD, the year the Normans invaded England under William the Conqueror. As England's new king, William insisted that trustworthy documents demanded signatures and dates, and English scribes basically lost their minds about it.

Signed, Sealed, Delivered

Signing a document seems perfectly obvious, right? If you want an important document to be trusted, you sign it and put a date on it. That lets people know you are a witness to the truth of what's in the document— your signature represents your testimony.

But before the Normans invaded, English people didn't even *use* paper contracts. If there were disagreements over who owned land, they would fall back to the trust they had built over years of knowing people. They'd get together a bunch of the oldest people in town and ask them "what's your memory of who owns this land?" And everyone else agreed the old folks' testimonial was *authoritative*: the elders were the source of truth. (At the time there was no scientific research that showed the limits of human memory: no understanding of what we learned in the chapter about bias, that group memory can also be swayed by a powerful story.) Asking elders was the way many communities agreed on truth worldwide (and it may still be, in some places). Other deals were sealed with objects: a sword, a ring, a cup, a staff cut from a tree on the land, or even pieces of someone's hair. These symbolic objects helped people remember the details of the deal.

Michael Clanchy (the scholar who did most of the medieval research I'm talking about here) shares a story about a contract made at the time when people were still deciding what made one trustworthy. To seal this contract for a monastery in Sussex, scribes and officials did the following: made the gift of a Christian gospel book and laid it on an altar, put a wax seal on the document, and had a couple of lords draw the sign of the cross on the document near their names.

They added the crosses for three reasons. One, they probably didn't know how to sign their own names. Even signing your name was a specialized skill that only scribes learned. Two, the cross symbolized their signing on behalf of their god, an act that asked Christian readers to trust the document more. And three, the people around them might not have trusted what was written in the document *or* the wax seal, so they had to add just one more thing to really drive it home.[1] Clanchy describes other ceremonies that would have gone along with the signing of this contract, like the signers making the sign of the cross on their chests, and pronouncements being made—behaviors that observers at the time could see in person, which would inspire their trust.

People might also write "in this year on this date in such and such a king's reign, I wrote this, and this right here is my signature" on a contract *in addition to writing their signature.* Signatures were not so common that everybody just accepted them as the evidence of truth.

The Bayeux Tapestry depicts William conquering the English. This section shows King Harold swearing his loyalty to William. Note that Harold is making it official by touching two holy relics. *Source:* Photo courtesy of Wikipedia editor Myrabella

And forget about dates. At the time, people didn't agree much on the right way to write a date. When did a new year start? (The Gregorian, Chinese, and Hebrew calendars still don't agree on this.) Should you write down what saint's day it is? Should you relate the date to a recent event, like the crowning of a king? Was it maybe even *blasphemous* to compare worldly business to important dates like the birth of Christ or the Resurrection, which they believed would happen in their lifetimes?

Tellingly, the scribe writing up the contract in Sussex included some excuses about *why the contract was even in writing at all*: "Because, it is appropriate that this should be brought to reach the notice of many ... lest in the process of time it be destroyed by ruinous oblivion."[2] Otherwise, presumably, putting the book on the altar, crossing yourself, and speaking the right words was enough to make it legal and trustworthy. It sounds as if he was thinking ahead to a time when all the trusted elders present and crossing themselves would be dead.

And he was right. More than 865 years later, what he wrote was still not destroyed by ruinous oblivion: Clanchy has passed it on and I am now passing it on to you. Congratulations, you've got the wording from a deed (dated 1153) to a salt pan—basically a salty hole in the ground. That's the power of written information. (The hole is probably long gone, or at least no longer salty.)

The scribe was pointing out an advantage of writing that other people around him maybe couldn't see: writing was as close to "going viral" as a document could be in that era. It would reach many more people than would see the ceremony. And yet human beings have always had a hard time trusting written information because of that same power: writing goes places that we do not. Because they can leave the people who wrote them, written words don't build trust in the same ways we naturally grow to trust others—by seeing their actions, and coming to expect that they will continue to act the same way.

The Normans' insistence that authoritative documents must have signatures and dates had scribes throwing everything but the kitchen sink at a document to make it "official." You can imagine them shaking their heads in confusion. How was everyone supposed to trust some letters on a piece of paper, rather than elders' memory or a sword? Most people didn't even know how to read or write!

Why Trust Writing?

Writing has been around since the sixth millennium BC—for more than seven thousand years—though different communities started writing at different times. For thousands of years, no machinery existed to produce writing—no computers, no copy machines, and no printing press. Writing was done by hand, and that meant a radically different experience of written information. There just wasn't that much written material *around* (and sound and video recording weren't invented until the 1900s!). Only very small groups of people in power, and their scribes (the people who did what their job title said: they *transcribed*) had the ability to read and write. The idea that every child should be taught to read and write wouldn't come around for hundreds of years.

Imagine living in a time when you trusted the memory of your elders, not writing, as the most authoritative source of truth. (For some of us, this may even have been the case in recent generations.) Now imagine that someone comes up to you during that time and says "I own this land—look, it says right here, on this piece of paper. See the signatures?"

That person's claim would seem laughable. Where are the trustworthy elders saying "Yep, that's been his land as long as I've been alive"? What's this flimsy-looking "paper" thing that looks like a leaf? What's that scrawl at the bottom? What even are letters?!

Believe it or not, books, legal documents, letters, and other written texts have long caused the same kind of panic you may hear about new media. (You know the panics I'm talking about—the ones where people fear change and freak out about a new technology, asking *Do video games damage children's brains? Will comic books open the door to the devil? Will the internet destroy society?!*)

Everywhere writing has spread, it has usually upset someone with the radical changes to society it makes possible by holding on to ideas for a long time, traveling great distances, and demanding new kinds of trust. Even the introduction of the alphabet made people uncomfortable with how it would radically change their world.

Source: Work Projects Administration Poster
Collection—Library of Congress

Here's an example from Socrates, again, in ancient Greece. He suggested that *writing itself* would corrupt the minds of youth.[3] How? He believed young people wouldn't need to use their own memories anymore. Socrates called writing "deceitful" because unlike people (unlike those elders remembering who owned the land), it couldn't respond to questions. And when Socrates was talking about this, he was citing even an older authority: Egyptian mythology. He wasn't the first to be concerned with the trustworthiness of writing.

Books, as we know them today, also disrupted people's lives and livelihoods in an earlier technology revolution: the one caused by the printing press. Books as we know them are a little less than six hundred years old. The invention of the printing press made it possible to mass-produce writing with machines. That meant many, many more people could get access to books, newspapers, and other written documents—and more people could make them. As you may remember from history class, the printing press went hand-in-hand with the Protestant Reformation—a major revolution in the Christian church, changing the systems of power and trust in different interpretations of the Bible. Christians alive then struggled to decide which interpretation they trusted, and which church they would attend.

Does This Touch on Your Family Tree?

Scout Law: "If I understand how communities decide what information to trust, I will be better prepared to identify bad information."

Let's go back to the family tree exercise we started earlier.

Take a look at the people you put on that tree. What messages did they communicate to you specifically about writing and reading? Did they keep books around, or did they scoff at reading?

What messages did their roles in the world communicate to you? If people in your family are teachers, professors, lawyers, or work in government jobs, you may have higher trust of books and the written word, because those are the bread and butter of that kind of work. If your family were immigrants, they may have stressed how important it was to do well in school.

Or did people in your family have land, jobs, their homes, or their freedom taken away from them by way of documents they were not allowed (or able) to read or sign? Were their families too poor to afford education, needing their children to work on the family farm or business? Were your ancestors forbidden to learn to read by their households or governments, because they were black, native, or female, or did they speak a language that was not the dominant language in your country? If you go back into family documents, did anyone sign their name with an X?

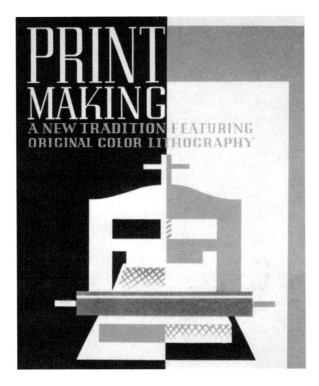

Like handwriting, mechanical printing spread through the world unevenly. *Source:* Work Projects Administration Poster Collection—Library of Congress

Can you trace these patterns forward? How did this shape your views of learning to read and write? Of how trustworthy books, newspapers, and other documents were?

Again, **change one thing** about reading and writing in your family tree. How might that have shaped your trust or mistrust of writing?

Rethinking Testimony

Today, we accept signatures as important to our trust in documents, and in the systems they're a part of. They uniquely identify the person agreeing to the document. They're a way to hold *someone* accountable for the truth of a document: if the signature is forged, or someone signs a bad contract, they can go to jail.

But imagine: today, we're essentially in the same kind of historical moment of decision as William the Conqueror's scribes.

If you've been paying attention over the past couple of decades, you may have noticed that how we accept signatures, as a society, has changed a lot:

- Will your doctor or bank accept your signature by email? By fax? Only by postal mail? Why?

- What kind of digital format would be acceptable for your signature? Just the scribble of your name on a trackpad?

- Or does it need some sort of code to go with that? What more is needed to trust that *you* actually signed it?

Then there's the issue of *deepfakes*—forged videos that make it look like someone is saying something they didn't say. One of the most famous is the video produced by comedian Jordan Peele, where his face and voice were digitally manipulated so it looked like Barack Obama was actually saying what Peele said. The video was a warning about the rise of the technology that makes deepfakes possible.

Many of us are inclined to trust videos—sometimes more than writing!—because as children we learned to trust personal testimony. In a deepfake, it may look like a person is vouching for the truth. But videos have never been a perfect copy of reality, even before deepfakes. Take a clip that spread on social media in 2019, where video of United States House Speaker Nancy Pelosi was slowed down to make her look drunk. Editing, whether done by hand or done by the machine learning behind deepfakes, has always meant that videos are not perfect records of events or testimony.

Deepfake technology isn't yet widely available, but it could be, soon. Although we have tools to identify when a video has been slowed down, cut, darkened, or otherwise edited (as I talked about in chapter 3), we don't have as many tools to catch deepfakes in the act. For a review of the tools we do have, see **keepcalmlogon.com**. We will need to develop these in order to regain trust in video's ability to capture reality.

These kinds of rapid changes to our trust are what a revolution looks like, at ground level. Its details are as simple as what our communities decide to accept as "the right kind of signature" on a document. And the side effects are chaotic: identity theft, deepfakes, and fake news, while we struggle to decide what is authentic and while malicious people take advantage of what we haven't agreed on yet.

We need tools to know who's really saying what in our digital lives—and who may be trying to trick us with faked "testimonies" or other recorded experience. In the next chapter, I'll go back and explore how we translate personal testimony into writing, and how we come to trust that recorded testimony is true—because online, that works differently than it worked in print. I'll discuss the ways that programmers, investigators, and the law—as well as the machines we log into—know who's who: addresses and certificates. These machine-based ways of knowing identity are powerful tools that can help you prove who someone is online. I'll also talk more about logins as a form of signature, and how opportunities for anonymity change our understanding of who someone really is—and how we can keep from being suckered by fake identities and the garbage they post.

13

A Toolkit for Online Trust

For years, one of the websites that ranked highly in searches for Martin Luther King Jr., a respected leader of the civil rights movement in the United States in the 1960s, was martinlutherking.org. The site—which is still online—mixes facts and fictions about King; it makes some horrendous claims (that black rappers want to rape and kill white people, for instance) and wild speculations (that Jewish people are involved in a Communist plot to overthrow the United States). The site was built by Stormfront, an online forum that claims white people are superior to other races.

How is this possible, you ask? How could people who have a bias against King own a website with his name in the address, and use that site to spread lies about minorities?

Why Would Anyone Trust What's on the Web?

In the past twenty years or so, the media have been full of excitement about the internet's ability to let everyone tell their own truth. The promise of sites like WikiLeaks, for example, is the route they offer around gate-keepers like newspaper editors, who might say, "We need to maintain our relationship with Congressman So and So; we can't publish anything that makes him look bad." Protesters around the world have been able to post their own frustrations and demands online, letting everyone know, directly, the changes they want to see in governments and corporations.

But from the martinlutherking.org example, we can see the downsides to not having editors or fact checkers built into the internet.

Online, the old ways we built trust in the written word don't work to stop rumors and bad science from spreading. There are people who scam each other, circulate hoaxes, and post fake products on shopping sites. There are plenty of places online where someone can comment anonymously or by using a fake name. More frustratingly, it's easy to copy and paste things. Just a few clicks, and you can look like the original creator of something you actually copied from someone else.

Many people have started to feel you can't trust anything you read on the internet. Wikipedia and search results take a particularly hard hit, with teachers warning students not to trust either as sources of truth. But the internet isn't *always* untrustworthy, right? Surely there's some information on there that is good.

In this chapter, I'll go over tools that can help us identify who is putting information up on a website, what their biases might be, and whether we should trust them. These tools help us with the following Keep Calm Scout Laws: "If I understand how news, books, and other media are made, I will be better able to identify bias," and "If I understand how communities decide what information to trust, I will be better prepared to identify bad information."

Start with these questions:

- Who runs the site?
- What evidence do *computers* need to make sure that the people who own the site are who they say they are?
- Who is able to post on a site?
- What evidence do *we* need to make sure that the people posting on the site are who they say they are?
- Looking at an individual account, picture, or piece of writing, can we figure out whether someone has posted the same thing somewhere else?

I'll explain what we use (instead of swords, wax seals, and written signatures) as evidence that we can trust who said something online: addresses, logins, digital signatures, and certificates. I'll talk about the ability to log in anonymously, and its pros and cons, and I'll offer some tools for identifying fake accounts.

Black people in the United States have long found the need to gather, confirm, and publish information for themselves. *The Negro Motorist Green Book* (sometimes titled *The Travelers' Green Book*) was published from 1936 to 1966, by a New York City mailman, Victor Hugo Green. Black travelers needed this information they could trust to get them to friendly businesses, or to help them avoid "sundown towns" where laws said people of color had to leave town by sunset or face arrest. How do our judgments about trustworthy information come from our specific needs? *Source:* Melvin Tapley

Who Owns the Site?

To find something on the internet you need to have an *address*, also known as a URL (uniform resource locator). Addresses appear at the top of your browser window, and in links that connect you to another address. Some of the same addresses that take you to web pages also form the second part of an email address (like gmail.com).

Let's take a look at what the address in this picture is made up of. The browser has made the *domain name*—the part of the address that reads something dot something else—darker, because it's the most important part of the address. It tells you whether this is the site you think it is. The domain name is followed by *.com*, the *top-level* part of the domain. (This used to be just .com, .net, .org, .edu, or country codes, but has now expanded to include a larger range of suffixes, like .shop or .bike.) The part of the address that tells you who owns the site is *always the top-level part and the part immediately to its left*—"youtube," in this case. That matters a lot: youtube.shadyvideos.com would definitely not be a YouTube site; it doesn't matter that "youtube" is in the name!

You can read other things in this address, too, some of which can be useful to you. As I mentioned before, *https://* tells you you're protected against eavesdroppers on your internet connection (as opposed to http, which is not secure). *v=*, in this case, means "this video is" the code that comes right after it. *t=* means "start playing this video at time" 137 seconds. You could change the number after *t=* to change when the video starts playing, or the *v=* number to watch a different video on YouTube.

Source: https://www.youtube.com/
watch?v=JvfOn6vUfTQ&t=137

Notice that nothing after *.com/* tells you who controls the content (which in this case happens to be a video from my series, *The Media Show*). YouTube has the ultimate say in whether videos stay up or go down here, because they own youtube.com.

Even though addresses are powerful tools, most of us ignore them by now. We may not even be aware that behind the scenes, apps on our mobile devices are also probably using addresses to contact other computers. Addresses are still the most powerful strings of letters and numbers on the internet, controlling who does and doesn't have access to posting or reading content online.

Someone, or some organization, pays for and controls each domain name. The Internet Corporation for Assigned Names and Numbers (ICANN), an American nonprofit organization, is the ultimate authority on who owns the domain; they license out the ability to sell domain names to *domain registrars*. When someone buys the rights to a domain from a registrar, the registrar keeps records about who owns the site. See **keepcalmlogon.com** for information on how you can do a "WHOIS" search to look this up yourself!

ICANN also manages the massive database of numerical addresses assigned to every device connected to the internet (if you've heard of IP addresses, those are the ones), so that the content of websites, email, signals sent from your web-enabled fridge or fitness tracker, and other internet data don't get sent to the wrong place.

If you can get information on IP addresses or domain names, you can get a clearer sense of

- where content is being posted from;
- where email is being sent from, and whether it is being forwarded or its origins are faked;
- where someone is visiting a page from; or
- who is managing a website.

Addresses are the tools that law enforcement uses to solve crimes (online and off). They're what digital security professionals use to figure out where hackers are coming from and going to. And they're what programmers use to build the very architecture of the internet we use every day. In short: understanding web addresses is powerful.

An address tells you who gets the final say over what a site is used for. And that can be useful when you're trying to understand its trustworthiness. It may take a little more digging to really figure out who owns a site; you may also need to research the owners of the company that controls the site. You might need to look into other interests the owners may have that may bias them—like a racist group, or a corporation that is attempting to make its product look better.

This can be useful if a whole site is spreading hurtful information. You can appeal to the owners to take the content down, or you can go further upstream: complain to the company that owns the *servers* the website is hosted on. This has happened many times over the years with Stormfront: after the 2017 white supremacist rally in Charlottesville, Virginia, for instance, people appealed to its webhost, which refused to host the neo-Nazi site anymore. (Unfortunately, after about a month or so, the site was up and running again on a different webhost.)

Sometimes, however, addresses get hijacked, taken over by criminals or protesters. Other times, someone with malicious intent gets between us and the address we're trying to reach—that's called a "man in the middle" attack. In those cases, how can we confirm that we're reaching the right address?

Uncrackable Code

You may have seen references to *certificates* online—for example, when you go to a website and your browser warns you that it has a bad certificate, and won't let you go there. Certificates are a special kind of digital "signature" that computers use to confirm that a website is controlled by the owner. When you see a certificate warning, it's possible that someone has tampered with a website, or is getting between you and the site you really want to see.

Certificates rely on *encryption* as a form of proof that a site can be trusted. You may have heard of encrypted email, messages, or other communications. Encryption is a part of the digital system that we trust to keep us safe from criminals and snoops. When we give our credit card number to a secure website, when we trust that a website is not going to download a bunch of malware onto our machine, or when we use a VPN to connect to our office, our devices and the servers they're connecting to make use of certificates and encryption to establish trust.

Both of these rely on trusting that there's *something that only you have*—not unlike trusting that only you can sign your name the way you do, or only you know your password (ahem ... don't share your passwords).

In digital systems of trust, another kind of verification that only you are supposed to have is *private keys*: huge numbers generated via *encryption,* which are so long and complicated that no computer currently in existence is powerful enough to guess what they are. When I say "you," here, I mean your device has it stored in memory. Keys can also be used to generate a *signature*, which can be added to email or a document to mathematically prove that only you could have signed and sent it.

Website servers, email servers, and other devices may also have their own private keys that they use to trust each other—which in turn protects you and your devices. When your computer tells you not to access a site because its certificate is bad, that means it's checked and it can't prove that the site has its private key. Someone else could have hijacked the site for malicious purposes, or is performing a man-in-the-middle attack.

This explains how machines determine whether to trust each other. But just knowing that a machine says a site is safe, or knowing who owns the site, doesn't let us know who's *posting* on that site. How do we figure that out?

Consistently Me

You're already familiar with the simplest key to knowing who someone is online: account names or logins. Your login serves to tell other human beings that you are probably the same person every time you show up and post something.

But logging in also tells *computers* that you are who you say you are— once again, because you have knowledge that only you are supposed to know, namely your password. (Which, again, is why you should not share passwords, and why stronger, non-guessable kinds of logins like multi-factor authentication are better at protecting your account.) It's how an online service knows to show you *your* files, and not someone else's, when you log in. It's how an app or website knows what things you're allowed to do, and what you're not.

"Now, wait a minute," you may be saying. "It isn't as simple as 'it's just me' online." Right: things are a little more loosey-goosey than that. (Just as they are with signatures—which can always be forged.) You may have more than one account on an app or service. You may create and destroy an account as you need to. And you probably still share account passwords with someone else (hello, absolutely everyone sharing their streaming video logins with their friends and family).

In the sense of basically confirming that you are who you say you are, though, your login works much of the time. That account confirmation takes everything we say when logged in and ties it to the same identity.

But because everyone's sharing their passwords (aaaaugh, don't do it!) and devices, stronger forms of "signatures" are needed when it comes to high-stakes digital transactions, like legal and financial ones. As our ways of confirming someone's identity have evolved—with your doctor, lawyer, or bank slooowwwly moving from demanding you fax things to being able to accept your signature online—so have criminals' ways of attacking your account name and password. This has become an arms race of sorts. It has cost the world economy millions of dollars in identity theft and chargebacks on credit cards.

Some financial transactions that involve a tremendous amount of money now demand you present an identity document like a passport, on a video call which clearly shows your face—essentially, taking a step back from trusting signatures to seeing and trusting your face and your control of the document.

What we have, now, is a spectrum of trust in identity—from posting anonymously in throw-away accounts; to accounts where you have the same name, but maybe never touch your wallet; to lower-value money transactions where you've connected a credit card, and can just tap your phone against another device; to those high-stakes transactions. On the low end, you may not even need to log in. In the middle, you may still be

OK with a user name and password. On the high end, you're doing a video call and showing a passport.

So, what about the low end of that spectrum—anonymous and fake accounts? Why do we even have those, if they're not trustworthy? Well, they have a long and storied history on the internet. Being on the internet didn't always require you to tie what you did online to your wallet and ID. Those who built the internet built anonymity into it because of their commitment to free speech.

Anonymity and the Internet

Scout Law: "I talk to different people in my life in different ways. It should be up to me to decide who I want to talk to, how, and when."

You may have seen a cartoon from the *New Yorker*, dating back to the early days of the public internet, in which two dogs are sitting in front of a computer. One is excitedly explaining to the other, "On the Internet, nobody knows you're a dog."

At the time this cartoon was published, in 1993, there were few real names or pictures online—just user names, which were often short because of limited memory space. But using short names meant you had fewer options to choose from; you had to make sure your name didn't conflict with someone else's. So many of us took on some sort of "handle" or nickname. Most of us didn't use our real names.

Hardly anybody back then ever posted a picture online. This may sound unbelievable now, but the internet was mostly made of words at the time—again, computers had less memory, and image files are much bigger than text files. The internet "pipe" was skinnier, so less could flow through it—connections were slower and less able to pass along data. A picture might take minutes if not hours to load through that skinny pipe. Video and music files are even larger, so they were even less common.

So, *we didn't have profile pictures.* Much less entire social media feeds. Much less streaming video! There was zero concern that someone would take a video of you doing something stupid and post it online.

For many of us online at the time, the *New Yorker* cartoon summed up the freedom we felt in our digital lives. We could say and do all sorts of dumb stuff, and it wouldn't stick around the internet to haunt us forever. We felt like we finally got to be valued for what we thought, felt, and how we acted toward others rather than what we looked like or how we dressed. Sometimes we ended up being more honest and trusting with people than we were in real life—and our internet friendships became more important to us than the people in our physical communities. All of this was priceless for teenagers feeling awkward. (And believe me, a lot of us who lived through those days feel really sorry for kids online now, in this age of selfies and photo filters.)

It was with the rise of Google and Facebook that expectations about whether you're required to *be you* on the internet changed. Drastically.

In 2011, Google began demanding that people who had accounts use their legal name. Facebook, which officially always asked people to use their legal name, began enforcing that in 2014. Once they collected this information, it was tied to everything else you put out there. They did this on purpose: knowing who you are, and associating it with the ads you click, is the Holy Grail for marketers.

For tons of people, real name requirements were a problem. This happened in part because Facebook made a total cock-up of figuring out whose names were "real." Robin Kills The Enemy, a member of the Rosebud Sioux group of Native Americans, was blocked from using her account because Facebook decided her name was a fake, even though it was on her driver's license.[1] Other users with long names were told they had to spell their names differently because they contained "too many words." Hiroko Yoda, a Japanese author, was blocked from making a Facebook account because they decided she'd taken that last name after the character in *Star Wars*.[2] Performers and writers known to huge audiences by names other than the ones on their IDs—including the writers Salman Rushdie and R. U. Sirius, and many drag queens—were told to change their account names to their ID names. Transgender people were threatened with the loss of their accounts if they didn't use their "dead" names.[3]

Alex Bayley gathered a list of reasons people disagreed with real-names policies:[4]

- "I am a high school teacher, privacy is of the utmost importance."
- "I enjoy being part of a global and open conversation, but I don't wish for my opinions to offend conservative and religious people I know or am related to. Also I don't want my husband's Govt career impacted by his opinionated wife, or for his staff to feel in any way uncomfortable because of my views."
- "This identity was used to protect my real identity as I am gay and my family live in a small village where if it were openly known that their son was gay they would have problems."
- "I go by a pseudonym for safety reasons. Being female, I am wary of internet harassment."
- "I've been stalked. I'm a rape survivor."
- "We get death threats at the blog, so while I'm not all that concerned with, you know, sane people finding me, I just don't overly share information and use a pen name."

Having online identities that can't be traced back to our physical bodies and legal names can be important for security, privacy, and sometimes publicity reasons. We may need to be anonymous to explore parts of ourselves that we're not ready to fully own—like living with a medical condition, coming out as queer, or deciding to change jobs. As young people, we may need the protection of anonymity so the things we post won't impact our future prospects, whether we're under age and posting pictures of our liquor shelf, questioning the religious beliefs we were raised with, or sharing stories about our relationships. It's important that we be able to choose who can know what about our personal experience and identity, and choose whether or not we want to maintain a consistent identity online to build trust in an online community.

But anonymity is a double-edged sword. As we saw in the cases of the Macedonian teenagers and Russian operatives during the 2016 US election, anonymity can be used as a weapon. Some people use it to explore their violent abusive sides, venting frustration and hostility and hiding behind an identity that is not theirs. Accounts not tied to real identities are also used to spread disinformation, disrupting our trust in our communities.

R.U.R. (Rossum's Universal Robots) was a Czechoslovakian play that introduced the word "robot" into the English language in 1921 (in Slavic languages, "robot" means "work"). The robots or "bots" we talk about online don't have physical bodies; they're just pieces of code. *Source:* Work Projects Administration Federal Theatre Project

Anonymous behavior ends up being some of the worst behavior on the internet.

Fortunately for all of us, there are time-tested ways to identify fake or anonymous accounts that are up to no good. Read on.

Signs of Fake Accounts

The 2016 American election was far from the first time someone tried to cause trouble using fake accounts.

Most people are familiar by now with the 419 or "Nigerian prince" scam that has arrived in most of our inboxes since our first days on the internet (and which is actually a continuation of "Spanish prisoner" postal letters and faxes sent to unsuspecting targets since 1898!).[5] A website for "Kaycee Nicole," created in 1999 by a woman in Kansas, convinced the internet that a college-aged basketball star was dying of leukemia. "Kaycee" received gifts from people around the world.

There were even prior attempts to sway elections. As early as 2012, Enrique Peña Nieto's campaign in Mexico tested out the use of bots to automatically post content in his favor and against his opponents. They manipulated the content of hashtag discussions on issues like energy. They even flooded tweets about safe exits and injured protesters during one protest against police brutality, making the hashtag unusable and putting protesters at risk.[6]

It's going to be increasingly important to identify fake accounts in order to make sure we're not being lied to, influenced, or drowned out by people who disagree with our political beliefs.

How to Keep Calm and Carry On

In your digital life, you've probably developed your own techniques for identifying fake accounts. Maybe you have a gut feeling that something is just "off."

Amelia Acker has studied fake social media profiles. She suggests the following guidelines for identifying them. Many of these are techniques people have used to identify internet hoaxes for years, and they may confirm your gut instincts. When you find a profile you think is fake, check for the following:

A SPY doesn't LOOK LIKE THIS

A SPY may LOOK LIKE THIS

DON'T TALK about

TROOP MOVEMENTS-SHIP SAILINGS
WAR WORK-MUNITIONS SHIPMENTS

Our opinions about who looks "shady" may not serve us when it comes to malicious people trying to trick us, as the Canadian government warned citizens during World War II. The same goes for fake online accounts: they may look like "our kind of people," the people we trust, but look for these telling signs to see if they're fake. *Source:* Canadian Wartime Information Board.

Take a look at the name of the account:

- Does the name include a lot of double letters in weird places, or random numbers?

- How do the screen name and user name compare?

- What comes up when you do a search for the user name or screen name on another platform?

- Compare this account with other accounts that are supposedly for this person on other platforms. Do they link to each other?

Look at the banner, bio, or profile pictures on the account:

- Is the profile picture a default? (On many sites, it's a generic "person" icon)

- Do a reverse image search (see **keepcalmlogon.com** for tools): Where else does this picture show up? Does it look like the user stole it from someone else?

- If you search for their bio in quotation marks, does it turn up somewhere else, like Wikipedia, or an account under another name?

Take a close look at the things posted on the account:

- Has the account been around for a while, or is it relatively new?

- If they're posting a lot of photos, do they also write something about them, or not?

- Is the bulk of what they post reposted from someone else? Or are they generating unique content? You may need to compare accounts or do a search to figure this out.

- Are the links they post shortened? What do they lead to? (Be careful when looking at a suspected bogus account: preview links, don't follow them.)

- Do they post a lot of duplicate stuff over time?

- Is there a location tag on the content? Where is it from? Does it seem to match up with where the account says it is posting from?

- Sometimes accounts get hijacked. Looking at the account over time, did it go dormant for a while, or was it deleted or suspended? Has there been a sudden change in the tone or language of what gets posted?

- Follow the money. If you can, figure out how often an account posted paid, promoted content versus free content.

Look at the followers:

- Do a lot of the followers look suspiciously fake?

- Do others comment on this account? Low to no comments can indicate the account is a fake.

- Do the followers make nonsense comments?

Finally, how do other people interact with the account?

- Are responses from followers unique, or re-pasted over and over?

- Are there a lot of auto-replies like "Thanks for the follow! Check out my page" posted by the account or by others?

- Does there seem to be a pattern of other accounts sharing this account's posts automatically?

- Who links back to this account? You may want to do a search for the address of the page itself to figure this out.

On its own, no one bad answer to these questions is necessarily a sign that the account is a bogus bot trying to trick you. But if you see a few bad indicators in one account, it's worth being suspicious of what the account is posting.[7]

Trusting One, Trusting Many

By taking apart the stories of a simple signature and a simple login, as I did in this chapter and the previous one, we can see the two kinds of trust I talked about in chapter 9 in operation. First, there's trust that *this person is who they say they are*, and the associated trust that, like the people we have trusted since we were infants, this person will continue to act more or less the same way. We trust that they are testifying to the truthfulness of the document. We trust that the person behind the account is the same one who logged in last time.

But there's also our trust in the *system of people and devices* surrounding the signature and the login. We trust the signature on a contract because *everyone has agreed* that when someone signs a document, they are vouching for its truthfulness, and if they are lying, other people will punish them. We trust a user account because we trust that the computers in the login process were given the password for that account, which only one person is supposed to have.

This gets us to the *trust in systems* we all rely on to survive in a complex modern world. Why do we trust people who are a part of these systems? We don't trust them all for the same reasons. And the internet is changing many forms of trust.

In part IV of the book I'll delve further into our trust in systems and authorities: in chapter 14 I'll look at professionals, the schools that train them, and the ways that they produce information that is considered *authoritative*. In chapter 15 I'll focus on books, no matter who wrote them, or whether they're fact or fiction; in chapter 16 I'll shift to journalism and the news, and then to new digital systems of information. I'll devote chapter 17 to Wikipedia, which offers a strange hybrid of professional-style information production and online tools like addresses when it asks us to trust its information. Algorithms, the subject of chapter 18, are their own kind of system, created by the choices made by people who build software; algorithms offer their own suggestions of what information to trust. In chapter 19, I'll talk about a major source of bias across all forms of communication: the need to make a profit. And finally, in chapter 20, I'll look at what lies ahead, and how we can (both individually and together) demand change, rebuild trust, and survive the digital revolution.

IV

WHY TRUST
THE SYSTEM?

14

Professions: Trust in Special Knowledge

The first conflict is over the distribution of knowledge: "Who knows?"
The second is about authority: "Who decides who knows?" The third is
about power: "Who decides who decides who knows?"
—Shoshana Zuboff[1]

"Professional" Authorities

I once taught the graveyard shift in a South Bronx after-school program:
a mandatory writing workshop for sixth-grade girls, in the fiftieth-worst
school in the city, at the very end of the day, on Fridays. Pretty much
nobody wanted to be there.[2]

The girls did whatever they could to distract me from talking about
writing. To this end, one day one of the girls, who was Puerto Rican, asked
me, "Why teachers don't talk ghetto?" That was how she described the
way she and her classmates talked—they proudly identified as "ghetto,"
and spoke with a rhythm, accent, and slang that would likely be familiar
to anyone who's seen depictions of inner-city New York on TV.

The other girls laughed. "Well, teachers don't 'talk ghetto' because
they're trying to 'be professional,'" I explained. "Do you know what 'professional' means?"

She startled me by doing a spot-on parody of Elle, the ditzy heroine of
the movie *Legally Blonde*. "Yah," said my student, flipping her hair. "It
means, like, you talk like this." She sounded like a "Valley Girl," the mate-
rialistic, mythical teenage girls who supposedly haunted the malls in the
suburbs of Southern California where I grew up.

I was floored. Her understanding of "being professional" was tied to
Elle being *rich* and *white*, and from someplace far away from her. Not
related to *professions*—you know, jobs that people do. (Which was upsetting. I wanted to support this kid in getting a better job, someday, and she
didn't think that was possible for someone like her.)

What Does "Professional" Mean?

What is a profession? Let's pick this apart. This is where we move from trusting someone because of who they are to trusting someone because of the system they're a part of—as we all do, growing up in modern society. This chapter and the next few that follow address this Scout Law: "If I understand how communities decide what information to trust, I will be better prepared to identify bad information."

A "profession" is a category of people whose opinions our communities may trust because of the way they do their work. Most of us think of "professional" as "doing a certain job for their whole career," or "having high status in a career," or something like that. Many of us learn from those around us to treat professions with extra respect, because of the *experience* and *social status* we feel these professionals have.

But sociologists who study professions think of them in a more specific way. When a regular old job becomes what sociologists call a "profession," the people doing that job come together and agree that they will hold each other to particular *standards*. Doctors are held to an ethical standard, and it includes the rule "First, do no harm." If a doctor harms or kills a patient, medical boards may take away their license to practice medicine. If lawyers violate the ethics of law, they may lose their license to practice law.

The standards professionals are held to and their relationships with their colleagues make up the system that holds up our trust. These systems ask professionals to write, think, and communicate information to each other and to us in particular ways.

In this chapter, I'll give examples of a few professions' standards: namely scientists, historians, and religious leaders. In chapter 16, I'll specifically go over the standards journalists are held to.

Here are three things professions have in common:

1. Each has a **well-defined, specialized body of knowledge**, which professionals defend as their own field of expertise against claims made by other groups.[3]
2. Licensing boards and formal associations **hold professionals accountable to their peers**.

3. Often a college or university acts as a gatekeeper to **professional training**. Without that training, it may take a lot of argument to call yourself a professional in that field, and people will likely not trust you.

These points are important to understanding *why* people trusted journalists, historians, and scientists as gatekeepers of "good" information. What trust we have in them rests on knowing that their training has taught them to check their information in a particular way, against certain kinds of evidence and the opinions of their peers. They have ways of *confirming* that what we're getting from them is good information, by holding each other to standards for how they gather, study, publish, and argue about that information.

We don't always think about this. For a long time most of us have taken the quality of professionals' information for granted. A lot of people still trust facts just because they're in writing! Or we trust things written by professionals because of *what* job they have, not based on *how* they develop facts and confirm them with their peers.

But at this moment in history, it's important to understand why we are asked to trust professionals. Their systems of training and creating knowledge are now being disrupted by technology.

It's useful to recognize how brief a time professions in general—and journalism and universities in particular—have been the gatekeepers of facts. Before the 1800s, there were only three jobs recognized as "professions" in Western society: medicine, law, and the clergy. Most sciences began to define themselves as professions in the 1800s. Journalism is even younger: it did not organize into a profession until a few decades into the 1900s.

In the scope of thousands of years of human history, that is very, very little time. Knowing how short the life of professions has been is a reminder: there's no guarantee that journalism or universities will endure, just like there's no guarantee we will keep reading and writing the same ways.

One last note: computer programming is barely a profession. Computer *science,* within universities, is generally held to standards that most academic scientists are. But computer *programming*—the work that builds the sites and apps we use every day—is new, disorganized as a system, and lacks university training as a "gatekeeper" to who can participate. Plus, computer programming is only just now developing standards of ethics to keep us safe. Compare this to civil engineering (the folks who design bridges and other buildings we use daily), which has long had high standards for safety and ethics. (Remember what I said about all computer code being broken? I'll talk about this a little more in chapter 18, on algorithms.)

Professional Basics

There are a few basic requirements that *all* professionals are supposed to stick to.[4]

Experts in a profession are supposed to keep an open mind. If another expert or someone from outside their field comes up with a new way of looking at something, they evaluate it based on what they already know. They think about the quality of the source. Then, they may *change what they assume is true* to incorporate this new information. They may decide another expert is no longer the authority on the topic. They are also supposed to stay critical: not to accept every new thing they read with open arms and total approval. They ask questions, gather evidence, and compare it with the evidence and arguments presented by people and media around them.

But let's talk for a second about what being "open-minded" and "critical" mean to professionals. Keeping an open mind and thinking critically is *not* the same as doing knee-jerk questioning for its own sake, rejecting "the system, maaaaaaan," or criticizing something because it's "mainstream." It's about gathering and comparing evidence.

Professionals are supposed to have some humility about what they do and don't know. While I was doing my doctorate, I found that the more I learned, the more I started to feel overwhelmed by the sheer volume of things I *didn't* know. When you study that much, you get this feeling of *whoa, this is way bigger than I can know on my own.* You learn you can't do *all* of the scientific experiments or *all* of the historical research by yourself. Same for journalism—journalists rely on each other's reporting to piece together a story all the time.

Reliable information comes from groups of people working together, not from individual geniuses working alone. Even geniuses need to be able to explain their work to their peers. And the fact that there *are* different groups of people working on building knowledge and information means that they're going to come up with different perspectives on the same subject. They may not all come to the same answer.

It doesn't always happen that professionals are humble or work together. Some people get stuck on constantly needing to "be the expert." But good academics will show some humility about how much there is in the world to know, and share credit for what they've done.

It's not only professionals who can be held to these standards! All of us can approach information this way, to determine if it is worth our trust. And that's what the American Library Association suggests in the guidelines I included in chapter 9, "The Roots of Trust."[5]

Those are the basics. Each professional field has its own requirements on top of that for building trustworthy information. Let's talk about a few of those.

Historians

Historians are expected to use many sources of evidence to tell the story of the time they are studying. (Or else explain why they are focusing narrowly on one source of facts.) And they will generally specialize in one part of history: say, medieval England, or medieval Spain, or women in the medieval era, or eras when there were revolutions ... you get the idea. They can get pretty specialized in the questions they personally research, though they are often asked to teach more broadly than their specialty.

A historian looks at *primary-source material*—eyewitness accounts from people who were actually there, trade records, legal papers, census records, even ruins of buildings—to tell the story of what was going on at the time. Two historians studying the same time period might come up with very different stories! Think about it—if one historian focuses on company records and newspaper reports about a labor strike, the resulting story might favor the company's side. Another historian who is studying journals of the strikers, and census data about who lived in their households at the time, might come up with a story that is much more personal to the strikers.

It's like when your sister and brother remember that your grandmother left her precious things to *them*, but your cousins remember something verrrry different . . . everyone has their own interest. You're going to need multiple perspectives to see the whole picture.

You may have heard people in your community calling themselves "amateur historians" to distinguish themselves from professional historians. Amateur historians might take care of a local museum or library, or give tours of some part of your community that they love and know a lot about. The difference between amateur and professional historians generally comes down to whether their writing is reviewed by other historians before it is published (if they publish writing at all), whether they had the same exposure to the breadth of material and ideas that professional historians have, and whether professional historians recognize that they are playing by professional "rules." Amateur historians do sometimes contribute new historical information. However, there is no guarantee that other historians have reviewed their work for accuracy.

This mural's depiction of the history of the waterfront of San Francisco, in the last project funded by the Work Projects Administration, sees that era from the perspective of workers who went on strike there. *The Waterfront*, mural by Anton Refregier. *Source:* photograph by Carol M. Highsmith

Scout Law: "If I work to understand where my own opinion comes from, I will be better prepared to protect myself from people who want to manipulate me."

Your family tree is a good starting place to think about how you feel about history. You may feel like you got fewer messages about history from your family than you did about, say, medicine or religion, but I bet you got a few. Start a new family tree with "history" in the trunk. Again, your jobs, schools, and social groups will be the branches; your family will be the roots.

For starters … did people in your family talk about their own history? Did you have family members around to talk about the past? How did what they said (or didn't say) influence how connected you felt to history?

How about your community? Were there historical landmarks or events to commemorate things in the past? Did you study the history of the region where you lived in school? Or did most of the historical events you studied happen somewhere else? How did this impact how you felt about learning history?

Did your family have particular touchstones in history they talked a lot about—battle reenactments, military history, migration from another country, or civil rights movements? What was present in their stories about history? What was missing?

Was your family's sense of history related to their understanding of their religious texts? How?

Did anyone in your family ever disagree with the history you may have been taught in school?

Again, do the **change one thing** exercise. How would your opinion and trust have changed if one of these people or institutions in your life had felt this way?

Religious Figures

Many religious scholars apply the same rules that historians use to religious texts. Their work can help us figure out when we're looking at fanatics or cults, rather than a long-lived tradition that will nurture our souls. Many religions have scholars who examine the evidence in the faith's central books and debate with each other about which evidence is sound and which is not.

For example, religious scholars look back at history and can see that over time plenty of people and religious groups have predicted the end of the world or the return of a prophet, and their predictions have not come true. Wikipedia has a great list of predicted apocalyptic events, which, as I'm writing this, stretches from 66 CE to dates thousands of years in the future. They include past failed predictions of Armageddon or the return of the Messiah by Tim LaHaye, Sun Myung Moon, Louis Farrakhan, the Jehovah's Witnesses, Menachem Mendel Schneerson, Nostradamus, Charles Manson, Brahma Kumaris, Chen Tao, Sir Isaac Newton, Jerry Falwell, Pat Robertson, Rasputin, and even Martin Luther.[6]

Doomsday predictions: everybody makes 'em but pretty much nobody gets 'em right. There's a pretty poor track record on "the world will end completely" predictions, so it might be a good idea to not listen to those. Or at least, to demand evidence, and ask what the person predicting doom gets out of making that prediction.

In the Abrahamic religious traditions—what Christianity, Judaism, and Islam are collectively called—historical work is done by Bible, Torah, and Qur'an scholars, who sometimes communicate with each other across religious boundaries because their books overlap. They may look at the dates described in these texts, and check the stories in them against other texts and historical knowledge. They may look at how many people confirmed what is reported in these books—they look for eyewitness accounts, as many of us would—and decide that reports from multiple eyewitnesses are more reliable than those that depend on the story told by one person. Buddhism and Hinduism also call out "testimony" like this as a source of truth.

Religious scholars may look at what kind of writing is in a religious text (what *genre*) and use that to decide which parts are important to follow. For example, ancient eyewitness accounts in the Bible (like those of the gospels in the New Testament) may be judged as more central to the faith than the parts that are clearly fantastical (like the book of Revelations) or written in the form of poems (like the psalms of the Old Testament).

There have been different translations of these books throughout history, and scholars of language called *linguists* also compare them to check whether the translations stay true to the teachings put forward by the founder of the religion.

Your mileage may vary. There are Christian sects, for example, which insist that each follower's personal reading or experience of the Bible is more important than the insights of the leaders of their church. Ultimately, it is up to each of us to seek further knowledge and perspective on our faith.

Your Family Tree and Religion

Returning to your family tree: add religious affiliations for the people you included, wherever you know them.

Some religious communities have an unshakable trust in their central book, and a deep distrust of anything written that does not conform to it or to the teachings of their leaders (like, say, science textbooks or fantasy novels). Some religious folks may mistrust interpretation of events in the media by reporters or experts, believing that it is crucial for each seeker of knowledge to do their own analysis and come to their own conclusions. Did people in your family or community feel this way? Where it feels relevant to you, write down how this may have affected your relationship to writing or other media that were *not* based on your central book.

Again, do the **change one thing** exercise. How would your opinion and trust have changed, if one of these people or institutions in your life had felt differently?

Scientists

There are many different kinds of scientists, from particle physicists to marine biologists, neurochemists to materials scientists, geologists to astronomers. Each of these communities of scientists works together to produce new information on highly specialized topics.

But there are some general rules about how scientists are supposed to make and spread information. You may have heard these rules from your science teachers at some point.

Scientists review what other scientists have written on a topic and write it up at the beginning of a report. Working from what they read, they come up with a hypothesis (or a few) about what they expect to see

Doctors also rely on scientific research in journals (not the same as articles about medicine you might read in the news or online). The warning signs of a medical fraud listed on this poster from the Great Depression still hold true today (though some reputable doctors now advertise). *Source:* Work Projects Administration Poster Collection—Library of Congress

when they try an experiment or do more observations. They then describe how they observed or did experiments, so other scientists can try the same process and see if they get the same results, or point to flaws in their process that may have screwed up their outcome. They write up what they observed or found in their experiments, often doing statistical analyses to check whether the things they found could be due to random chance. Checking for the same results, analyzing methods, and analyzing for random chance are checks for *validity* (whether their methods really found what they said they would) and *reliability* (whether the phenomenon they're looking at is something that will reliably keep happening). Finally, they sum up what they learned and put it in the context of work that other people have done, suggesting more work their field may still need to do or questions that need answers.

With some tweaks to this process, researchers who study people, like linguists, sociologists, anthropologists, psychologists, and economists produce new information in similar ways.

Scientific specialties have additional standards, on top of these, to which they hold each other's writing. A doctor friend gave me an example of how different these standards can be between scientific fields. Her team did research on artificial heart valves. Because their project straddled two scientific fields—medicine and engineering—they got very different responses from different journals when they went to publish. Engineering journals sent back their paper with the comment, "Why are you talking about all this medical research in the literature review?" Medical journals wrote back, "This is fine, but we don't need this diagram of how you engineered the valve." Each journal wanted to see certain kinds of evidence from these professionals, and not other kinds, to know their work was trustworthy.

Your Family Tree and Science

Returning to your family tree, let's think about some factors that may have influenced whether the people around you trusted science and medicine:

- Did you have doctors, nurses, or scientists in your family?

- Did anyone in your family have a health condition that shaped how you related to hospitals, scientific research, or medicine?

- Did anyone in your family insist on "natural" or "traditional" healing remedies? Do you know why?

- Was someone's trust or faith in science or medicine shaken by a particularly bad experience? For example, was your community subjected to unethical medical experiments, as black men in Alabama were exposed to syphilis and not treated in the Tuskegee experiment? Or were women you knew given thalidomide during pregnancy, which caused birth defects? Or was there a toxic spill in your area, where a company involved made sure that medical and media reports said there were no effects and they were not responsible?

Again, do the **change one thing** exercise. How might your opinion and trust have changed, if one of these people or institutions in your life had felt this way?

How Professionals Write

Books are one kind of information put out by professionals. I'll talk more about them in chapter 15. But professionals write in other formats, too, including journal articles and less formal communications, such as interviews and opinion pieces in newspapers, or in casual posts on social media.

Journal Articles

The trust built up among scientists, historians, doctors, lawyers, and other researchers is usually tied to publishing articles in *journals*. Each field usually has a few journals. Don't confuse these with the regular magazines that most of us read, as I once heard a cat owner do at a veterinarian's office. She was referring to something she read in a science-related magazine, and made it clear she thought this magazine was how veterinarians communicated new information about medical advances to each other.

Generally, it's not. Scientists may keep up on general advances *outside* of their field through news articles. But a news article isn't shaped like a journal article. Instead of literature reviews and hypotheses, a news article will start out with what scientists found. This can leave the impression that the information is much more "final" than the scientists themselves feel it is. Or the journalist may put the research in the context of a larger, more entertaining story about the researcher and who they are, the history of the field, or some big idea, as Malcolm Gladwell has done in his books *Blink* and *The Tipping Point*.[7]

But when it comes to judging the quality of information in their area of expertise, experts will look to their specialized journals.

One of the requirements of these journals is that other professionals support the evidence in the article, which the authors need to demonstrate by referring to previously published work in their field. Yep, when teachers demand to see references and citations in your papers, it's not just that they want you to prove you've read stuff; it's also part of a professional tradition of proving that there is more to your argument than your own desire to spout random thoughts.

Articles in scientific journals usually take the shape I mentioned earlier: they start with literature reviews and hypotheses, describe the study, talk about findings, and come to conclusions. Other professional journals may ask that articles be structured in different ways.

I don't mean to say that the shape alone—or publication in a journal, for that matter—is the only indication that the information in an article is authoritative. As an extreme counterpoint, I give you the classic article "Chicken Chicken Chicken: Chicken Chicken," published in the *Annals of Improbable Research*. Here's an excerpt from the article's conclusion:

> Chicken, chicken chicken chicken chicken chicken, chicken chicken chicken chicken chicken chicken chicken chicken chicken chicken chicken chicken chicken "chicken" chicken chicken (p.p., chicken chicken, chicken chicken!)[8]

At least ... I *think* that's the conclusion. It's certainly positioned and formatted correctly for the conclusions section of a journal article, after other sections with serious-looking graphs and flowcharts. But every word in the article is "chicken," as is the title of that section. (The *Annals of Improbable Research* encourages teachers to use the parodies of scientific articles in its pages as teaching tools, to help students think critically about what makes research trustworthy.) So, there you go: an example of how shape alone should not have you saying, "Well, that *looks* like serious science ..."

In sum: expert research is usually presented in articles that have a particular shape in order to help the reader dissect their analysis easily. But a "scientific journal article" shape, on its own, does not mean information is trustworthy. Anyone judging an article needs to dig into the arguments and analyses and compare it to other information before deciding that it is authoritative and trustworthy. And they may need the help of others in the article author's community to understand whether they trust the findings of that article, and why.

When Professionals Speak Casually in Tweets or Talk Shows

So, how about when authoritative people write in less formal or more casual ways? Like in a letter, an editorial, or social media?

Again, that depends. Generally, this casual chatter won't have gone through as much of a filter as what they write for their colleagues. But then, there are moments when scientists might put some of their early findings from a study up on their websites, talk about their past research, or make informed comments about others' research or issues in the news.

Staying in Their Area of Expertise

We may trust professionals' expertise on a subject. But it's not a good idea to trust information that comes from professionals *just* because they're professionals. You want to know that they're well respected for their work by others who do the same work; that they are open to new information, but also think critically about it; and that they're making observations about stuff within their area of expertise.

Even though professionals may be expert in one subject, that doesn't make them expert in every subject. We may trust computer programmers for authoritative advice on fixing our computer, but not listen to their medical or dating advice.

Even *within* medicine, you may not want to trust a specialist in one field to comment on another field. For example, Dr. Oz, who has made a career out of spreading health advice on TV, is trained as a heart surgeon. But in the *British Medical Journal*, a panel of other doctors found that more than half of the things Dr. Oz recommended on his show were not backed up by research from other medical professionals—particularly when it came to topics like diet and cancer, which are not in his specialty.[9]

Similarly, a lot of the writing that claims black people are mentally or genetically inferior to white people (the idea of "white supremacy," as espoused by Stormfront, the group I mentioned in chapter 13 that runs martinlutherking.org) was not done by authorities on brains or genes. A major supporter of those ideas was a physicist, William Shockley.[10] His work on radio circuits won him the Nobel Prize—but that didn't mean he had spent time carefully going over literature on psychology, genetics, neuroscience, education, sociology, or any number of other fields that had better information about race and intelligence than he did. In fact, it may have meant that he specialized and *didn't* read what others had written. But eventually, professionals who had studied those subjects spoke out about the flaws in Shockley's claims. That's how professional conversations are supposed to go: correcting bad information with better information.

You Might Be Asking . . .

"So how do I know if I should trust information from professionals?"

How to Keep Calm and Carry On

Here's a brief checklist to go over when you encounter information from professional authorities:

- Has this information, whether in a journal article or other format, been reviewed by other professionals?

- Do its creators reference work by other professionals?

- What claim—like a degree or training—do its creators have to their expertise?

- Are they speaking about their field of expertise?

- Do they present evidence for the claim they are making?

- Do you think the evidence really supports the claim?

- If it's a piece of research, how broad or narrow is the question being asked?

- Did the research answer that question, or some other question?

- Did the research follow the legal and ethical guidelines of the field?

- Are the creators of the information using neutral or biased language?

- Do they acknowledge the limitations of their research?

Fighting Authority

Looking back to how these professionals appear in the family trees of our opinions, each of us may find the roots of our trust or distrust. We all grow up in particular communities with particular needs, beliefs, histories, and ways of socially relating to others. These social patterns shape how we relate to media and information, and how we relate to the people who create them. Our communities have different reasons for deciding who is an authority, and whose word counts most, in what situations.

You Might Be Saying ...

"I have a problem with authority! I don't trust what the people you're talking about say!"

How to Keep Calm and Carry On

Everyone's trust or distrust of certain information has its roots in a real need or worry—either our own, or a need or worry further back in our family tree. I want to acknowledge that.

Sometimes we worry that life (as we know it) will be completely disrupted if we trust information from the news, from scientists, or from other professionals. Some religious communities may feel this way about any text or medium that does not align with their central text.

Sometimes we or our ancestors might have been told that our first-hand experience of the world was not as important as an authority's view of the world, because we came from a rural area, or were poor, or not from the "right" religion, or were not white. Sometimes this led to changes in schools, government activity, jobs, or other parts of our lives— changes that damaged our families. Of course that built mistrust. Once bitten, twice shy.

But even if you don't trust professionals or the "mainstream media," you should also understand what standards they use to claim they are trustworthy. Because once you know those, you can look for the proof that they did what they said they were going to do to earn our trust. You can judge them (as well as information that disagrees with them) by the standards they have, or even by the standards for other information, to see how well their claims hold up.

You don't have to pour your heart and your beliefs into any of the strategies for judging information I'm presenting. Use mindfulness: just

A reminder about the power of books. This poster called attention to a special collection of the New York City Library, which later became the Schomburg Center for Research in Black Culture. *Source:* Work Projects Administration Federal Art Project

try out the strategy, and observe where it takes you. Use these strategies as tools. See what it gets you to apply a new standard for trustworthiness to different forms of information.

And once you know the evidence and methods experts use to demonstrate trustworthiness, you can begin to ask questions about what they've said. If you fight like they fight, you gain the powerful tools that powerful people use. If you reject these ways of asking questions and demanding evidence, you're leaving money on the table; you're putting yourself at a disadvantage when powerful people in the society we live in highly value the authority of scientists, doctors, journalists, and other professionals. Relying on these tools, there may be ways to fight for better information. Your family and ancestors may not have had these tools to defend themselves from media, politicians, or unethical scientists or doctors. But you do.

Now, authority doesn't mean everyone else is *forced* to agree with the ways professionals and other authorities claim to be trustworthy. You could, for example, insist every document have a stick-figure picture drawn on it instead of your signature, in order for it to be usable in court. Or you could cast doubt on the authority of a scientific paper backed by thousands of scientists, claiming there was a "conspiracy" behind its findings.

Even if we're not *forced* to trust authoritative information, it can be *costly* to disagree with authorities about what is true. It may cost us our freedom (go to jail), our money (pay a fine), or more often, our reputation (as when suddenly, instead of being a respectable coworker, you're "that weirdo in accounting who keeps insisting it's legal to sign his reports with a stick-figure picture," or people don't want to talk to you on Facebook anymore because you keep saying climate change is a hoax). Each of us must decide, but weigh the consequences to our lives and loved ones.

Before we leave the subject of the printed word, let's talk for a moment about another form of trusted written information, a common medium for professionals to work in: books.

15

Books

Here's some other books you might enjoy. But … you don't have to take my word for it.

—LeVar Burton[1]

Why Did We Trust Books?

When I was seven, I *loved* the comics page in the paper. I particularly loved *Bloom County*. This was really a comic for grown-ups, with lots of political commentary. In my defense, the comic also had lots of appeal to a seven-year-old: it had a gross-looking cat who was constantly barfing, a talking penguin, one kid who was terrified of the Giant Purple Snorklewacker in his closet, and another who had a talking computer that could perform almost magical acts of hacking.

Our second-grade teacher wanted us to keep track of how many pages we read, and to read a certain amount. So I reported back that I'd read dozens of pages of the biggest *Bloom County* collection I owned.

She told me that book didn't count.

Looking back, I still think she was wrong. Here are a handful of words I learned the definitions to, at age seven, because they were in *Bloom County*:

apartheid

antiquated

extremities

belfry

annihilation

euphemism

foreshadowing

obsolescence

Machiavellian

turpitude

Where does the idea come from that there are some books that everyone is "supposed to read"? *Source:* Work Projects Administration Poster Collection—Library of Congress

Clearly, it's not like I learned *nothing* from the comic . . .

There has always been "common knowledge" or "folk wisdom" about what reports, books, and other media to trust or not trust. Do any in this list sound familiar?

- "That's not the kind of book you should use in a book report, honey. That book's only for fun."
- "I always listen to 98.9. Those talk show hosts tell it like it is!"
- "I don't like that paper. It's a sensationalist tabloid. I read the *Times* instead."
- "You can't trust the mainstream (or lamestream) media."
- "That book isn't very biblical."
- "Fanfiction isn't REAL writing. You're stealing their characters!"
- "Freedom of the press is guaranteed only to those who own one." (This one's from journalist A. J. Liebling.)

When we are young, teachers and parents may encourage us to trust some shapes of texts or media and not others—like my teacher telling me comics didn't "count." Or they may want us to rely on the word (and position) of an expert—professor, military general, or preacher—to clue us into whether some information is authoritative. This is easier for us than having to research the claims the article is making, or the background of the writer.

But in a world where it is getting ever easier for anyone to put any information out there, it's up to all of us to think harder about whether something we read, hear, or see is trustworthy, no matter what shape it comes to us in.

As I mentioned earlier, understanding how information is *made* and *spread* within our communities is critical. It can empower us to fight fake information, rebuild trust in our communities, and help us thrive in our careers.

In chapter 14, I went over some of the ways scientists, historians, religious leaders, and other professionals are expected to build trustworthy, authoritative information. In this chapter, I'll delve into how those practices and others apply specifically to books.

We'll continue working on the family trees of our opinions in this chapter. Look for exercises where you will add more information about your family's relationship to written information, fact and fiction, and textbooks.

The Process of Publishing a Book

Scout Law: "If I understand how news, books, and other media are made, I will be better able to identify bias."

Have you ever heard someone scoff about a book, saying "Oh. It's *self-published*"? Like somehow that made the book garbage?

Trash talking about self-published books is one of the things that the digital revolution is changing. With Amazon and other outlets making it easier for people to mass-produce a book without going through a publisher, we're going to see more and more self-published books. The social status of self-published books is already changing. There are a lot of books that have gone from being self-published to being distributed by major publishers. Hugh Howey's science-fiction *Dust* trilogy comes to mind.

When I first started talking about writing a book, some of my friends in tech were skeptical about how I wanted to do it. I started looking for an agent, because I knew that could help me find a publisher. That's when a friend asked, "Why not just write the book and put it up online? The agent and the publisher are just going to take your money and tell you to change the book."

Well, I answered, as a writer, I expect that my conversation with an editor is going to make my article or book *better*. Working with an editor means working to check that more people will accept that the claims you make are accepted as truthful by most people—and this goes for newspapers and TV newsrooms as well. Producing a book with a publisher generally involves copyediting and some amount of fact checking to confirm the claims the author is making are not false. If I were just off on my own, I might misremember things, or make wild claims.

When authors make references to other books, the way professionals do, it can also demonstrate that they're not making stuff up. They're presenting readers with evidence, if they want it, so readers know the author is not some lone wackadoo inventing stories that sound seductive.

When I was negotiating this book with publishers, they explained to me the process of how the book would be peer reviewed. They were eager to get the book out to other experts in my field to make sure I wasn't misrepresenting anything or making false claims. Publishers run books in front of everyday people, too, to see if the readers connect to the author's message and style.

Of course, this isn't always the case. Some publishers don't check their books with other experts, and some will spend less time and money on editing. Then the only barriers to publishing false (or also plagiarized) information are legal consequences like lawsuits, or public accusations. These can pressure publishers to ensure a thorough fact-check, or even to pull a book from the shelves if the false information becomes public after it's been released. In countries with stricter laws about defamation, a government might take action to stop a book from being published—which could end up censoring legitimate, truthful information.

Ultimately, there are still possibilities that untrue information could be published in a book, whether self-published or printed by a well-known publishing house. It's worth understanding what measures are in place at a given publisher to ensure that doesn't happen.

How to Keep Calm and Carry On

How do we know whether something written in a book is trustworthy or not? In nonfiction books, there are a number of helpful clues:

- Does the author refer to other books to back up claims? And are those books also making good, backed-up claims?

- Is there some clue about the source of the writer's authority? For example, the EdD after my name tells you I got a doctorate in education.

- How well known and established is the publishing house?

- Can you learn what its fact-checking practices are?

- Is the publishing house owned by a company that has other interests in the topic at hand? For example, if it's a book about the production of a given movie, does the company own the studio that made that movie?

Fact or Fiction?

Whether writing in books was even *supposed* to be true, or whether it was made up, has been a source of tension for a long, long time. The Christian church, in particular, has long had a tense relationship with the idea of fiction. A monk at Canterbury in 1121 wrote, "It is a shocking thing for anyone knowingly to write what is false in sacred histories, for the soul of the writer is slain every time they are read or listened to."[2]

The classic opening line of a fairy tale tells readers to suspend disbelief and immerse themselves in stories of witches, wolves, and wayward children. *Source:* Whitley, Works Projects Administration Poster Collection—Library of Congress

So writers who penned a fictional story or poem in earlier eras usually made an explicit note of it, including some lines toward the beginning, like, "Hey, there might be some lies in here," or "I'm not here to tell the truth." Imagine J. K. Rowling setting out at the beginning of every *Harry Potter* book by saying, "What I'm writing down here isn't real. People can't fly, dragons don't exist, you can't turn invisible or kill someone by pointing a wand at them."

Today we don't feel the need to do that. We have the *genre* known as fiction, and when we pick up a fiction book (past the age of, say, seven) most of us understand we're not reading something that actually happened.

But in medieval Europe, fiction that was just for fun was new idea. There were traditional legends to teach your people's history, and religious texts, and official written records of ownership, but writing down your own stories was seen as … weird. And maybe pointless. Think about it: if most of the people you knew (who knew how to write) were supposed to be working on official paperwork or sacred texts, on pain of torture of their immortal soul, it might be startling and confusing to encounter a book that they wrote *just for fun*.

People didn't have as much leisure time at that point in history, either; everyone had to work hard just to produce enough food to survive. Who was going to settle down to read a good murder mystery, much less write one?

Some Christian sects still worry about the difference between fact and fiction, and they warn their followers not to read *Harry Potter* books, watch *Star Wars*, or play *Pokémon*. They point to parts of the Bible that warn against spreading myths, the presence of "pagan" imagery in fantasy books, or the impact fiction may have on people's minds. But other sects are less concerned. They note that the Bible itself contains fictional material, which is used to teach spiritual lessons.

It's worth understanding the historical reasons why religious traditions may be suspicious of fiction. They're linked to past limitations on who was allowed to learn to read and write, and who had time to do it. Like the family tree of our own opinions, the roots of concern about fiction may run deep.

It's worth making a note on your family tree about how your family has related to fiction:

- Did adults in your family read to you when you were small?

- Did they themselves read books for fun?

- Did you grow up in a family that rejected fiction in favor of religious texts?
Consider: How may this have impacted your relationship to other writing? Your sense of what to trust, and what not to?

Textbooks

Textbooks are in a funny kind of bind. If they're being taught in school, *somebody* has decided they're trustworthy, right? And yet, there have long been battles over what should go in textbooks, or what has been put in textbooks and shouldn't be there. Most of us are just given textbooks by our teachers, and we are expected to absorb them and then spit them back on tests. We're never told *why* we are supposed to trust these books.

I'm going to let you in on some secrets about how textbooks are made.

First of all, it's worth pointing out again that a textbook is not the exact same thing as the knowledge produced by a scientist or a historian. They're usually overviews of a whole field of that knowledge, written at a level that is easy for students of a given age to understand.

Textbooks are generally written by people who research history, science, psychology, economics, or whatever topic at hand, sure. (Although having worked at textbook publishers myself, I can tell you that a lot of the work of writing a textbook, including preparing new editions and creating exercises, may not be done by the authors listed on the cover. A lot of us doing the grunt work on textbooks were students at schools of education, or English majors; we weren't specialists.)

But when they're writing textbooks, scientists, historians, and other scholars don't do the same things they do when they're writing for their colleagues. Textbooks tend to include a broad overview of concepts and facts that are considered pretty "settled." When scientists or historians are still hashing out the details in ongoing arguments—say, whether

Pluto is a planet, or how a government has treated a particular ethnic or religious group—textbooks don't necessarily treat them as *arguments*.

This doesn't necessarily mean what's in a textbook isn't true (although there have been plenty of cases where things in textbooks are not true). It's just that most textbooks don't reflect the fact that our knowledge of history, science, literature, and math change over time. They present their subjects as a done deal—something that every scientist or historian agrees on. And they don't always agree! When a scientist or historian presents new arguments backed by solid evidence, even long-held theories and facts in textbooks can change.

Memorizing facts isn't the same as doing the work of historians or scientists. But it's often what textbooks ask students to do. The work that historians and scientists do involves asking *questions*, testing hypotheses, doing research, and presenting arguments based on what they found in that process. Training kids to memorize is not the best introduction to understanding things the way scientists and historians do—because memorizing is not their day-to-day work! Neither is anything remotely resembling standardized tests. *Asking questions, doing experiments, analyzing evidence,* and *making arguments* is closer to real research.

So if you were skeptical about things you were being told to memorize or felt like your history or science classes raised more questions than they answered, good news: you were already closer to doing science and history the authoritative way. Even if you didn't get a good grade (or got in trouble!) because you asked those questions. Even if your question was "why do I have to learn this when it seems so irrelevant?"

There are ways to produce textbooks that bring students closer to thinking like scientists, historians, and other scholars. In his book *Teaching What Really Happened* (which is subtitled *How to Avoid the Tyranny of Textbooks and Get Students Excited about Doing History*), the historian James Loewen says he wants to see history textbooks teach students "to scrutinize how a given piece of history came to be. Who wrote this book? Who put up this marker [commemorating a historical event]? Who *didn't* put it up? What points of view were omitted?" This means less emphasis on memorizing facts, and more emphasis on asking questions and gathering evidence.[3]

Unfortunately, history classes (like many other classes) face a challenge in trying to teach that way: standardized tests. Standardized tests are big part of why our schools rely so heavily on textbooks. Most textbooks emphasize memorization of facts because that's what students will be tested on. The more that governments and educational institutions use standardized tests to measure student growth, the harder it is to base a curriculum on students' questions, thinking, writing, and research. Giving a score to the quality of a student's writing is much, much harder than scoring based on which bubble they filled in.

As long as standardized tests are what students, teachers, textbooks, and schools are held to, there is little incentive to choose textbooks that emphasize research skills and critical thinking. Teachers who want to teach critical thinking or research skills have to do so *on top of* memorization of what will be on the test—which means fitting even more into crammed courses, and doing at least twice as much work.[4]

The process of getting a textbook approved is also where things can get further from the truths that researchers uncover. In the United States, committees of teachers, superintendents, and people in government typically have the authority to approve textbooks. Those people—particularly politicians—may have beliefs about what students should know that differ from what scientists, historians, and other professionals think people should know.

James Loewen lays out the textbook approval process in another book, *Lies My Teacher Told Me*. Although his textbook *Mississippi: Conflict and Change* ultimately won an award for best Southern nonfiction when it came out in 1975, publishers had been hesitant to publish it and the Mississippi textbook approval board refused to approve it for use in schools. Why? Loewen reports: "It contained too much 'black history,' included a photograph of a lynching, and gave too much attention to the recent past, according to the white majority on the rating committee."[5] To even make this book available for teachers to choose, Loewen and his coauthors had to sue the state under the First Amendment.

There's an even sadder example, this one about poor-quality science textbooks. Richard Feynman, one of the greatest physicists of the last century, developed theories of quantum mechanics and did research leading to nuclear weapons. Feynman tells a story about a time he was invited to review physics textbooks for the state school board of California.

Feynman found a number of errors in the textbooks that didn't match up with the latest knowledge in physics or math. Worse yet, at one point his committee was asked to review books that had nothing but blank pages. The publisher had missed a deadline, and was asking committee members to review those books based on the publisher's *descriptions* of the books—not on the content of the books, which wasn't finished yet.

This is an extreme case. But political pressure on state educational boards often shapes what appears in textbooks. For example, pressure from religious groups led to the publisher Holt's decision to take out any mention of gay people from their high school health textbook. Pressure to avoid talking about safe sex led the authors to offer weak advice, such as "go out as a group" and "get plenty of rest," when talking to teens about how to avoid sexually transmitted diseases.[6] This political pressure can make for gaps in readers' understanding.

When it comes to textbooks, the majority wins—and in the United States, that means states with the biggest populations of students: California. Florida. New York. And Texas. These states represent the largest markets for textbook publishers. As a result, when it comes to content, they tend to get what they want, because textbook publishers want to win large contracts for their school districts.

The short and long of textbooks is: Teaching is a lot of work. And the more writing, research, and questioning students do, the more work it is for teachers to grade and comment thoughtfully on their writing. Most American teachers are trying to do their best within a system that wants to see students spit back information they memorized, rather than think critically about information they encounter. And textbooks provide the easiest way to give an overview of what will be on a test, or to introduce a large field of research in a short period of time.

Textbooks have their place. But they're just a start. And most of them won't have you do the critical thinking you need to survive an information revolution.

How We Value Information

Scout Law: "Trust, and the information we trust, belong to us. They are resources we build in our communities, together, for each other."

By now it should be clear that "just always true" is never really the case about things we read. What we accept as trustworthy may be different depending on *our own current need* for information.

We may use different books for book reports, reading "for fun," teaching a class, or developing our spiritual lives. The same goes for the news, or for information we find online. Or think about how you choose a movie to see: when it comes to talking trash about the new blockbuster, you may just spout anything you heard from someone's comment online or on the morning show. But when it comes to actually deciding which movie to go to, you might deliberately look for reviews from someone whose opinion you trust. Your need for more trustworthy information can be more serious: you might trust home remedies or the healing power of prayer in the first week of a bad cough, but if it keeps going for a couple of weeks, you might decide a doctor's help is part of some higher power's plan for you.

For any information you go looking for, ask yourself:

What do I trust this information to do for me?

In the next chapter, I'll cover the reasons why we do (or don't) trust journalism, another profession that shapes much of the information we receive. The news bears the curious burden of needing to be "fair and balanced." (But have we always expected this to be the case?) Just as with books and information from other professionals, understanding how the news gets produced, and what its gaps and weaknesses might be, is crucial to understanding what we might trust.

Keep looking back to your opinion's family tree as we discuss how print, broadcast media, and websites developed people's trust over the years. Even if you're aware of them, earlier influences on your opinion shape your current information needs. Understanding how biases in new information resonate with your personal biases is critical at this moment in history— particularly when it comes to "fake news."

16

The News

Never forget that your obligation is to the people. It is not, at heart, to those who pay you, or to your editor, or to your sources, or to your friends, or to the advancement of your career. It is to the public.

—Ben Bagdikian, to his UC Berkeley journalism students[1]

Why Did We Trust the News?

In March 2018, the Seattle TV station KOMO aired an announcement that caused a national uproar. Two anchors (who were called A and B in an article on the sports blog *Deadspin*), read the following statement:

B: Our greatest responsibility is to serve our Northwest communities. We are extremely proud of the quality, balanced journalism that KOMO News produces.

A: But we're concerned about the troubling trend of irresponsible, one-sided news stories plaguing our country. The sharing of biased and false news has become all too common on social media.

B: More alarming, some media outlets publish these same fake stories ... stories that just aren't true, without checking facts first.

A: Unfortunately, some members of the media use their platforms to push their own personal bias and agenda to control "exactly what people think." ... This is extremely dangerous to a democracy.

B: At KOMO it's our responsibility to pursue and report the truth. We understand Truth is neither politically "left nor right." Our commitment to factual reporting is the foundation of our credibility, now more than ever.[2]

That sounds reassuring, right? In this time of questionable content, it's nice that at least one station stood up for journalistic values of even-handedness and fact checking. They're not the only ones who have made statements like this. Fox News has for years declared itself the home of "fair and balanced" reporting. The UK news outlet the *Guardian* touts the thoroughness of their researching when asking readers to subscribe. The *Washington Post* suggested its support of fair, democratic discussion by changing its motto to "Democracy Dies in Darkness." Most news outlets want you to think about them as fair.

So why was there a massive uproar about the statement these anchors read if this is such a popular idea?

Because the exact same statement had been read, word-for-word, at dozens of news stations, which made it sound like it was definitely not an independent, free-thinking decision voiced by reporters dedicated to a local community.

Fox stations, CBS stations, NBC stations, and ABC stations broadcast the speech. One journalist at *Deadspin* edited together video clips from all of these statements—and the result was unsettling, with the voices of anchors sounding like a creepy mass echo of each other. Dozens of journalists repeated, "This is extremely dangerous to a democracy. This is extremely dangerous to a democracy. This is extremely dangerous to a democracy."

What was going on? Who had told all of these anchors to say the exact same thing? We're talking four different networks here, not just Fox or ABC. Who was in control?

Although different networks provide the *content* for these stations, Sinclair Broadcast Group *operates* each one of them. Sinclair owns 193 stations around the United States, reaching millions of viewers. And it has become known for sending "must-run" orders to its stations, insisting that anchors and programmers air their news segments, infomercials, documentaries, and other content—most of which align with the views of the Republican party. Some are even further right, venturing into news items about the "deep state," a concept that is popular among conspiracy theorists.

Sinclair has even delivered orders on how anchors should dress while reading the statements about biased news: "Avoid totally red, blue and purple ties, the goal is to look apolitical, neutral, nonpartisan yet professional. Black or charcoal suits for men ... females should wear yellow, gold, magenta, cyan, but avoid red, blue or purple."[3] Sinclair knew that even the way anchors dressed could give viewers a sense that they were Democrats or Republicans. And they wanted to control that message— ironically, to make it look like their reporters were not subject to a particular point of view.

One Sinclair reporter was bothered by the biased way he was being told to interview everyday people for news segments. He was being fed questions that assumed how the people on the street who he was interviewing would respond, pushing them into an answer that they might not want to give and shaping how the report would be delivered. "I'd ask loaded questions like, 'How much do you disagree with Obama this year?'" he said. The question starts by assuming the interviewee disagrees with Obama, and doesn't ask what they actually think. "It was disguised as real journalism. But I'm a Republican, and I was still pissed by it."[4]

Is this always how news works, whether print, online, on TV or in radio? Isn't journalism supposed to be fair and balanced? Or was that always a lie?

As scientists and historians do with books, journalists ask us to trust their articles and broadcasts. Journalists aim to earn our trust in some of the same ways, mainly through their professional training and the ways they create and spread information. The Sinclair incident upset people because it violated one of the usual expectations of crafting news: that journalists should be allowed to use their independent judgment on the situations they're reporting without being subject to orders from the companies that employ them.

In this chapter, I'll go over the reasons why news claims to be trustworthy. Then I'll talk about some sources of bias that can take away from that trust, like ownership, which can change what a news organization does and doesn't report. And even if we think it is likely that a news outlet has a particular political leaning or conflict of interest—or we have no way of knowing what that leaning or conflict is—we can be mindful of the solution proposed in any individual article or editorial, and consider it on its own merits. And we can still hold news organizations to the standards that originally earned our trust.

News Becomes a Profession

As it turns out, if you asked one of your ancestors who lived in the 1800s why anyone would trust newspapers, they might say, "That's a really good question!" And then they might give you a lecture about the danger of believing what you read in "that rag." Or they'd box your ears ... or

1896: The *New York Times* tries real, real hard to break free of the "yellow journalism" era of the early 1800s.
Source: De Yongh, Library of Congress

something. Because it wasn't always the case that news even tried to be fair or accurate. Journalism changed to gain the public trust.

There have always been "different kinds" of newspapers. Some focus more on crime; some on business; some on international news; and some on "lifestyle" content like celebrities, or "human-interest" stories. Some papers never make a secret of their political bias. In many countries, a certain paper will be known for supporting one politician or political view—or will even be owned by politicians.

So where did we get the idea that the news needed to be "fair and balanced"? This wasn't even always the case in the United States. Around the time of the American Revolution and for some time afterward, papers in the United States were also known and expected to be the mouthpiece of a particular candidate. Hamilton had his paper; Jefferson had his.[5] News outlets have at times been owned by powerful people with interests in other industries like mining, steel, film, or technology. That ownership can also impact whether the news reported is really fair or balanced.

The idea that news might *not* lean in one direction or another didn't come to the United States until about sixty years after the Declaration of Independence. The 1830s shaped the news as we know it. James Gordon Bennett set out in the *New York Herald* to report news and "support no party ... care nothing for any election, or any candidate from president down to constable."[6]

But "care nothing for any election" came with a price: a focus on junk instead of reports on the corporations or politicians who were making decisions that affected readers' homes, jobs, and health. Bennett and other publishers at the time had their own bias, summed up in the old adage "If it bleeds, it leads," which is still applied to the news today. They favored true crime, tragedies, and bizarre stories that would capture readers' attention. This peaked in the competition between Joseph Pulitzer and William Randolph Hearst in the 1890s, where their rush to print hoaxes and scams earned their papers public scorn and the label "yellow journalism."[7]

Sound familiar? Papers of the 1800s were *full* of "fake news." Why? For exactly the same reason why the internet is full of hoaxes and clickbait headlines. They draw people's attention. And when you have people's attention, advertisers will pay you for it. I'll talk more about that in chapter 19, on profit.

Journalism as a profession began in the 1900s. Before then, pretty much any kid out of high school who could demonstrate he could write could get a job at his local newspaper. (And it was mostly boys—with great exceptions like Ida B. Wells, Nellie Bly, and Ida Tarbell, journalism, like many jobs, was effectively closed to women.)

By organizing as a profession, journalists were essentially asking the public to trust that they would gather and present their information using special methods to ensure that it was accurate and not biased. Becoming a profession meant people applying for news jobs or calling themselves journalists started having to show that they had been trained in special journalism *skills*. With the help of those who were already working as journalists, colleges and universities began organizing classes and departments to teach students these skills.

Like science, history, and other professions, journalism holds its members to ethical standards to remain worthy of the public's trust. There are a number of these from different organizations. The Society of Professional Journalists puts its guidelines in four groups.

1. Seek truth and report it.
2. Minimize harm.
3. Act independently.
4. Be accountable and transparent.[8]

Other organizations go into more detail about standards they demand for journalists.

- Respect the truth, and the right of the public to truth.
- Ensure what they write or broadcast is accurate, not biased, and not presented out of context.
- "See that the public's business is conducted in public." In other words, support transparency in government and corporations, exposing wrongdoing and misuse of power.

- Avoid financial, political, or personal conflicts of interest—like investing in the businesses they are covering, campaigning for candidates, or accepting gifts—and disclose their own and the news outlet's conflicts of interest.
- Make a clear distinction between what is news, and what is opinion or advertising.
- Only report facts they know the origin of, including identifying their sources.
- Protect the identities of sources only if there is a pressing need to keep them confidential (for example, if a source's job or life is at stake), in which case the journalist must respect that need at all costs while explaining why confidentiality is necessary.
- Use fair methods to gather news.
- Publicly correct errors in their reporting.
- Give people accused in a report the opportunity to respond.
- Respect the rights of those who they report on.
- Be aware of discrimination spread by news outlets, and work to correct that.
- Observe common standards of decency.[9]

In the United States, ethical codes point journalists to the First Amendment. The founders of the country gave the people free speech, and journalists are supposed to uphold that right with integrity, and defend it against anyone who wants to "exploit the press for selfish purposes."[10]

Anything that presents itself as "news" can be held to these standards. And anyone who writes it should be, too. If you're concerned that certain news is biased, only presenting one side of a story, or spreading falsehoods, you can actually make use of journalism's own rules and standards to get a sense of whether your perception is correct—or whether you've just chosen to believe what jibes with your own opinion.

In fact, I think it's a great self-defense technique to check any information by journalism's standards. What happens when we demand that scientists make clear when their funding causes a conflict of interest? What happens when we ask to see our history textbooks presented in context?

What if we hold religious blog posts or politicians' campaign promises accountable for giving accused people the opportunity to respond?

The ethical standards journalists are supposed to be held to aren't just pie-in-the-sky guidelines. News outlets and their reporters are supposed to *do* specific things to make sure they are upholding those rules. Today, because they are also worried about fake news, and the public's fading trust in them, many news outlets are working harder to show what they do, to earn trust.

Journalists have a massive toolkit to find and verify information. Just about every tool and resource used by other professions I describe in this book—from science journal articles, to website ownership searches, to eyewitness interviews, to ferreting out fake social media profiles—gets deployed by good journalists, too. Let's go over some of the things journalists do to seek the truth.

Attribution

You may have heard the term "off the record." It originates in journalism. When people ask to go "off the record," it means they will tell the journalist something, but they do not want it reported. People speaking to journalists might say this because they don't want to lose their job, worry about their reputation or that of their friends and family, or even fear violent retribution or being jailed for speaking out.

If they are OK with going "on the record," they are willing to let the journalist report what they said and attribute it to them—so we can know it was them, and determine if we trust their statement. If they want it reported "not for attribution," they're OK with it being reported, but with the journalist listing them as "an anonymous source." The ability to quote anonymous sources speaking off the record gives journalists the ability to share information that they couldn't otherwise talk about. In Washington, DC, it is pretty common to have sources speak on condition of anonymity because many US government officials' jobs could be at risk if they speak out without approval from their department.[11]

Journalists can still make good use of off-the-record information without even mentioning they used an anonymous source. They might use the

"Extra, extra, rea d all about it!" The cry of newspaper sellers in earlier eras was the ancestor of today's attention-getter: "breaking news." *Source:* Work Projects Administration Poster Collection—Library of Congress

information as "background." This might mean they go to another source to see if they could confirm, without exposing the first person. Off-record information could also give journalists some new questions to ask.

But there's an obvious problem with using anonymous sources: you can't prove who said something or trace back evidence for the story. And this could leave a reporter wiggle room to slip questionable information into a news article. Over the past few years, a number of prominent news organizations, including the *New York Times*, the *Intercept*, *BuzzFeed*, and the Associated Press, have been more public about their anonymous source policies.[12] The *Times* has tightened theirs, requiring reporters to get approval from their department heads and reveal the identity of their source to their editor. Here's the *Times*'s standard, according its executive editor Dean Baquet:

> Anonymity should be, as our stylebook entry says, "a last resort, for situations in which the Times could not otherwise publish information it considers newsworthy and reliable." That standard should be taken seriously and applied rigorously. Material from anonymous sources should be "information," not just spin or speculation. It should be "newsworthy," not just color or embellishment. And it should be information we consider "reliable"— ideally because we have additional corroboration, or because we know that the source has first-hand, direct knowledge.[13]

Confirming with Other Sources

"Additional corroboration" is another key idea in journalism. Journalists are supposed to verify and triangulate: rather than take one person's eyewitness testimony as the gospel truth, they are supposed to check that testimony with someone else. And then with another person ... and maybe another. They're supposed to figure out if a source is *reliable*. See the pattern here? They're supposed to do this, just as scientists, historians, religious scholars, and other professionals are.

Reliability here is not exactly the same as how scientists think of it, but it's related: If you ask other people or other sources of information, will they tell you the same thing? If you ask the same people more than once, will *they* say the same thing every time?

The Poynter Institute for Media Studies suggests the following checks on reliability for journalists learning to check facts:

- If people claim to be experts (like scientists or other professionals), journalists need to verify this is true. They may check in with a university to see if the experts work there or earned the degree they said they hold. If sources say they have extensive experience doing a certain kind of work, journalists should check with the colleagues those experts claim to work with.

- Like scientists looking for the "methods" section of a journal article, journalists should also look for things that demonstrate that people making claims are "showing their work."[14]

- Is the claim coming from a company or industry organization? "Follow the money" is a guiding principle in journalism. People might not speak against their own financial interests, and this can bias their claims. I'll talk more about this in the upcoming chapter on profit.

- Who's involved? Journalists will also check ownership of websites as well as parts of a website that may show who's involved with an organization.

- Journalists and fact checkers may look for the "About" section of an organization's website to see if its mission may have a clear, even openly stated, bias in a particular political or financial direction. And then they might dig deeper.

How to Keep Calm and Carry On

Scout Law: "If I understand how news, books, and other media are made, I will be better able to identify bias."

Journalists aren't the only ones who can confirm information with other sources. With the internet available, we can all do a little more digging and see how information from authoritative sources compares to what we see in the news. For example, you can find another way to find the facts about crime and politics in your community, state, or country. Or, as I described in chapter 13, you can look into who owns a site or search for fake profiles. Here are a few more tools.

- Get police statistics. Make sure they actually come from a police department or crime-reporting organization—there's a lot of bad "I saw it on the internet" kind of information floating around about crime.

- Compare news written inside your country with news that comes from a foreign news source.

- Additional information on how to check on the authoritativeness of specific photos can be found in the earlier chapter on relationships online.

Journalistic Privilege

Along with the ability to use anonymous sources, another support reporters and their sources have for bringing the truth to light is "reporter's privilege" or "journalistic privilege." This refers to the right that reporters have in some countries not to be forced to testify in court about who gave them information, or to turn that information over to law enforcement. This protection makes it more likely that sources will talk to journalists, without fear that they will be outed.

The way this privilege works varies from state to state in the United States, and from country to country. And unfortunately, this right, which is supposed to protect a key role of journalism in democracy, is under attack from a number of legal decisions.[15] Take a look at **keepcalmlogon.com** for organizations that are working to ensure journalists have this protection.

Separation of Opinion and Advertising from News

Traditionally, in newspapers and broadcast news, it was agreed that opinion pieces should be put in a clearly marked section of their own. Many of the highest-regarded news organizations still do this.

Advertising, similarly, was separated out into sections that looked different. The field of public relations (PR) and the information it produces has made distinguishing between news and not-news seriously challenging. Organizations or companies sometimes produce their own PR articles and send them to news organizations, which sometimes pick them up word-for-word without making it clear they did so. At other times, they pay for this placement.

With the advent of the internet, this line has blurred. News, opinion, and advertising may all appear on different parts of a page (like the sidebar or additional links following a news article), or even end up on sites far from the one that originally produced them.

Covering a "Beat"

Beat reporting is one way that a news outlet strengthens its ability to thoroughly and deeply cover an issue. Reporters might be assigned to education, city hall, or science as a "beat," meaning that's all they cover. These reporters build up a large contact list of people in their subject, preferably ones with different perspectives: for example, someone on the schools beat might be in regular touch with principals, teachers, experts on child behavior, members of the local board of education, and parents. Beat journalists go back to their contacts regularly to cross-check stories they are working on, and ask them if there are new issues coming up that might matter to their community. In the process, both readers and sources come to trust that they are knowledgeable.

Fact Checking

Fact checking is another of the activities that are important to making sure the news is not being faked. Sometimes journalists will fact check for themselves; sometimes there is someone else hired by their company to check their work. It is the fact checker's job to make sure that the stories and statements reported are correct.

Here are some fact-checking questions recommended by the Poynter Institute, which focuses on improving journalism, as well as by PolitiFact and Africa Check, two organizations dedicated to fact checking:

Was this a significant statement, or did the person making it misspeak?

There's always the possibility that a quote came from someone who said something in the heat of the moment, and it doesn't represent what that person really meant. In these cases, it's useful to have a fact checker go back to confirm the quote with the person it was attributed to, and see if they stand by it.

Can we verify this statement?

Fact checkers will break down a statement into parts, in order to think about whether those parts are can be verified as true or not—because all human beings say things that are a mix of fact and opinion.

Here is an example of three statements from the Poynter Institute's course on fact checking, and their demonstration of how to think through the truth contained in each one:

- "The unemployment rate has decreased by two points in the four months since I became president."
- "The private sector's confidence in my government has led to a two-point decrease in the unemployment figures."
- "Without my government, we wouldn't have seen unemployment fall by two points."

The three sentences are predicated on the same basic fact: The unemployment rate has decreased by two percentage points over a four-month period. That is verifiable through a national statistical agency. The second claim injects a claim about causation: It was the private sector's confidence in government caused unemployment to go down. This gets trickier: Businesses are often polled about trust in the government's economic policies; and job data can be broken down to detect whether the decrease in unemployment was due to more jobs or more people dropping out of the labor market, and whether these jobs were created in the public or private sector. But correlation is not causation, as the old warning goes.

The third claim is more clearly an opinion: There is no way to know what would have happened to the unemployment rate, had the country been governed by someone else. It is worth noting that such a claim can't be supported in facts, either, so the speaker is playing with truthfulness.[16]

Journalists are supposed to keep track of these different kinds of claims and treat them differently. Journalists should not treat the statement "Without my government, we wouldn't have seen unemployment fall by two points" as if it were true. They should look for the source of the statistic on unemployment and mention it. And then it's their job to press the politician claiming responsibility for the improvement in unemployment to be more honest, and to do research on business and job data.

You, too, can look at a news report the way fact checkers should, to see whether the journalists have done their job. How easy would it be to prove or disprove each claim they include in their article?

It's worth keeping in mind that it is generally not illegal in the United States for anyone to lie to you. Politicians, news anchors, teachers, your neighbors—not anybody. There are exceptions: for example, when someone is on the witness stand in a courtroom. When it comes to claims made about food and drugs, claims about what someone can say are regulated.

There are also laws against defamation, or saying something untrue about a person, but the wronged person has to prove the person telling the lie about them knew it was a lie and meant to harm them. Even then, you might be surprised at what people and companies can get away with.

In fact, United States court decisions have actually *protected* lies as free speech. Why? As Garrett Epps summed it up in a piece for the *Atlantic*, "the cure—government control of what can be said in politics—is far worse than the disease." Courts have decided that there is too much danger that people saying truthful things could be intimidated or silenced if everything people say is put on trial as a possible lie. It would leave less room for valid criticism.[17]

If we didn't check this fact, what would be the impact?

Some facts are really important to check, for public safety, while others are less critical. Each news outlet has its own standards for thinking about the impact of getting a fact wrong.

When I was an intern at *Sunset Magazine*, fact checking was part of my job. I learned that the magazine took fact checking so seriously that if a reporter wrote "Jennifer's blonde hair streamed behind her in the wind," I had to call Jennifer and ask if her hair was blonde. Obviously, this fact was not likely to get *readers* in trouble, or even the magazine; it seems unlikely Jennifer would complain if we described her hair color wrong.

But the legend was that there was a very serious reason for being that precise. *Sunset* included a travel and outdoor-life section, and would sometimes suggest hiking trails to readers. My editor said that at one point, they hadn't fact checked the trail route—and readers had ended up on a military bombing range! Thank goodness, nobody was hurt.

You can see why a news organization might care a lot about checking its facts. In addition to upholding the truth, there are legal consequences for false reporting. The company might get sued for damages, like in the case of the bad trail route.

In the case of reporting on public figures, there are *libel and slander laws* that news organizations are held accountable to. Internationally, these are known as *defamation* laws. Slander is something untrue someone says; libel is something untrue someone writes down or publishes, including fake images. Everyday citizens can sue a news outlet if it puts out untrue statements about them that cause them harm. Public figures can, too, but there is a stronger standard in their case: they have to demonstrate that what the news outlet said about them was malicious and operated with a "knowing or reckless disregard for the truth."

Because there is a long history of news outlets being held to defamation laws, you can generally trust that professional news organizations work to make sure what they report is correct, lest they get sued for a lot of money. As a news intern, one of the first things my editors insisted I read had to do with libel. They could have guessed that I'd already learned about libel in college, but their concern was so serious they wanted to make sure they covered their bases.

There are also some questions journalists and fact checkers may ask about the sources of information being reported:

Is this an *original* source?

Here, you may start to see a pattern! When journalists ask if something is an original source, they are asking some of the same questions historians, scientists, lawyers, and theologians do. Here's what they mean by "original" or "primary" sources:

- testimony from someone who experienced or witnessed an event, including oral histories;
- other direct evidence from the event (like the evidence police would find at a crime scene, for example);
- autobiographies or memoirs; and
- results of a scientific experiment or other academic research.

Balance across an Entire News Outlet

Now that you've got a clearer picture of the parts of professional journalism that encourage us to trust the news, you have a few tools to gauge the truthfulness of individual news articles based on strategies journalists use themselves. There are also some ways you can gauge whether an entire news outlet is reliable. Is "yes" the answer to the following questions?

- Does the outlet issue corrections?
- Does it have fact-checkers on staff?

You can also look at the mix of what the outlet is publishing, to think about whether some issues are not being covered, or to check the accuracy of what its reporters write:

- Take a look at a news site's list of "most shared" stories. What are the top stories about?
- Look past the first page. Is there news that impacts your community, including its schools, courts, police force, roads, and local business?
- Politically, which side are the outlet's editorials on?
- Again, as in chapter 11, ask: Which kinds of people are represented in this outlet's reporting? How are they represented? Whose voices are heard? Whose are not?

And finally, it's useful to keep an eye out for the kind of unusual protest over a station's policies we saw at Sinclair. From the reports about Sinclair's must-run demand, we learned their reporters and station managers were in a tough position: many of them had signed contracts that said they couldn't work for any of Sinclair's competitors for six months, *and* if they quit they would owe the company up to 40 percent of their salary.[18] When journalists are under pressure to say exactly what their company wants them to, even if it conflicts with fair and accurate reporting, the public deserves to know.

What I've covered in the last few chapters has mostly pre-dated our digital lives. The way information is spread online has its own unique characteristics—and its own systems that support (or don't support) our trust. I'll devote the next two chapters to some of the systems that build our online information: the special case of the crowdsourced encyclopedia Wikipedia, and algorithms, which are like recipes that sites and apps use to serve up information.

17

Wikipedia

The Special Case of Wikipedia

I've talked about the information that can help us decide whether we should trust websites, like addresses and login names. I've also talked about the ways that professions, like science, journalism, and history, work for our trust. Somewhere in between, the internet generated a kind of knowledge unlike any the world had seen before: Wikipedia. Sure, it's "shaped" kind of like an encyclopedia—it's in the name. But the ways people around the world build information on Wikipedia, and the way the site demonstrates the truthfulness of its information, are unique. People who have been in school during the last twenty years have probably been warned by their teachers at some point that Wikipedia is not a good source of information. But I want to make the case that because it's transparent, it's not actually all that bad—if you know how to look into what's trustworthy.

Why Trust an Encyclopedia Edited by Random Strangers?

Scout Laws: "If I understand how news, books, and other media are made, I will be better able to identify bias"; "If I understand how communities decide what information to trust, I will be better prepared to identify bad information."

Why is it many teachers are leery of Wikipedia?

Anyone can post anything to Wikipedia. That's the idea of the site: it's the world's source of information, created by anyone in the world who wants to edit and add to a page. *You* can post to Wikipedia, right now! (To find out how, check out **keepcalmlogon.com**.) But then again, Wikipedia isn't the *only* place online where anyone can post anything.

There are downsides to anyone being able to post anything. (I've described some of them earlier.) The history of Wikipedia is littered with

Roll up your sleeves—we can all help Wikipedia
be more trustworthy! *Source:* Tom Morris,
work derivative of "We Can Do It!" poster by
J. Howard Miller

stories of vandalism and other malicious or misleading editing of the
site's content. The volunteer editors who work to keep vandals at bay
don't always have a chance to revert bad changes right away. And there
are a few other drawbacks that I'll get to in a minute.

But I'm going to make a case that Wikipedia is not as bad as many teachers would have you believe. No, you definitely don't want to use Wikipedia
(or any encyclopedia!) as your main source for a research paper. No, you
don't want to rely on it for medical advice or legal advice. And yet Wikipedia

can be a fine place to start finding relevant sources, and can help you get to a wealth of images, sound files, and other resources from libraries and museums around the world, whose staff are sometimes given the job of posting their collections (like most of the images in this book!) to the site.

More importantly, unlike much of the information we encounter online, Wikipedia *does* have rules about determining what is a trustworthy fact and what kind of evidence is good enough to support the facts. They put those rules on their page for anyone to view. And the history of who has changed a page, adding or removing information, is also visible to anyone who wants to find it, along with comments from people who have edited or are watching the page. Because of this, Wikipedia, if used correctly, can be a more trustworthy source of information than much of the rest of what you find online.

The Five Pillars

Wikipedia has five "pillars" that serve as guidelines for people who are adding to or reading their site. The first two are useful in helping us think about the claims Wikipedia makes to "being truthful":

Wikipedia is an encyclopedia

Wikipedia is not a soapbox, an advertising platform, a vanity press, an experiment in anarchy or democracy, an indiscriminate collection of information, or a web directory. It is not a dictionary, a newspaper, or a collection of source documents, although some of its fellow Wikimedia projects are.

Wikipedia is written from a neutral point of view

We strive for articles in an impartial tone that document and explain major points of view, giving due weight with respect to their prominence. We avoid advocacy, and we characterize information and issues rather than debate them. In some areas there may be just one well-recognized point of view; in others, we describe multiple points of view, presenting each accurately and in context rather than as "the truth" or "the best view." All articles must strive for verifiable accuracy, citing reliable, authoritative sources, especially when the topic is controversial or is on living persons. Editors' personal experiences, interpretations, or opinions do not belong.[1]

Let's break down what the pillars are trying to do to keep Wikipedia truthful:

Because Wikipedia is not an advertising platform, it should not be a place where the content is only there to make someone money. This doesn't mean that companies don't sometimes edit Wikipedia to make their companies, products, or stock price sound better than they should. Politicians have also been caught editing their own pages to make them sound better. But Wikipedia encourages editors to identify people who have a conflict of interest and question or remove changes they made to an article. Those people can sometimes be identified by the IP address they're editing the site from (see? Addresses come into play again) or by the group of pages they've chosen to edit.

Because Wikipedia is not a soapbox or vanity press, it should not contain personal testimony, or writing in which people ramble on about their pet projects or issues. Editors are encouraged to take anything like that down. (And if *you* find something like that in a Wikipedia article, you can flag the article to be edited, or even fix it yourself.)

Saying that "Wikipedia is not a newspaper" points out some of the things Wikipedia does not do. Wikipedia's volunteer editors are not supposed to do personal investigation or interviews to come up with the information they put in articles. Wikipedia does not emphasize the latest breaking news; rather, it focuses on providing a big-picture summary.

The "neutral point of view" guideline encourages editors to leave their personal feelings about an issue at the door. The encouragement to describe, but not argue for, multiple points of view should help editors overcome bias. Different perspectives on Wikipedia should be shown as perspectives, rather than as facts.

You Might Be Asking . . .

"OK, so that's what Wikipedia says it does. How do I actually know whether to rely on the facts I see in an article, though?"

How to Keep Calm and Carry On

The pillars are only guidelines. And, ultimately, it's possible that the trustworthiness of any article could be damaged by someone defacing the article, or by an overzealous volunteer editor with an ax to grind.

More usefully for those of us trying to understand how true a Wikipedia article is, each article has information that can help make it clearer *what was actually done* to create it. When you're relying on Wikipedia, look for the following.

- **Criticisms.** When a Wikipedia article is about a historical subject or a theory, it will often have a section titled "criticisms" or "critique." These sections will give you a perspective on other authorities who have pointed out flaws in the main information in the article. For example, check out the many and diverse criticisms on the page for "cultivation theory," which I talked about in an earlier chapter. I often jump to the "criticisms" section first, to see how seriously I should take an idea. These criticisms don't necessarily tell me I should dismiss an idea entirely—just that I should be careful how and where I use them.

- **Citations.** Just like a scholarly book, Wikipedia articles should have links to other web pages, news or scholarly articles, or books that back up their claims. I've made use of these in writing this book! Generally, when you're using Wikipedia as a source, you don't want to cite it; you want to dig deeper into the articles and books in the citations.

- **History.** Arguably the most fascinating part of Wikipedia is the "History" page linked at the top of an article, which lets you see every change that was made to the article over time. This includes links to the old content and the changed content, the date the edits were made, and the IP addresses and/or user names of the people who made the edits. If the users who edited the article were logged in and have a profile, you can take a look at other articles they have edited, see some information about what they know and do in the rest of their lives (are they a professor? a retired history buff? an activist? someone whose goal is just making Wikipedia better?), and even take a look at discussions other people have had with them about edits they have made, maybe arguing or asking for more information.

- **Talk.** Like the History section, this link at the top of a Wikipedia page gives background on changes that have been made, or should be made, to the article. In here you'll find discussions between editors about whether there is enough evidence to make a claim, whether someone appears to have a conflict of interest or is posting their personal opinion, and so on.

Given what you see in those four places, what do you think about the trustworthiness of specific claims in the Wikipedia article you're looking at?

Like all sources of information, Wikipedia is what it is. It's not just fact, it's not just truth. But its editors are held to rules that help them, and you, move in the direction of the truth. Its great strength is making its rules clearer and more accessible to everyone than the rules in journalism, academic research, or fields like politics or advertising where there are even fewer rules.

Wikipedia's Blind Spots

That said, some of the site's rules leave it with blind spots.

Wikipedia's rules make it hard to capture information about traditions that are largely oral, based on firsthand testimony of the sort I described in chapter 12. When I was trying to put more information about traditional African dance styles up on Wikipedia, I ran smack into the rules. Wikipedia doesn't have guidelines for determining how factual oral traditions are—and that's how most of the knowledge about traditional African dance is passed around, by conversations with dance teachers and choreographers. If I were trying to improve the articles, I would have to cite news articles, which may not do deep research because the reporters don't have the time, or anthropologists or missionaries, who might have cultural biases that would keep them from understanding the dances the way the dancers do (though anthropologists also have rules intended to steer their research clear of their own biases).

Wikipedia is also made weaker by its reliance on textbooks. Wikipedia's rules ask contributors to rely on sources of information that pull together a number of sources themselves, rather than citing "primary research" when adding facts to the site. Textbooks are one of the aggregate sources of information Wikipedia says are appropriate. "Primary research" includes articles written by researchers who specialize in a topic and may be shedding new light on it—but the rest of the field hasn't agreed with them yet, or written their findings into the kind of overviews that Wikipedia thinks are the best sources of information.

One college professor ran into this shortcoming when he found a mistake in Wikipedia, and tried to correct it. Timothy Messer-Kruse studies and teaches labor history. He noticed that the Wikipedia page for the

Haymarket riot, where a bomb was thrown at an originally peaceful labor protest, contained a strange claim. The trial of the anarchists who were accused of the bombing lasted six weeks—and yet Wikipedia said that during that trial, no evidence was presented connecting the defendants with the bombing.

Messer-Kruse had studied primary source material from the trial, and he knew this was wrong. Forensic chemists presented analysis of the metal shrapnel from the bombs. One hundred eighteen witnesses were called. They described meetings where attacks were planned, and secret messages placed by conspirators in radical newspapers. So, Messer-Kruse changed the Wikipedia page to describe the evidence.

His changes were removed within minutes. The person reverting the changes pointed to Wikipedia's "undue weight" rule: minority views should not be given more weight than majority views.

In other words, because years of textbooks and other overviews of that historical era said there was no evidence presented in the trial, Wikipedia's rules said Messer-Kruse couldn't change the page to reflect the facts he had found in court testimony and scientific evidence from the time of the trial. Messer-Kruse linked to the testimony from the trial, which the Library of Congress had put online. Still no luck; Wikipedia editors pointed to the undue weight rule and changed the page back to the original.

Even when Messer-Kruse published a book on his research and corrected the page again, Wikipedia editors held him to the undue weight rule. One wrote, "If all historians save one say that the sky was green in 1888, our policies require that we write 'Most historians write that the sky was green, but one says the sky was blue.' ... As individual editors, we're not in the business of weighing claims, just reporting what reliable sources write."[2]

So the good news is that Wikipedia articles are supposed to be held to standards for evidence, and the site is very clear about what those standards are. The bad news is the blind spots in those standards. Messer-Kruse is going to have to wait until other scholars mention his findings in textbooks and other historical overviews before Wikipedia will treat the facts he found in original documents from the time of the trial as true.

This engraving, with portraits of the defendants in the Haymarket trial, was distributed among labor activists, anarchists, and socialists. *Source:* Walter Crane

18

Algorithms, or Digital "Soup" Recipes

In 2014, Facebook did one of many creepy things it would do over the next few years: it played with people's emotions—literally.

Without getting permission, Facebook filtered 689,003 users' feeds based on words they and their friends used that related to different emotions. For one group of users, it didn't show posts with words that indicated negative emotions like sadness or anger. For another group, it took out posts with positive emotional words.

The result? Facebook researchers saw what is called *emotional contagion*. People who only saw negative posts also put things in their feeds that were negative, spreading bad vibes like the flu. The opposite happened for those who only saw positive posts.

Source: Work Projects Administration Federal Art Project

When the researchers published a paper on this study, outcry was swift. Digital rights activists, journalists, and political figures called the experiment "scandalous," "spooky," and "disturbing." Would manipulation of Facebook feeds be able to channel people's emotions to get them to buy advertisers' products, even if they weren't interested in them? Or change the outcome of an election?[1]

It's probably clear to you by now that social media, shopping sites, apps, and other places in your digital life change the order of what they show you. What may be less clear to you is *how* they are changing things they show you, and *why*.

The simple explanation for *why* sites change the order of what they show is that they are working to turn a larger profit. I'll talk more about that in the next chapter. But that doesn't explain *how* they are changing the order of rankings in search, say, or posts in your social media feed. The *how* involves algorithms. Those algorithms are written by people. And I'd argue we should know a lot more about those algorithms, the people who code them, and their motives before we put our trust in them.

Algorithms: Made of People

Algorithm: a big, difficult-sounding math word. Let me simplify it by explaining that an algorithm, in computer code, basically acts like a recipe. It's a set of rules in a particular order that produces a particular result. So, for example: out of all the onions in your kitchen, choose the largest one. Cut it in quarters. Then cut those quarters in quarters. Are they now too small to cut again? No? Then cut the pieces in half. Yes? Put oil in the pan and turn the heat to medium. Put the onion pieces in the pan. Cook. Are the onions browned on one side? No? Leave them longer. Yes? Stir until the browning is even. Did you burn the onions so they're inedible? Yes? Throw it all out and go back to step one. No? Add the onions to the other ingredients. Et cetera.

Notice that in this recipe, there are steps that aren't "true" so much as "matters of human judgment": Are the pieces too small to cut, or are you going to obsessively chop until they're smaller? What is "browned" and what is "burnt"—is this inedible now, or does that one person you're cooking for really like the burned bits? The same goes for algorithms: they also have human judgment built in. Think back to the example where

Facebook engineers decided that the "news" meant "politics, crime, or tragedy." They could just as well have said "things that happened yesterday," "things that happened in your city," and "scientific discoveries"—and that would have put a totally different set of stories, images, and videos in your feed. Same goes for the emotion experiment. Two different recipes produce two different kinds of soup.

For most of us, it looks like algorithm recipes are just magic. Shopping sites know what brands we like! Music sites play a great series of songs in a row! Search engines just come up with the right answer! We're told some algorithms can even identify where crimes are likely to rise! We ask our devices' systems a question, and they just make life easier for us.

But the reality is, it's not magic:

Algorithms are made of people.

OK, that sounds a little weird, especially if I'm talking about recipes. What I mean is that algorithms are just rules written by people, like any other system. But you can tack "is made of people" on the end of any fancy new tech idea to remind yourself it's not magic. Search engines are made of people. Smart assistants and voice recognition are made of people. The blockchain? Looks like it's made of math, ultimately made of people. (And of other people's computers, the same way "the cloud" is.)

As we've asked with other systems: Why should we trust the system of people that produces these algorithms? I'm going to argue that right now, we shouldn't, always. We don't know much about these recipes, or the human judgment that went into them. There aren't yet enough legal requirements forcing companies to be clear about them. And as I'll explain, there are places where magic-looking algorithms hidden from the public eye can have serious negative impacts on our lives. They can spread violent content and extreme ideas. They can make the biases we talked about earlier even worse. They may only show us content that agrees with us. Or in some cases, they pass judgment on people's financial status, or even their freedom. In this chapter, I'll touch on search engines, YouTube, and social media, but I'll also dive deeper into systems that can have a more serious impact on our lives: image recognition, credit scoring, and even algorithms which decide whether our résumé gets looked at when we apply for jobs.

Some Work Projects Administration posters, like this one, sent overly simplistic messages to build public confidence in complicated processes. Today we often talk about the "magic" of search engines or voice-recognition systems without fully understanding the systems of code and people behind them. *Source:* Work Projects Administration Poster Collection—Library of Congress

The Frighteningly Life-Changing Magic of Tidying Up the Internet

Most algorithms we encounter online are intended to narrow down the digital firehose we drink from, turning it into a drinking-fountain-like trickle rather than soaking us and knocking us over.

So how do they know what to show? In this current era of social media, what we see often draws on data we gave to the system. This includes information we gave intentionally, like our name, the city we live in, our jobs and interests, and links to our family members. But it also includes our actions: when we re-post, click, or like things, hide them from our view, or move on to another page. It includes the data in trackers and cookies.

Sound familiar? When social media algorithms make choices based on the social networks, preferences, location, and interests we feed them, we give them the biases from our family trees. And they continue to develop these biases by customizing our feeds based on things we've clicked on or liked in the past. They're likely to cut out content that doesn't agree with us, and this can keep us from developing trust in people who may have different viewpoints from ours.

As I mentioned in chapter 11, Eli Pariser, an activist on the left side of the political spectrum, noticed that even though he followed a number of conservatives on Facebook because he wanted to know what they were thinking, there was a point at which Facebook stopped including conservative posts in his feed. Was this because the company had a bias against conservatives? No—the opposite was happening to conservatives, who didn't see liberal posts. This all came about because Facebook had changed its algorithm to prioritize the kind of content people were already clicking on, reinforcing everyone's biases.[2]

This kind of selection by the algorithmic soup means we keep seeing more of the things we already believe. On YouTube, this gets even more alarming; the author Zeynep Tufekci noted that the more she clicked through videos for a political topic, the further YouTube took her down a path of radical ideas in the same vein, diving into conspiracy theories and even calls to jihad. "Intrigued," she writes, "I experimented with nonpolitical topics. The same basic pattern emerged. Videos about vegetarianism led to videos about veganism. Videos about jogging led to videos about running ultramarathons."[3]

Filtering by your own preference is more automatic than traditional newspapers, whose editors deliberately choose news they feel is most pressing to some group of people and push it to the top of the page. Today, even news sites have flirted with using an algorithm to change the order of what you see.

Social media sites often explain they are doing this so we will "get to see more of the stuff we love." But "love" on those sites is often defined as "stuff you click or comment on," in these cases. Does that sound like "love" to you? Or obsession? Boredom? How about hate-reading or hate-watching something, for the sheer pleasure of making fun of it? Arguing with someone you think is wrong? It could be any of the above, and not every system we encounter online is smart enough to know the difference. This is a crucial reason why I recommend not re-posting information about mass shootings or other human-caused calamities online: each re-post is essentially a vote for the shooter, telling the site's algorithm you want more people to see this, and you want to see more like it yourself. It's a vote that the company should keep posting more things like this, and advertising next to it, making more money with every click. It's a vote that is likely to spread extremism to more angry young people.

And this makes for a fast race to the bottom. Algorithms often get set up to produce content that draws on what is making the most money by attracting the most attention, and that's when things get really dark. A seller on Amazon called Solid Gold Bomb had an algorithm generate T-shirts that began "Keep Calm" (yep!) and then added random words afterward, waiting to see what sold. When a shirt sold, he'd print it. The owner, Michael Fowler, figured people would look for shirts that said things like "Keep Calm and Nurse On." Registered nurses, or breastfeeding mothers? The algorithm didn't know and didn't care. Fowler was just excited by the possibilities of suddenly having more than ten million possible designs to sell to customers.[4]

What the algorithm developed instead were shirts that said "Keep Calm and Rape a Lot," or "Keep Calm and Knife Her."

On YouTube, parents are starting to voice concern about the random garbage the site's algorithm gives their kids when they click through to characters they know and love. Toddlers watching nursery rhymes or

Disney videos have ended up following links to disturbing low-rent videos featuring their favorite characters—for example, Peppa Pig drinking bleach or Elsa from *Frozen* bleeding as Spider-Man breaks her arm.[5]

Consider the impact of algorithms with results like these. What could happen to your relationships with your friends and family if social media ran more emotion experiments like Facebook's? Human beings have a huge range of emotions in our face-to-face interactions with each other. We may offer love and support over a death in the family, commiserate over an ugly breakup or a loss by a favorite sports team, work together to get justice when our workplaces infuriate us by treating us wrong. On social media in particular, we may see the early warning signs if a friend is depressed and considering suicide. The choices algorithms make may not be the same ones we'd make to support our friends and family.

Because Facebook's emotion experiment raised so much anger, it seems unlikely that social media will try the exact same algorithmic scheme again. But if social media sites do manipulate our feeds to filter out negative emotions like sadness, depression, and anger, they take away opportunities for us to take care of each other in hard times.

Who benefits from the algorithmic tidying-up of our feeds? Is it only done so advertisers will have a friendly place to make money without people bringing down each other's moods? Is this what we really want?

You May Be Asking . . .

"OK, so they're controlling what's in my feed. What can I do about that?"

How to Keep Calm and Carry On

Scout Laws: "If I understand how news, books, and other media are made, I will be better able to identify bias"; "I talk to different people in my life in different ways. It should be up to me to decide who I want to talk to, how, and when"; "If something digital is not doing work for me right now, I can turn it off."

Along with the earlier tips on conserving your attention by reducing alerts and setting "off" times, there are also ways to ensure you see more of the stuff you want to and less of the stuff social media sites want you to. There are a few general things you can try:

Like the market, a search engine depends on a complex system of behind-the-scenes sources in order to deliver the goods.
Source: Work Projects Administration Poster Collection—Library of Congress

- Look for the settings on an individual post or account. If you feel like you're hearing too much from some people, groups, shows, companies, types of posts, and the like, and not enough from the ones you care about, see if there are ways to "mute" the noisy person from your feed. That can make it so instead of having what they post pushed to your feed, you can just go check in on theirs when you feel like it. I'm at a point where I've muted pretty much everyone I know on Facebook and a lot of them on Twitter (with the exceptions of people who I worry about).

- Muting usually doesn't give your friends an indication you aren't "listening" to them, which is nice, because it doesn't become a big hairy deal. But if you don't mind them knowing, and you need stronger medicine to make stuff go away, you can often block certain accounts or even terms from coming up in your feed.

- If advertising is getting too heavy in your feed, look into the settings for your account and see if there's a way to adjust sponsored content specifically. For example, Facebook currently gives you a way to wipe out all of the things it thinks it knows about your interests.

Next, let's talk about search algorithms. Like editors of newspapers or books, they are part of a system that decides what we see first when we go looking for information.

Search Soup

Much of the time when we go looking for information online, we start with a search engine. A lot of us don't go much further than the first search result, or the first page of results. Often, we feel like the first results are fine for our needs.

But how do we know that first result is trustworthy information? How do we know that the search engine really gives us the best result first?

There are no guarantees that the information is true, or even useful for the needs that may have sent us looking. Search engines aren't in the business of determining whether information is accurate or not. Rather, what they give us is a picture of how *valuable* they estimate the information to be.

A search engine keeps an *index* of all the sites its *crawlers* (bits of code) have found as they move from page to page around the internet, like spiders on a web. The index is a database that keeps a condensed, ranked record of every written word, link, and image on every page (not audio or video—not yet at least). When a word appears on a page a lot of times, the page's rank for searches of that word may increase. This was an early way that search engines used to rank sites. Today, it's only one ingredient in the "ranking soup."

Every search engine has its own algorithm for deciding what results will be most valuable to us based on what we entered into the search bar. Unlike many such "recipes," we do have some idea what goes into search algorithms. Google's PageRank algorithm has been written about a lot; it was made while its creators, the Google founders Larry Page and Sergey Brin, were still students. So that part, at least, is not as protected as the rest of the company's "secret recipe."

Beyond PageRank, the secret Google recipe is protected because it is very, very, *very* valuable. Like, billions of dollars, "driving the value of the entire tech industry" valuable. Search is what drives people to websites—and when people show up at websites, advertisers want to be there too, to capture their attention. In fact, search companies came up with one of the first profitable business models online: helping advertisers understand who was going where, and using that information to sell ads.[6]

What would happen if people knew exactly how search algorithms work? For one thing, they could copy the search-soup recipe and sell it themselves. It's argued that that competition would discourage people from doing the work it takes to develop the best soup possible. But it would also be easier to do things to a website to make it rise to the top of search results even if it shouldn't be there—and that might make for an arms race where consumers lose.

Because understanding algorithm soup is so profitable, there is an entire industry known as search engine optimization (SEO) that makes fairly educated guesses about how search engine algorithms work. SEO specialists poke and prod at search engines until they figure out how much of the different ingredients each one uses. Search engine companies also share parts of their recipe with the public, particularly with businesses who want to understand how to get the attention they need by being findable in search results. To get a look at sites where SEO experts and search engine developers talk about how search works, check out **keepcalmlogon.com**.

So, what is in search engine algorithms? First, let's get a common misconception out of the way. Many people mistakenly believe that search engines rank websites based on how many people click on them, as if clicks through to the site were "votes" for that site. This isn't true!

Think for a second about how that would work: for starters, how would they start out the rankings before anyone had clicked on any sites? More importantly, using clicks for rank would just keep giving votes to the same sites. The top ranked sites would keep getting seen and clicked on as people decided they didn't need to dig any deeper into the search results, and they'd just keep getting ranked as more and more popular. There would be no way for new, good-quality sites to move up into the first page of search results where people would see them. (Note that this sets search apart from social media feeds, where clicks might be counted as votes—which gives an advantage to posts and people who are already popular.)

Instead, the main ingredient in most modern search engines is something like PageRank, the innovation that made Google a huge success. PageRank uses the links *to* a website—the links themselves—as votes for how important the page is. By looking at which page links to where, search engines estimate which sites are most valuable to the people doing the linking. For each page, Google's PageRank algorithm doesn't just look at how many links there are to that page. It also looks at how many pages link to the pages doing the linking. PageRank also looks at the rank of pages that link to a page. Ultimately, then, there *is* a popularity contest underlying search—but it's about who links to who, not how many times people click.

Besides PageRank, what else is in that soup? As of 2005, Google looked at over one hundred factors to rank pages in search.[7] Today, these factors include:

- links on the page;
- the writing around those links;

- the date the site was updated or the post went up (newer content is favored over older content—which isn't always great if you're looking for an old page);
- metadata, aka information Google may have added to the record about that page in its index (for example, if a site is known to contain adult content or a lot of spam);
- information from Wikipedia or other trusted sites, which Google may use to help sum up a subject for you;
- what language the site is in;
- the site you usually go to for searches (if you spend a lot of time on Amazon or Facebook, Google will move results from those pages toward the top of the results pile);
- the device you're using;
- your location, if you have it turned on;
- searches you recently did.[8]

At its heart, search engine ranking is doing its best to figure out what you meant when you wrote your search query. But other factors, like driving profitable traffic and serving the mainstream, also influence what the results serve you.

By "serving the mainstream" I don't mean search engines are politically biased, necessarily. I just mean they are trying to serve the largest number of people. Basically, when search results only in *one* ranking of the most popular things, it becomes a popularity contest.

The clearest way to show how this could be problematic was pointed out by Danny Sullivan at the blog Search Engine Land: when someone does a search for "football," should your top-ranked result be about what Americans call "football," or about what pretty much everyone else in the world calls "football"—what Americans call "soccer"? How would you decide? Should you base it on how many people in the world use each word? Split it up? Base what you show on where the searcher lives, or where they are right now? What if it's an American doing a search for football when they're traveling in the UK?[9]

Back in 2008, when I was researching my dissertation, I noticed that some of this search engine popularity contest was biased toward programmers: the people who make the most links, because they build webpages. And programmers were interested in programmer things, like programming languages, science, and entertainment genres they liked (say, science fiction or games).

Even to this day, the bias toward technical people can be found in some parts of your search results. When you do a search for "python," or "python eggs"—or even "eggs of a python"—the top results are about the programming language Python. If you're a kid in primary school trying to do a report on snakes, or figure out what to feed your pet, you're going to have to be more careful with your searches than a programmer. Same thing happens when you google "ruby" or "ruby gem"—that's also a programming language, so have fun when you're researching birthstones or engagement rings.

Ultimately, the developers of search engines know there isn't one right answer for *everyone* in the world—but they know that like most people, you're likely to make do with the first answer they give you. And you're going to be frustrated if you're in Australia or India and you get results about the Super Bowl when you wanted to get the dates of a local match. This is why search engines are eager to make use of your own information, like geographic location, language, and past searches: it makes it easier for them to guess the one right answer *for you*. But of course, when a "personalized" search algorithm also incorporates other things it knows about you, the way social media algorithms do, it can reinforce your own biases.

So, there you have it. Search engines are built in ways that incorporate human biases—those of the people who build the internet's links, sites, and algorithms, and your own biases, built in when search engines started to customize search based on what they knew about you. This is one of many, many reasons why it's a good idea to dig further than the first result a search engine turns up.

But now that you know this about search engines, you're in a better position to look more closely at search results than you were before. For tips to make search engines serve up a recipe that suits your purposes, see **keepcalmlogon.com**.

From Search and Social Media to Society

Algorithmic bias in social media may seem bizarre and easy to spot. Bias in search may seem less important in an age where personalized search tailors your results to you based on what you like. But let me tell you what happens when algorithms are built into our financial and work lives. Because once it hits you at that level, you may not be as delighted by the "magic" of perfect searches anymore.

For example, when you last applied for a job, you may not have been aware of algorithms that threw your résumé out before it could even be looked at. Job application systems look through résumés for exact keywords—not words that mean the same thing, not acronyms, and maybe not even plurals of the word! They rate the quality of the application based on that score, and pass along the highest-scoring applications to the people looking at them. A human being may never look at a low-scoring application.[10]

Companies with a more serious impact on your life—like banks, credit bureaus, and law enforcement—use algorithms to predict what you will do next. Companies that aren't even related to these companies—like social media—may be selling your data to them.

Or you may just give your social media data to them yourself. Some credit services ask to pull data from your social media accounts, or even scrape your call and text message history. Then they build algorithms based on signs that may seem outrageous as a basis for judging that someone's good to pay them back. Are you connected to someone on social media who defaulted on a loan? Statistically, you're more likely to default on a loan if you have a connection that did—so kiss your loan prospects goodbye. Do you type in all lowercase letters, OR ALL UPPERCASE ONES? One company figured out that ALL CAPS people are more likely to default on a loan, and started restricting loans to people they saw typing this way on social media. Make racist comments online? Another lender is trying to figure out how that is related to your credit decisions.[11] So think twice before giving credit or other finance sites access to your social media (and this includes signing in to them from your profile).

Generally, what these algorithms are trying to do is predict *risk*. Not risk to you. The risk that you pose to someone else—the company offering you the loan or the apartment, or in the case of law enforcement, the risk that you will commit a crime.

Algorithms in software made to recognize images or voices have turned out to be biased by the "machine learning" training done by software developers in Silicon Valley and Redmond—and they are overwhelmingly white, male, American, well educated, and well-off. "Machine learning" requires information for computer systems to learn. At a basic level, "face recognition" is made up of some developers in an office somewhere, taking a big batch of pictures and telling the computer, "That's a face." If there aren't any people with dark skin in the office to take pictures of, or people who don't have the same accents as educated white American men, they're going to have a harder time recognizing other people.

The voice command systems that help drivers interface with their devices without getting distracted initially had a harder time under-standing women—and even men with British accents.[12] More troublingly, face-recognition software has a harder time recognizing people with dark skin. In one early, highly publicized case, an HP "smart" camera system failed to recognize black people's faces as faces at all.[13] Google's photo ser-vice assigned the tags "gorilla" or "monkey" to some black faces until the company removed those tags.[14] Face recognition systems also fail to make distinctions among darker-skinned people. With the increasing rollout of this software in police databases and body cameras, darker-skinned peo-ple are at risk of being misidentified, wrongfully jailed, or even killed.[15] Because of the way these algorithms were developed, are they really wor-thy of our trust?

Social media and search companies are having to reckon with the ways that targeted ads—which use algorithms that draw on your personal data—may violate US laws against discrimination in housing, jobs, or credit. In 2019, Facebook reached a settlement with the American Civil Liberties Union and the Communications Workers of America (CWA), declaring it would change its system so its algorithms would not exclude anyone from seeing job postings or housing listings based on "protected status"—information about their gender, age, race, or other legally protected aspects of who they are.[16] This was not something Facebook had thought to build in automatically. It took collective action from the CWA and other groups to make sure Facebook's algorithm did not discriminate when it knew that users belonged to groups like "new parents," "Kwanzaa celebration," "active seniors," or lived in a zip code known to others in a community as "a bad neighborhood."[17]

Where's the List of Ingredients?

When we buy processed food in the store, it generally comes with a label that tells you what's in it: facts about the levels of vitamins, sodium, or carbohydrates, and a list of the ingredients. In many countries, laws require manufacturers to put these labels on food, to protect consumers.

Here's the thing about computer algorithm soup: right now, there aren't many laws requiring companies to make clear what goes into their recipe. Or to keep dangerous ingredients out of the soup.

No laws requiring a site or app to tell us if it's playing with our emotions. Or what ingredients it thinks make up the "news." Or if it's deciding to salt your feed with more of the same things you already clicked on—even if that means making your biases stronger. Thankfully, as I write this, San Francisco has banned the use of face-recognition software in its city agencies, including law enforcement; other cities are expected to consider similar bans. But we have little insight into what makes up face recognition algorithms, or those that shape our job applications, legal systems, or credit ratings.[18]

To some extent, algorithms solve problems caused by the technology itself. Are there too many posts in your social media feed? Has context collapse made it impossible to sort out the different parts of your life? Are too many items showing up in your shopping-site search results? We didn't have these problems before the digital revolution offered us more than we could ever eat. In this case, algorithms are sort of like preservatives in bread or cereal: before our great-grandparents started to buy "shelf-stable" processed food that would sit around forever, we didn't have artificial additives to keep food from rotting. The overwhelmingness of our feeds was a product of the need to get as many people on the site as possible, so it could be profitable. And the algorithms were the preservative. In social media, algorithms prioritize certain people over others without asking us. Is that really something we want them to do?

I've referred to profit often in this book. In the next chapter, I'll more thoroughly lay out the ways in which turning a profit can impact our digital lives—and detract from the trust we may want to put in media, digital or otherwise.

You Might Be Asking . . .

"I'm tired of all this online mystery meat! But can I really avoid algorithms?"

How to Keep Calm and Carry On

Scout Laws: "I talk to different people in my life in different ways. It should be up to me to decide who I want to talk to, how, and when"; "Control of my digital and media life should be *mine*."

When it comes to social media, at least, one option we all have at our command is our consumer choice. There are many tools to communicate with our friends that don't rely on algorithms. Most email, chat apps, and forum software don't algorithmically mess with the order of what they show us. As I suggested in the earlier chapters on our communications and attention, switching to small-group chat channels can lessen our online stress in addition to getting us away from algorithms.

When it comes to web search, shopping sites, finance, or government services, though, it's going to be harder to avoid algorithms. Here is where we all need to step up. We need to demand more clarity from tech companies, finance companies, and governments on what goes into the algorithms that shape our lives. We should push for laws and oversight to ensure fairness and quality in algorithms that could discriminate. Like San Francisco, we may even be able to halt the use of some flawed algorithms, like face recognition, in our communities. For more on where to get involved in efforts like these, see **keepcalmlogon.com**.

19

Beware the Profit Motive

Jacob Silverman, the author of *Terms of Service: Social Media and the Price of Constant Connection,* made the following comment on the Facebook emotional contagion experiment I mentioned in the last chapter:

> Facebook cares most about two things: engagement and advertising. If Facebook, say, decides that filtering out negative posts helps keep people happy and clicking, there's little reason to think that they won't do just that.[1]

In the last chapter and the one on bias, I talked about human sources of bias. There's one more source I didn't cover there, because it's so big, and so pervasive, that it deserves its own chapter: the need to make a profit.

It makes sense that a company—or even a nonprofit, or government!—needs to have income to keep it going. Employees need to be paid for their time, so they can eat, put a roof over their heads, and care for their families. Electricity, paper, and other resources for putting out information need to be paid for. The same holds for any app developer, TV broadcast station, or book or magazine publisher. Information producers will make decisions based on what to produce based on will keep income rolling in, so they don't have to close.

The need to turn a *profit*, on top of that income, puts additional pressure on the shape and content of the information. In for-profit organizations, that profit goes to investors, and to the leaders of the company (in the form of bonuses).

How does the need to make a profit shape what we see? How can we be mindful of the changes it may make? In this chapter, I'll discuss some of the ways in which the need to make money changes what we do and don't see in our social media feeds, in the news, and in the products made by media companies.

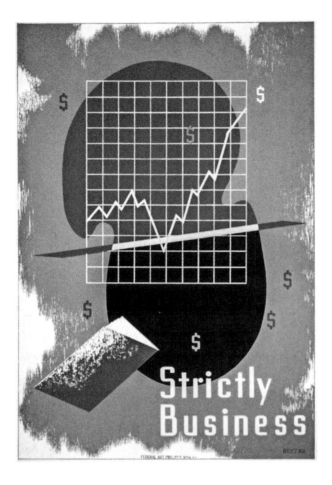

Whether charting slumps or skyrocketing prices, media companies—all companies!—keep their eye on the bottom line. *Source:* Buczak, Work Projects Administration Poster Collection—Library of Congress

How to Keep Calm and Carry On

Scout Law: "If I understand how news, books, and other media are made, I will be better able to identify bias."

The first questions you should ask yourself when being mindful of any media you are consuming, from websites, to TV news, to games, to books, are:

- Do you pay for this product?

- How does it make its money?

  The answers to those questions may inform what you do and don't end up seeing. Then ask:

- Who profits from these media, and from my participation in them?

- Is the benefit a public one, or does it enrich private individuals?

  Finally, it's worth thinking about what your options are:

- What other choices could you make to use media?

- If you want to leave a web service and take what you've created with you, can you do that? How?

  In this chapter, we'll explore these questions.

Do You Pay for This Product? How Does It Make Its Money?

Originally, nations invested trust in TV and radio stations by requiring them to apply for *licenses* in order to broadcast. In the United States, licenses for broadcast are granted with the expectation that broadcasters will make use of our airwaves in ways that don't conflict with one another technically (say, interfering with one another's signals) *and* that they will broadcast *in the public interest*.

But since the beginning of TV and radio, *private interests* have shaped what we see and hear—interests that benefit only a few people, not the general public.

What are those private interests? The shadow state? An international banking conspiracy?

Nope. Just ads.

You don't need to go digging for secret schemes to find the force that shapes what gets broadcast and what doesn't. The answer has been hiding in plain sight the whole time: it's about profit. Same thing in magazines, newspapers, and online.

There have always been ways in which companies influence the content at media outlets they own. Companies may have a financial interest in airing some things and not airing others. And with the majority of media owned by a tiny number of companies, this can mean we see more from a smaller number of people with interests that may not match ours.

You Might Be the Product ...

There's a saying that goes, "If you're not paying, you are the product." This could mean one of a few things. In the case of broadcast media, "you are the product" because TV or radio stations deliver your attention right into the hands of advertisers. Today, with apps and subscription websites that sell your data, sometimes you're literally paying for the service as well as being the product.

It gets really obvious that you're the product when you look at advertising industry publications like *Adweek* or *Advertising Age*. In those pages, network owners like Bravo or ABC and producers of individual shows talk about audiences as packages of people with particular characteristics, like "women over 21" or "empty-nesters." They promise they can "deliver these audiences" to anyone who advertises with them, mentioning things like "return on investment" and the likelihood that those audiences will purchase products advertised on their favorite shows. Media-industry ads like these often leak into the streets in New York, as well: you're walking down the street and suddenly a bus-stop ad is trying to sell you a tween girl who is "choosy and trend-conscious." Frankly, it's creepy.

Ratings and Metrics

Media companies aim to increase the number of people visiting, watching, reading, listening to, and interacting with their content. The more they have, the more viewers they can sell to advertisers. This is measured with statistics called *metrics* or *ratings*. Since the early days of television and radio, there have been commonly agreed-upon ways of gathering ratings. For many years, statistics gathered by Nielsen Media Research have been the standard for measuring who was listening to which radio stations or watching what TV shows. Nielsen counts audiences in a number of ways, including asking a subset of the population to use special gadgets to determine what's on around them. These gadgets either attach to your

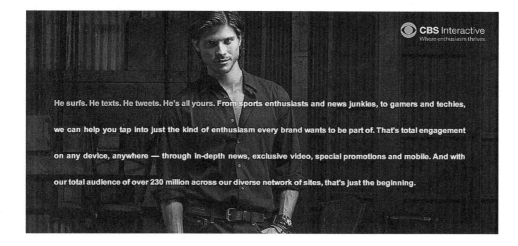

Ads like these, usually part of "upfront" campaigns by media companies, are often the starkest representation that you, as the audience, are the product. How would you feel about networks talking as if they have a right to sell you? *Source:* CBS Interactive, with thanks to Gladys Santiago for her curation of upfront campaigns on Flickr

TV or radio, or you wear them, and they sense broadcast signals around you. Surveys and focus groups are other tools Nielsen uses.

On the web or on a phone, it's easier for software makers to keep track of what people are looking at. Software developers can track which pages get loaded, when people stick around, where they go next, and when they stop using the site. They can also embed pieces of code to let them know when ads, posts, or videos are loaded; how far down a page people get; whether they go on to purchase products that were advertised; whether they come back later, and other, more detailed information that keeps track of who a given viewer is. (Think back to the example in chapter 7 about the "stalker shoes.")

Who wants to know this information? Again, it's not just TV producers or website developers. Information about who is looking at what media is of the greatest interest to advertisers who are paying the media producers to place ads next to their articles, videos, shows, social media posts, or games. What they want to know is who prefers which products: Coke or

Pepsi; diet or regular; flavored seltzer, coconut water, or kombucha. Then they want to sell more of those products.

Because there's more and more competition for our attention in the digital revolution, advertisers increasingly don't care whether people have viewed the content they're advertising next to. They're pushing for knowing who has *actually watched their ads*. Not that they don't care at all about the content. When it recently became clear that ads are showing up next to social media posts by hate groups, or disturbing videos, advertisers have pushed sites to remove that content.

The Impact of Ads

The advertising that appears around the apps, websites, news, and shows you consume can actually change what you see, particularly in broadcast and print media.

Broadcasters may shift their content to support the viewpoint of the companies that pay them to air ads, covering topics they might otherwise not have paid attention to, or avoiding topics that might hurt the advertiser's profits. Newspapers sometimes signal to advertisers that they will not let bad news pollute the air around their ads. "*USA Today*'s Positive Journalism Creates a Positive Environment for Your Advertising," read one brochure sent from that paper to potential advertisers.[2]

Then there's the stuff where companies just straight-up pay to put their products right into the show or feed you're looking at—product placement and paid content. Cars and soda cans in TV shows and movies are among the most common product placements—if you see a logo, it's almost guaranteed that someone got paid to show that product there. In the United States, paid content is regulated by the Federal Trade Commission (FTC); media producers are supposed to make it clear they received money to feature products or content, so that we don't end up thinking they're offering their unbiased opinion. But this doesn't always have an immediate effect. For example, the group Truth in Advertising found over a hundred unidentified paid product placements in the Kardashians' Instagram feeds in 2016.[3]

Ads are under some requirements to be truthful; in many countries, they cannot outright lie. In the United States, the Better Business Bureau is responsible for making sure advertisers do not make false claims about a competitor's product. But they do not have any obligation to protect the truth beyond that. The FTC can prosecute advertisers for "false and misleading" advertising. They can demand that advertisers not omit important information or lie. The FTC has particular regulations in place to protect vulnerable groups like children and terminally ill people. But the FTC only cares if the claim has a *material* impact on the promises made in the ad. An advertiser can still make false claims about the location where an ad is shot or the person endorsing the product—those aren't considered to have an impact on the truth of the claim.

However, the FTC is made up of people appointed by the US president—and as a result, if the president has promised to go easy on business, those appointees may not bother to pursue any claims about false advertising.

Making a Profit on the Internet

On the internet, "you are the product" means that your data and your attention are both being mined by companies to sell. Social media sites gather your birthday, gender, location, and other personal information and connect it to information about what you click on, whose posts you respond to, and which groups you join. This information is hugely useful to companies who want you to buy their products, so they will pay social media sites to place ads on the pages you're looking at, based on what your data says about you. Again: you're the product.

This hasn't always been the case. At times, people have paid for the service with their own money instead of paying for it with their attention and data. In earlier days of the internet, most people paid for an internet service like AOL, CompuServe, or Prodigy both to bring the internet to their house and also to provide entertainment and news. Ads were not as common; the services ran on people's monthly payments, so they didn't rely as heavily on advertisers.

When it became clear that the internet had the potential to reach a tremendous number of people, that changed. Venture capitalists began to pour money into internet companies, figuring the companies would figure out how to make a profit as they went along. Many companies began to capture and sell user data (something they're still trying to get the right balance on today).

And companies began figuring out ways to make advertising viable online. Banner ads quickly proved problematic; people tended to ignore them. Companies have also tried sponsoring search results, providing products to bloggers and YouTube personalities to review, and figuring out the right rhythm of posting updates about their products to social media and email. All of these strategies aim to turn a profit.

Profiting in Shady Ways

To this day, advertising online has been problematic. Google reports annually on "bad ads," which some advertisers try to place with Google despite the fact that they go against its rules. Some commit *ad fraud*, generating fake ads and bids to make more money. But some of these ads deliver malware to your computer. And some take you to phishing sites that ask for and then steal your sensitive information. (This is another important reason to use ad-blocking software!) Google blocked 100 of these malicious ads per second in 2017 (that number went down to 75 in 2018).[4]

Some companies used other questionable means to look more profitable. At one point it was discovered that as many as 48 million Twitter accounts—10 to 15 percent of all users—were bots.[5] But Twitter initially refused to take those accounts offline. Why? As a company, Twitter's value comes from how many users it has, and their connections to each other. If it were suddenly to acknowledge that one out of ten of its users wasn't real, its stock price could tumble. Unfortunately, it is in Twitter's interest to continue to allow fake accounts that spew ads, fake news, political propaganda, and other low-quality content into their system.

"But all media need to make money! There's no avoiding that!"

How to Keep Calm and Carry On

Completely avoiding media, sites, or apps whose producers need to make money would be difficult. But you can choose services where profit off of your attention is not the #1 motive. If you want, you can avoid services that mine your data for profit, or even ones that serve you ads.

- Some services' business models still rely on user payments instead of ads.

- State-funded and nonprofit public broadcasting is available in many countries, and may also fund related websites. The cool thing about our current historical moment is how easy it is to find these services from other countries, as well as our own!

- Email can be ad-free—but know if, like Gmail, the service mines your email for data.

- Many group text options, chat channels, and online forums don't show ads. Some of these you may even be able to run yourself. Look for "open source" software.

- Do some digging to learn about the business models of any site, app, or service and whether they're selling data about you. (I know some parents who make their kids write a paragraph about how a game makes money before they let them download it!)

  For specific suggestions, see **keepcalmlogon.com**.

Editorial Soup

Just like algorithms do today, broadcast stations, magazines, and newspapers have always manipulated the order of what they show to maximize their profit. Consider, for example, reality shows and news that keep plugging what's "coming up next" on the show, so you watch all the way through—including the ads.

Did you know that newspapers decide how much they print based on the so-called *news hole*—the amount of space they have left *after* they lay out the ads? That has been the simplest way that profit has shaped the news. Sometimes articles get cut just because there isn't enough money from ads to print on more paper. Online, news sometimes goes unreported because there's only so much money from ads, and only so much money to pay reporters.

Same on American TV: you only have so much news broadcasting, because stations only show as much as they have to in order to meet their obligation to serve the public, and it has to be fit in around the advertising needed to pay for the station to operate and to turn a profit.

What news is profitable? Remember the "if it bleeds, it leads" rule from the section in chapter 2 on "mean world syndrome"? That holds doubly true for TV news. Videos about awful things happening capture people's attention: like a car wreck, we have a hard time looking away. So car wrecks are more common in TV news than information we might need to make better choices as voters—for example, that the city council has just approved tax cuts for a big-box store that is going to threaten the business of local mom-and-pop stores and drive down wages in local jobs. Think for a second: How often have you seen city council or state government news on your local TV channel? City council meetings are hella boring, really. Particularly when it comes to visuals. Literally nothing is on fire or going over the speed limit the wrong way on the freeway.

This puts video news in a bind. On TV, news shows are less interesting to advertisers than entertainment shows. Advertisers don't want their products to appear alongside news about real people dying or issues that upset a big part of the community. They also don't want to advertise alongside city council meetings, because they assume nobody will be watching. So basically, the financial pressure on TV stations is to get the right news balance of visually interesting things on fire and attention-grabbing car chases, a bunch of heart-warming stories about hero pets or athletes helping disabled kids, weather, and sports, and after *that* ... whatever the station has budget for and what fits in a half-hour time slot. Which is not much. The low profitability of news in light of the profitability of other violent content was the plot of the 1976 movie *Network*, in which a news anchor is laid off and has a breakdown. Then his network combines the anchor's breakdown with a bunch of sensational content in a new TV show—to get higher ratings.[6]

Consolidation

There's another way, beyond advertising, that profit shapes what we see. Who owns the media companies, how many companies they own, and how ownership crosses industries—like, for example, Time Warner owning cable channels, magazines, and film studios—can shape what we do and don't see.

How profit has pressured the media has changed a lot from the 1990s onward. The 1990s were an era of media *consolidation*: big media companies kept buying smaller media companies, until most of what was left was huge media companies. Five or six companies dominated media, making the market less competitive. In the United States, the Telecommunications Act of 1996 made it so one company could own multiple news outlets in one market. Earlier, this had been banned: if a company could own a significant portion of the news that was available to a town, people believed this *monopoly* would limit the range of ideas available to the public, and squelch democratic debate.

But since 1996, the trend has leaned more and more toward monopoly. In 2003, the Federal Communication Commission (FCC)—an agency made up of people appointed by the president, not elected by the public— voted to make it legal for a company to own both a newspaper and broadcast outlets (radio and TV) in one media market.

One of the unintended consequences of this trend is that news organizations are under pressure to make as much profit as other companies owned by media conglomerates, like TV and radio. And this is a huge problem for news organizations. Just as news tends to get lower ratings and page views than entertainment content, it also turns less of a profit.[7] Newspapers' profit margins range from single digits to percentages in the 20s.[8] Compare this with TV profit margins, which have been 40 to 50 percent.[9] Same with books, which tend to make profits between 2 and 3 percent. In the consolidation of the 1990s, large media corporations bought many publishers, which pressured them to produce books with more widely popular content.[10]

Consolidation changed news reporting. If you remember the HBO show *The Wire*, you saw this story play out (though you may not have known it was happening both behind the scenes, and on-screen). *The Wire*'s creator, David Simon, was a reporter who left the *Baltimore Sun* after the Tribune Company, based in Chicago, bought the newspaper from the Times-Mirror Company, owner of the *Los Angeles Times*.

As a reporter, Simon specialized in in-depth stories about social issues, like the ones he told in *The Wire*. Unfortunately, these stories take a lot of time to research and write, and that means the paper must invest a lot of money in a reporter who isn't turning in as many articles daily. In *The Wire*, we also saw editors who were interested in covering things on the cheap, or else investing in prize-winning stories that turned out to be fakes.

Simon has said that "out-of-town ownership is a disaster" for newspapers. He saw the management of big media conglomerates as only driven by profit, not by a desire to serve the community.[11]

Pressure to turn a bigger profit means making some changes that unfortunately hurt the news we receive.

First, to make news production more "efficient," news companies often get rid of the jobs we rely on to verify the news—the ones I talked about in chapter 16. Fact checkers are often the first to get fired. The fact checkers who are left sometimes have to cover a lot more news, making it harder to do their jobs.

And as for reporting the news far away, like in a state senate, the nation's capital, or places around the world? Companies that owned more than one news outlet closed bureaus far away because they were too expensive. Or they made it so one reporter covered Iraq or Beijing for several news outlets.

Consolidation can also hurt news reporting when conflicts of interest arise. When a negative report on safety and hiring at Disneyland was produced by one of its investigative reporters in 1998, ABC News scrapped the project. ABC is owned by the Walt Disney Company, which presumably did not want negative reports to make parents fear for their children and perhaps avoid the theme park, causing it to lose money.[12]

Cross-promotion can also influence what we see in the media, putting content in that we otherwise might not have heard about (but which maybe is not really important to us). For example, CBS News in Los Angeles and Chicago had their anchors wear leis and give the Hawaiian weather report to draw attention to their revival of the show *Hawaii Five-O*—not newsworthy to audiences in that area, simply an advertisement taking up news time.[13] *NBC Nightly News*, meanwhile, devoted a segment to Boeing testing its planes in 2012. Boeing is the exclusive sponsor of the app for NBC's *Meet the Press*, and to top it off, at that time, NBC was partially owned by General Electric—which makes engines for Boeing.[14]

"So you're saying there's a conspiracy in the media?"

Nope. It doesn't need to go as far as being a conspiracy to have influence on what you see.

"Conspiracy" has a very specific legal definition: it's "an agreement between two or more people to commit an illegal act." Nothing I'm talking about in this chapter is illegal. It's not illegal to force a news reporter to report on or cut a story. It's not illegal to prioritize your company's content over content from other companies. It's not illegal to mix up your social media feed or pump it full of garbage. If anything, these actions are maybe unethical. Nobody is going to jail for them.

How to Keep Calm and Carry On

Scout Law: "If I work to understand where my own opinion comes from, I will be better prepared to protect myself from people who want to manipulate me."

When you come across a conspiracy theory about the media, check your emotions first. Go back to the mindfulness exercises in the first few chapters. Many people turn to conspiracy theories after frightening events or because of messages from their "family trees."

Then, ask yourself, "How does that work?" Go back over the "What Is the Solution?" exercise from chapter 11 on bias, and run it for claims made about the conspiracy (like "Jews control Hollywood" or "the government is covering up reporting about 9/11"). How would the people involved accomplish what you think they do? Check again: Is what you're suggesting really possible? How much money, time, control, and organization would it take to pull off? If it were happening, who would know about it? What would they say about it? Could they go public?

In the last several chapters I've described the trustworthy ways that information producers like journalists and scientists look for and present *evidence*. Our trust in them is based on things you can see in the information they present to you, and confirmed by their colleagues who have worked to make sure that information is valid and reliable. All of this information is out in the public for you to find! You might have to stop and think or do a little research, to find this information, but it's not secret.

This is what I mean by evidence: facts that can be *confirmed* through *multiple sources*, some of which are *legally binding*. When you look at a conspiracy theory, ask: Does this offer recorded evidence of things that actually happened? Or is its evidence made of things the theorist sees in the media that *seem* to be related to each other?

Think like a journalist—go back to chapter 16 for some guidelines. Figure out how you could triangulate a claim based on other sources of information. Are there statistics out there? Seek out sources that disagree. What do they say is happening? Keep in mind that you can probably trust the credibility of people speaking against their own interests more than those who are speaking about something that will benefit them. Which means the first step is figuring out what the speaker's interests are.

Media ownership information can be confirmed using a number of sources, including ownership databases from your state government. People *can* go to jail for lying about their companies—there are laws about that. Rely on this information for solid details about who controls which media outlets.

Monopoly: It Ain't a Game (or a Conspiracy)

Conspiracy usually isn't the right term for the oversized influence that a small number of people and companies have over what shows up in the media. *Monopoly* is a much more fitting term. The journalist and news critic Ben Bagdikian has said that the way the news outlets operate together is

> not the result of a conspiracy. Dominant media members do not sit around a table parceling out market shares, prices, and products, as is done literally by OPEC. The five [at the time, in 2004] dominant media firms don't need to. They share too many of the same methods and goals.[15]

Robert McChesney, a media industry critic, disagreed about price-fixing, saying media companies do sometimes act like "cartels":

> Like all oligopolists, these firms rarely compete in the area of price. They use their economic and political power to advance their interests and to dominate consumers.... Corrupt policy-making has crafted regulations to suit the less competitive markets desired by dominant commercial interests.[16]

Media companies still compete to have higher stock prices, higher profits, and more viewers than each other. They may have the same people on the boards of their companies, and they may lobby Congress together to make laws that are favorable to all of them. And this is also currently legal in the United States.

Monopoly is what happens when one business entity controls enough of a market that it can determine what products are available, at what price (like in the board game by the same name, when you own all the properties of the same color, put up houses and hotels, and start gouging other players for rent). If you've lived through your cable company playing games with what channels or games you have access to, you've had a taste of this. Worries about the end of net neutrality are also about media monopolies being able to slow down your internet speed or make you pay more to view media that are not produced by their company.

The difference between conspiracy and monopoly is a subtle distinction, but it's worth making if we want the media to change. In a conspiracy, people acting to fix prices or put out bad information do so in secret. In a monopoly, theoretically, much of what they do should be visible to the public, through legal means or getting involved in the business.

The problem with calling a monopoly a "conspiracy" is that it doesn't help us understand where its power comes from—or how we could fight that power.

You Might Be Asking ...

"OK, so how do I figure out who's profiting from a media outlet?"

"Do [the information creator's] interests coincide with the interests of most citizens, of our society as we see it?" This was the question asked by the Institute for Propaganda Analysis. It is still relevant today.

Who benefits from a media channel and the information being spread by it? It is worth looking into whether someone is making a *financial profit* from a piece of media. It is also worth thinking about whose life is made better or worse by the *messages* in a piece of media—for example, whether the message contains a stereotype about a group of people, or fails to represent another group at all.

How to Keep Calm and Carry On

Find out who owns a channel, newspaper, site, or other media outlet. These days, that information can often be found on a channel's Wikipedia page, but you can also go to the About page on a given channel's own website and look for phrases like "is a subsidiary of" or "our parent company"—those indicate ownership by another company or person.

States also offer public registries of ownership on their websites, where you can look up the actual, legal information on who owns a company. The websites for *Variety* and the *Hollywood Reporter* can also turn up a lot of information about which company makes which shows, and *Advertising Age* has information on partnerships between products, channels, and other properties. And as discussed in the chapter on how we know who's who online, you can also do a WHOIS search for information about who owns a website.

Then there are other questions to ask: Do these media outlets own products, properties, or other channels? How has that ownership impacted what does and doesn't get shown on the news, in entertainment properties, or in advertising in the channel? What are the political leanings of the owners?

Just as you did when looking for fake accounts online, find out if a message has been repeated elsewhere. For example, the Sinclair Broadcasting example in the news chapter, or a press release that has been picked up and used verbatim across news outlets. If it has been repeated, see who else appears to be spreading and benefiting from it.

Walling Up the Garden for Profit

About five years ago I decided to quit Facebook. My sister was about to have a baby, and she was sending me worried messages that she might need to switch jobs, which would disrupt her health insurance. I just thought to myself, "Facebook is making money off this conversation. I'm really not OK with that." It was the final crack in the dam. I'd been frustrated with how addictive Facebook felt, and I just wanted out.

But getting off social media means losing a lot—which is why many people don't feel like they can do it. Why is this the case?

Facebook is what people who build the internet call a "walled garden." (This is not the same idea as fencing in your digital security "victory garden.") The "walled garden" metaphor kind of explains itself: if you're in a garden with walls around it, it's not easy to have a conversation with people outside the garden, or share a picnic with them. The nice-smelling roses and trees bearing delicious fruit inside the garden are reserved for the people who can get inside the walls. Similarly, if you're within the walls, you're not seeing what is happening outside the garden.

Once upon a time, AOL was considered one of the internet's walled gardens. For many years, people who paid to connect to AOL could get AOL content, find other AOL users, and not much else. Paying for the service got you inside the wall. People who didn't subscribe to AOL couldn't see AOL websites or get into its chat rooms.

Facebook's wall is different: instead of paying to get in, you are supposed to give your real, legal name. But that is a kind of payment: knowing who you are, where you live, what you're interested in, and who you know is worth money to Facebook, because they can sell advertisers access to your feed and certain information about you. That's Facebook's business model: you are the product.

Another aspect of Facebook's walled garden is that when you decide to leave it, you can't really take what you built inside the wall with you. Facebook will give you a download of your pictures, videos, and posts, and contact information for your connections (as long as those people have provided it). But that doesn't amount to the same thing as what Facebook gives you within that wall: fast, easy ways to find and chat with your connections, and access to their updates. Those things ultimately belong to Facebook. Not to you or your contacts.

This is one last decision we can make when it comes to sites that may be profiting off us: whether we want to be able to take our stuff with us when we want to leave.

How to Keep Calm and Carry On

Scout Law: "Control of my digital and media life should be *mine*."

Knowing that some sites are walled gardens, we can make more informed decisions before we even join. We can decide whether we want to garden within their walls or not.

When you're making an account for the first time, look for something like "control over your data" in the terms of service, or poke around the "getting started" page to get a sense of what you'll be able to do with your data.

You can't take *exactly* what you build within a walled garden with you, but you can often take a lot of it. Look into the settings for your account to see if it's possible to download your content, then take a look at what was downloaded to see if there's anything else you may want to grab before you shut an account down.

There may be additional tools for pulling your information off a site. See **keepcalmlogon.com** for recommendations.

20

Going Forward . . .

In this book, I've mostly focused on things we can do *individually* to make our digital lives better—ways we can take small steps for self-defense, and conserve our sanity and trust.

Source: Work Projects Administration Poster Collection—Library of Congress

Some people might think I did not focus enough on what tech companies, media companies, and governments are doing (or not) that makes these problems worse. I would not, for one minute, say we should give companies or governments a pass for failing to protect our information, exploiting our data for profit, allowing hate speech and harassment to flourish on their sites, or making us addicted. Quite the contrary.

We have important work to do in the next few years to keep companies accountable. We should vote with our feet when we can, leaving sites when their bad choices about data use or moderation outweigh the benefit we feel we're getting from them. We should demand clear answers about what companies do with data that ultimately *belongs to us*—we produced it, it's about us. And we should work with our elected officials to hold tech companies to higher standards. See **keepcalmlogon.com** for ideas of where to start.

But bad behavior by faraway coders, corporations, and governments, I know, feels impossibly overwhelming sometimes. Heck, I work in tech and I *still* have a lot of learned helplessness when it comes to the really technical stuff. And it never feels like there's enough time to call my representatives in Congress.

This is why I took a "secure your own oxygen mask first" approach in this book. It's not just that we need to de-stress, or take back our attention, in order to have time to make better choices. We also need knowledge of how the systems around us work. That knowledge can empower us to act. As I said in the Keep Calm Scout Laws, it can help us survive attempts to manipulate us, misinform us, or bias us.

Ultimately, none of us can do this alone. We will have to work together to demand change from tech companies. Workers at companies like Google and Uber have already begun to organize; they deserve our support. So do our neighbors when they organize against unfair government handouts to tech companies. (It's not just New York offering to allow a helipad for Amazon's proposed office—did you know that from 2011 to 2019, Twitter didn't even have to pay payroll taxes to the city of San Francisco?)[1] There are efforts underway to demand that tech companies be clearer about how they use our data; the General Data Protection Regulation in the European Union was a good first step, but just saying "We collect cookies" isn't

Source: Work Projects Administration Poster
Collection—Library of Congress

enough information for most of us to understand what that really means. And it could also benefit diversity in the media voices we hear if we push our elected officials to break up monopolies in media both old and new.

The hardest of the things we need to do is to work together to rebuild trust in our communities. In the United States and in some other countries, political opinion has become so polarized that family members don't feel they can speak with each other. We have fallen out of agreement on which sources of information are trustworthy, and why. Our trust in information has been damaged by the first couple of decades of the internet, as we have run around blindly trying to understand changes to our trust in news and books as well as new sources of information, like public comments and Wikipedia. But as I stated in the Scout Laws, trust is something that belongs to us, something that we build together.

I hope this book can help start discussions in our communities about what information we trust, and what information we should distrust. At the 2019 Internet Freedom Festival, one attendee in a workshop on trust said, in a moment of frustration, that violent extremists "just need to go to church more often." Given the festival is home to a diverse international group that includes many Muslims, Jews, Hindus, Baha'i, atheists, and people from any number of other creeds as well as Christians, this seemed like a strange statement. So, he elaborated: one thing we know about extremists is that they *don't talk to the rest of their communities enough*. Checking in with others around us gives us perspective on the beliefs we're building, and an understanding of how our views might be harmful, or may not achieve the ends we want.

And spending time with others who aren't like us is the best way to build trust and empathy. When we see the pain, sadness, or joy on their faces, our mirror neurons kick in, effectively helping us feel what they feel—and understand better why they may not feel the same way our family or community has raised us to feel.

So, even though I arranged the exercises on trust and our "family trees" to be done individually, there is tremendous benefit in discussing them with those who don't see eye-to-eye with us. Ultimately, the best way to heal deep differences is to empathize with those we disagree with, clarify any misunderstandings we have of each other's worldviews, and forge a vision of what action we can take to improve our communities.

As always, check **keepcalmlogon.com** for ways to connect to groups that are working on issues described in this book, from fighting corporations' misdeeds to helping our communities rebuild trust.

It's a funny thing, to be writing a big, long book in (and about!) a historical moment where the lion's share of our daily information comes to us through a lightweight stream of letters, numbers, addresses, algorithms, and pixels. I've had moments when I've wondered, why the heck am I doing such a weird, throwback thing as to kill a bunch of trees and make people read for more than a few minutes at a time?!

But here's the thing about a book:

It has one publication date (unlike your nonstop social media stream).

It asks that you think about a topic at length (again, side-eye to your social media stream).

It makes for a comforting weight in your hand (OK, OK, not if you're using an e-reader. But an e-reader can still let you focus, away from ads and notifications).

And as such, it makes for an object and an event we can all reflect on, mindfully, together.

What I wanted to do, by writing a book, is start a conversation. To bring everyone together to talk about how to defend our communities from attention sinks, stress, theft, harassment, and the erosion of our trust and safety by misinformation.

I'm looking forward to the book tour. Hope to see you in your town. And in a few online AMAs or livestreams. And an email, if this book sparked some realizations for you.

But I hope you'll understand if it takes a moment for me to get back to you. Remember that broadcasting (like publishing a book) puts us in touch with more people than the human mind is equipped to cope with.

And I hope you'll understand if I keep my notifications off. I hope you'll give your stressed-out attention a break by turning off yours, too.

Notes

Introduction: Surviving the Digital Revolution

1. Moussa Abdoulaye, Simon Allison, Will Baxter, and Amy Niang, "Boy Scouts in a War Zone," *Mail & Guardian*, January 3, 2019, http://atavist.mg.co.za/boy-scouts-in-a-war-zone.

2. Shunryu Suzuki, quoted in James H. Austin, *Zen-Brain Reflections: Reviewing Recent Developments in Meditation and States of Consciousness* (Cambridge, MA: MIT Press, 2010).

3. Matthew Lieberman, Naomi Eisenberger, Molly Crockett, Sabrina Tom, Jennifer Pfeifer, and Baldwin Way, "Putting Feelings into Words: Affect Labeling Disrupts Amygdala Activity in Response to Affective Stimuli," *Psychological Science* 18, no. 5 (2007): 421–428, https://doi.org/10.1111/j.1467-9280.2007.01916.x, cited in "Putting Feelings into Words," UCLA Newsroom, 2010, http://newsroom.ucla.edu/stories/putting-feelings-into-words-155536.

Chapter 1: No One Is Born "Good" at Technology

1. B.D.A. New Technologies Committee, "Typefaces for Dyslexia," *British Dyslexia Association*, 2015, https://bdatech.org/what-technology/typefaces-for-dyslexia/; Lauren Hudgins, "Hating Comic Sans Is Ableist," *Establishment*, February 23, 2017, https://link.medium.com/khr50U3kbZ.

2. Luz Rello and Ricardo Baeza-Yates, "Good Fonts for Dyslexia," paper presented at the 15th International ACM SIGACCESS Conference on Computers and Accessibility (ASSETS 2013), Bellevue, WA, USA, October 21–23, 2013, https://doi.org/10.1145/2513383.2513447.

3. Don Norman, *The Design of Everyday Things* (New York: Basic Books, 2013).

Chapter 2: Look for the Helpers

1. Fred Rogers, "Tragic Events," Fred Rogers Productions, 2018, https://www.fredrogers.org/parents/special-challenges/tragic-events.php.

2. Bruce D. Perry and Maia Szalavitz, *The Boy Who Was Raised as a Dog, and Other Stories from a Child Psychiatrist's Notebook: What Traumatized Children Can Teach Us about Loss, Love, and Healing* (New York: Basic Books, 2017).

3. Maxwell King, *The Good Neighbor: The Life and Work of Fred Rogers* (New York: Abrams Press, 2018).

4. John Gramlich, "5 Facts about Crime in the U.S." Pew Research Center, 2019, http://www.pewresearch.org/fact-tank/2018/01/30/5-facts-about-crime-in-the-u-s/.

5. Jessica Schneider, "Hate Crimes Increased by 17% in 2017, FBI Report Finds," *CNN*, November 13, 2018, https://www.cnn.com/2018/11/13/politics/fbi-hate-crimes-2017/index.html.

6 Howard Kurtz, "Doing Something Right; Fox News Sees Ratings Soar, Critics Sore," *Washington Post*, February 5, 2001, https://web.archive.org/web/20160311190746/https://pqasb.pqarchiver.com/washingtonpost/doc/409058280.html?FMT=ABS&FMTS=ABS:FT&type=current&date=Feb%205,%202001&author=Howard%20Kurtz&pub=&edition=&startpage=&desc=Doing%20Something%20Right;%20Fox%20News%20Sees%20Ratings%20Soar,%20Critics%20Sore.

7. Park Elliott Dietz, "Mass, Serial and Sensational Homicides," *Bulletin of the New York Academy of Medicine* 62, no. 5 (1986): 477–491. https://www.ncbi.nlm.nih.gov/pmc/articles/PMC1629267/.

8. Adam Withnall, "New Zealand Shooting: Jacinda Ardern Vows Never to Say Name of Christchurch Mosque Attacker," *Independent*, March 19, 2019, https://www.independent.co.uk/news/world/australasia/new-zealand-mosque-attack-jacinda-ardern-name-terrorist-christchurch-a8829136.html.

9. Anne Lamott, *Bird by Bird: Some Instructions on Writing and Life* (New York: Anchor Books, 1995).

Chapter 3: Conserving a Valuable Resources

1. Catherine Price, *How to Break Up with Your Phone* (New York: Ten Speed Press, 2018), 102.

2. Matt Taibbi, "How Reading the News is Like Smoking," subscriber post on Taibbi's *Hate Inc.* newsletter, December 19, 2018, https://taibbi.substack.com/p/how-reading-the-news-is-like-smoking.

3. Price, *How to Break Up with Your Phone*; American Academy of Pediatrics Council on Communications and Media, "Media and Young Minds," *Pediatrics* 138, no. 5 (2016), https://doi.org/10.1542/peds.2016-2591.

4. "Our Letter to the APA," Children's Screen Time Action Network, 2018, https://screentimenetwork.org/apa/.

5. Tristan Harris, "The Slot Machine in Your Pocket," *Spiegel Online*, July 27, 2016, https://spon.de/aeNqr.

6. Christina Xu, "Convenient Friction: Observations on Chinese UX in Practice," presentation given at IxDA, February 7, 2017, https://vimeo.com/209792795.

7. Jennifer Dimas, "Anticipatory Stress of After-Hours Email Exhausting Employees," *Colorado State University Source*, July 27, 2016, https://source.colostate.edu/anticipatory-stress-of-after-hours-email-exhausting-employees/.

8. Katie Beck, "France's Battle against an 'Always-On' Work Culture," BBC *Capital*, May 8, 2017, http://www.bbc.com/capital/story/20170507-frances-battle-against-always-on-work-culture.

Chapter 4: Conversation Breakdown

1. Sara Kiesler, Jane Siegel, and Timothy W. McGuire, "Social Psychological Aspects of Computer-Mediated Communication," *American Psychologist* 39, no. 10 (1984): 1123–1134, https://doi.org/10.1037/0003-066X.39.10.1123.

2. David Mikkelson, "Fact Check: Americans with No Abilities Act," *Snopes*, November 15, 2014, https://www.snopes.com/fact-check/americans-no-abilities-act/.

3. Kiesler, Siegel, and McGuire, "Social Psychological Aspects of Computer-Mediated Communication," 12.

4. "Dunbar's Number," Wikipedia, last updated August 12, 2019. https://en.wikipedia.org/wiki/Dunbar%27s_number.

5. "Obscene, Indecent and Profane Broadcasts (consumer guide)," Federal Communications Commission, last updated September 13, 2017, https://www.fcc.gov/consumers/guides/obscene-indecent-and-profane-broadcasts.

6. James Poniewozik, "The Decency Police," *Time*, March 20, 2005. http://www.time.com/time/magazine/article/0,9171,1039700-1,00.html.

7. Shira Karsen, "What Happened after Janet Jackson's 2004 Super Bowl 'Nipplegate' Incident," *Billboard*, October 23, 2017, https://www.billboard.com/articles/news/super-bowl/8007041/janet-jackson-justin-timberlake-2004-super-bowl-what-happened.

8. I don't mean the Facebook groups that are sometimes huge groups created by the company. I mean the ones created by someone you know. I also don't mean forums or public comments where anyone can sign up. Those are also prone to social drama.

9. Reed Albergotti, "Inside Facebook Decisions on Subscriptions, Content Policing," *Information*, February 4, 2019, https://www.theinformation.com/articles/inside-facebook-decisions-on-subscriptions-content-policing.

10. Sheera Frenkel, "Facebook Says It Deleted 865 Million Posts, Mostly Spam," *New York Times*, May 15, 2018, https://nyti.ms/2GjHtHY.

11. KJ Dell'Antonia, "Facebook is Stealing Your Family's Joy," *New York Times*, April 12, 2019, https://nyti.ms/2X3CELO.

Chapter 7: "They Already Know Everything … and There's Nothing I Can Do"

1. Minna Sugimoto, "Former Beauty Queen Sentenced to 20 Years for ID Theft," *Hawaii News Now*, May 4, 2001, https://www.hawaiinewsnow.com/story/14574603/former-beauty-queen-sentenced-to-20-years-in-prison-for-id-theft/.

2. Brian Krebs, "Kansas Man Killed In 'SWATting' Attack," *Krebs on Security* (blog), December 17, 2017, https://krebsonsecurity.com/2017/12/kansas-man-killed-in-swatting-attack/; Brian Crecente, "Suspect in Fatal Swatting Case Confessed after Arrest, Says Detective," *Variety*, May 22, 2018, https://variety.com/2018/gaming/news/tyler-barriss-hearing-swatting-1202819348/.

3. Dan Tynan, "The Terror of Swatting: How the Law Is Tracking Down High-Tech Prank Callers," *Guardian*, April 15, 2016. https://www.theguardian.com/technology/2016/apr/15/swatting-law-teens-anonymous-prank-call-police; Jason Fagone, "The Serial Swatter," *New York Times*, November 24, 2015, https://nyti.ms/1NpF6WF.

4. Lincoln Spector, "How to Turn Off Windows 10's Keylogger (Yes, It Still Has One)," *PCWorld*, September 4, 2015, https://www.pcworld.com/article/2974057/windows/how-to-turn-off-windows-10s-keylogger-yes-it-still-has-one.html.

Chapter 8: Safer Relationships, Online

1. http://modelmugging.org.

2. "Preparations before a Date," *Model Mugging*, 2019, http://modelmugging.org/crime-within-relationships/preparations-before-a-date/.

3. Tactical Technology Collective, "Investigating Instagr.am: More than Meets the Eye," *Exposing the Invisible*, 2019, https://exposingtheinvisible.org/resources/obtaining-evidence/more-than-meets-the-eye-investigating.

4. Natasha Felizi and Joana Varon, "Send Nudes!" *Coding Rights*, 2015, https://www.codingrights.org/send-nudes/.

5. "Acquaintance Rapist Behavior: Who Is the Date Rapist?" *Model Mugging*, 2019, http://modelmugging.org/crime-within-relationships/acquaintance-rapist-behavior/.

6. Tiffany Kaitlyn, "Personal Tracking Apps Are Not for Women," *Vox*, November 16, 2018, https://www.vox.com/the-goods/2018/11/13/18079458/menstrual-tracking-surveillance-glow-clue-apple-health.

7. Lincoln Spector, "How to Tell if Your Android Phone Has Spyware," *PC World*, 2016, https://www.pcworld.com/article/3085112/android/keep-spies-off-your-android-phone.html.

8. "Awareness for Crime Prevention," *Model Mugging*, 2019, http://modelmugging.org/crime-prevention/awareness/.

Chapter 9: The Roots of Trust

1. Craig Silverman and Lawrence Alexander, "How Teens in The Balkans Are Duping Trump Supporters with Fake News," *BuzzFeed*, November 3, 2016, https://www.buzzfeednews.com/article/craigsilverman/how-macedonia-became-a-global-hub-for-pro-trump-misinfo

2. Philip Howard, "How Political Campaigns Weaponize Social Media Bots," *IEEE Spectrum*, October 18, 2018, https://spectrum.ieee.org/computing/software/how-political-campaigns-weaponize-social-media-bots.

3. Samantha Bradshaw and Philip N. Howard, "Troops, Trolls and Troublemakers: A Global Inventory of Organized Social Media Manipulation" (working paper, Computational Propaganda Research Project University of Oxford, Oxford, 2017), http://blogs.oii.ox.ac.uk/politicalbots/wp-content/uploads/sites/89/2017/07/Troops-Trolls-and-Troublemakers.pdf.

4. Soutik Biswas, "The Indian Policewoman Who Stopped WhatsApp Mob Killings," *BBC*, September 25, 2018, https://www.bbc.com/news/world-asia-india-45570274.

5. Bruce D. Perry and Maia Szalavitz, *The Boy Who Was Raised as a Dog, and Other Stories from a Child Psychiatrist's Notebook: What Traumatized Children Can Teach Us About Loss, Love, and Healing* (New York: Basic Books, 2017).

6. Linda Weber and Allison I. Carter, *The Social Construction of Trust* (New York: Springer Science & Business Media, 2003).

7. Robert D. Putnam, *Bowling Alone: The Collapse and Revival of American Community* (New York: Simon & Schuster, 2000).

8. Weber and Carter, *The Social Construction of Trust*.

9. Association of College and Research Libraries, "Framework for Information Literacy for Higher Education," American Library Association, February 2, 2015, http://www.ala.org/acrl/standards/ilframework.

Chapter 10: Trust and Our Opinions' Family Trees

1. Thanks to Media Education Lab and Renee Hobbs, "Teaching about Propaganda: An Examination of the Historical Roots of Media Literacy," *Journal of Media Literacy Education* 6, no. 2 (2014): 56–67, https://doi.org/10.23860/JMLE-2016-06-02-5.

2. Violet Edwards, *Group Leader's Guide to Propaganda Analysis* (New York: Columbia University Press, 1938), 1.

3. Clyde Miller to Members of the Progressive Education Association, November 15, 1937, obtained from records of the Institute for Propaganda Analysis, New York Public Library

4. Clyde Miller to Members of the Progressive Education Association.

5. Alfred McClung Lee and Elizabeth Briant Lee, *The Fine Art of Propaganda; A Study of Father Coughlin's Speeches* (New York: Institute for Propaganda Analysis & Harcourt, Brace and Company, 1939), quoted in Renee Hobbs and Sandra McGee, "Teaching about Propaganda: An Examination of the Historical Roots of Media Literacy," *Journal of Media Literacy Education* 6, no. 2 (2014): 56–67. https://digitalcommons.uri.edu/jmle/vol6/iss2/5.

Chapter 11: Bias? We've All Got It

1. Steve Buttry, "Verification Fundamentals: Rules to Live By," in *Verification Handbook*, ed. Craig Silverman (Maastricht, the Netherlands: European Journalism Centre, 2013), 13–17, http://verificationhandbook.com/downloads/verification.handbook.pdf.

2. We are all permanently indebted to Weird Al Yankovic and the other creators of the movie *UHF* for giving us the "drinking from the firehose" metaphor.

3. A. J. Agrawal, "What Do Social Media Algorithms Mean For You?" *Forbes*, April 20, 2016, https://www.forbes.com/sites/ajagrawal/2016/04/20/what-do-social-media-algorithms-mean-for-you/.

4. Eli Pariser, "Beware Online 'Filter Bubbles,'" filmed March 2011 in Long Beach, CA, TED video, 8:58, https://www.ted.com/talks/eli_pariser_beware_online_filter_bubbles/transcript.

5. Anil Dash, "The Year I Didn't Retweet Men," *Medium*, February 12, 2014, https://medium.com/the-only-woman-in-the-room/the-year-i-didnt-retweet-men79403a7eade1.

6. Brian L. Quick, "The Effects of Viewing *Grey's Anatomy* on Perceptions of Doctors and Patient Satisfaction," *Journal of Broadcasting & Electronic Media* 53, no. 1 (2009): 38–55, https://doi.org/10.1080/08838150802643563.

7. Olivier D. Serrat, "The Five Whys Technique," *Knowledge Solutions* (Manila, Philippines: Asian Development Bank, 2009). https://www.adb.org/publications/five-whys-technique.

Chapter 12: In Writing We Trust?

1. Plato, *Plato's* Phaedrus, trans. R Hackforth (London: Cambridge University Press, 1972). Cited in Clanchy, *From Memory to Written Record*, 294–295.

2. Clanchy, *From Memory to Written Record*, 296.

3. Clanchy, *From Memory to Written Record*.

Chapter 13: A Toolkit for Online Trust

1. Associated Press, "Facebook No Friend to American Indian Names," *Bismarck Tribune*, February 8, 2009, https://bismarcktribune.com/news/state-and-regional/facebook-no-friend-to-american-indian-names/article_5a4a204a-2764-5b77-8fee-7d84eef3f6c7.html.

2. Lisa Katamaya, "Japanese with Common Last Name Yoda Denied Facebook Account," *BoingBoing*, August 26, 2008, https://boingboing.net/2008/08/26/japanese-with-last-n.html.

3. "Real-Name Policy Controversy," Wikipedia, last updated March 16, 2019, https://en.wikipedia.org/wiki/Facebook_real-name_policy_controversy.

4. Bayley, at the time of Google's real-names decree, went by a different name.

5. For a really entertaining history of spam that goes all the way back to Spanish prisoner letters, see my colleague Finn Brunton's book *Spam: A Shadow History of the Internet*.

6. Erin Gallagher, "Mexico: Articles about Bots & Trolls," *Medium*, January 1, 2017, https://medium.com/@erin_gallagher/news-articles-about-bots-trolls-in-mexican-networks-7b1e551ef4a6.

7. Amelia Acker, "Data Craft: The Manipulation of Social Media Metadata," Data & Society's Media Manipulation Research Initiative, November 5, 2018, https://datasociety.net/output/data-craft/.

Chapter 14: Professions

1. John Naughton, "'The Goal Is to Automate Us': Welcome to the Age of Surveillance Capitalism," *Guardian*, January 20, 2019, https://www.theguardian.com/technology/2019/jan/20/shoshana-zuboff-age-of-surveillance-capitalism-google-facebook.

2. I previously wrote about this for *Bitch* magazine; the article appears in Lisa Jervis and Andi Zeisler, *BITCHfest: Ten Years of Cultural Criticism from the Pages of* Bitch *Magazine* (New York: Farrar, Straus and Giroux, 2006).

3. Think of midwives versus OBGYNs, or chiropractors and acupuncturists versus mainstream doctors. Over the years, there have been disputes between these fields about which of them can claim to be the trustworthy. I went to a great talk once on how hypnotism won out over "mesmerism" in mainstream psychology; see Alison Winter, "Mesmerism and the Introduction of Surgical Anesthesia to Victorian England," *Engineering and Science* 61, no. 2 (1998): 30–37, http://calteches.library.caltech.edu/3945/. You may be familiar with hypnotism, but less aware that "mesmerism" basically meant waving your hand over someone else's until they fell into a sleep-like state, leaving them vulnerable to the same suggestions made by hypnotists.

4. Here, I am working from the ALA standards for assessing information: Association of College and Research Libraries, "Framework for Information Literacy for Higher Education," American Library Association, February 2, 2015, http://www.ala.org/acrl/standards/ilframework.

5. Association of College and Research Libraries, "Framework for Information Literacy for Higher Education."

6. "List of Dates Predicted for Apocalyptic Events," Wikipedia, last updated August 4, 2019, https://en.wikipedia.org/wiki/List_of_dates_predicted_for_apocalyptic_events.

7. For a better picture of how academics might talk about the topics in *The Tipping Point*, check out Everett Rogers's book *Diffusion of Innovations*, from which *The Tipping Point* borrows liberally.

8. Doug Zongker, "Chicken Chicken Chicken: Chicken Chicken," *Annals of Improbable Research* 12, no. 5 (2006): 16–21, https://www.improbable.com/airchives/paperair/volume12/v12i5/chicken-12-5.pdf.

9. Christina Korownyk, Michael R. Kolber, James McCormack, Vanessa Lam, Kate Overbo, Candra Cotton, et al., "Televised Medical Talk Shows—What They Recommend and the Evidence to Support Their Recommendations: A Prospective Observational Study," *British Medical Journal* 349 (2014): g7346, https://doi.org/10.1136/bmj.g7346

10. Hatewatch Staff, "The Biggest Lie in the White Supremacist Propaganda Playbook: Unraveling the Truth about 'Black-on-White Crime,'" Southern Poverty Law Center, June 14, 2018, https://www.splcenter.org/20180614/biggest-lie-white-supremacist-propaganda-playbook-unraveling-truth-about-%E2%80%98black-white-crime.

Chapter 15: Books

1. LeVar Burton famously used this catchphrase when he hosted the PBS show *Reading Rainbow*.

2. Michael T. Clanchy, *From Memory to Written Record: England, 1066–1307* (Malden, MA: John Wiley & Sons, 2013), 320.

3. James W. Loewen, *Teaching What Really Happened: How to Avoid the Tyranny of Textbooks and Get Students Excited about Doing History* (New York: Teachers College Press, Columbia University, 2009), 68.

4. Loewen, *Teaching What Really Happened*, 68.

5. James Loewen, *Lies My Teacher Told Me: Everything Your American History Textbook Got Wrong* (New York: Simon & Schuster, 2007), 313.

6. Dan Quinn, "Another Example of How the Texas Textbook Wars Undermine Education Far Outside the Lone Star State," *Texas Freedom Network*, September 13, 2012, http://tfn.org/another-example-of-how-the-texas-textbook-wars-undermine-education-far-outside-the-lone-star-state/.

Chapter 16: The News

1. John Nichols, "Ben Bagdikian Knew That Journalism Must Serve the People—Not the Powerful," *Nation*, March 17, 2016, https://www.thenation.com/article/ben-bagdikian-knew-that-journalism-must-serve-the-people-not-the-powerful/.

2. Timothy Burke, "How America's Largest Local TV Owner Turned Its News Anchors into Soldiers in Trump's War on the Media." *Deadspin*, March 31, 2018, https://theconcourse.deadspin.com/how-americas-largest-local-tv-owner-turned-its-news-anc-1824233490.

3. Scott Pierce, "Owner of Three Utah TV Stations Orders Anchors to Read Statement Denouncing 'Fake News," *Salt Lake Tribune*, March 8, 2018, https://www.sltrib.com/news/2018/03/08/kutvs-owner-orders-anchors-to-read-statement-decrying-fake-news-from-national-outlets/.

4. Jonathan Beaton, "I Quit Working for Sinclair and They Sued Me. Here's Why I'm Fighting Back," *Huffington Post*, April 6, 2018, https://www.huffpost.com/entry/jonathan-beaton-sinclair-suing_us_5ac60f6fe4b09ef3b2441237.

5. James M. Fallows, *Breaking the News: How the Media Undermine American Democracy* (New York: Vintage Books, 1997).

6. Don R. Pember, *Mass Media in America* (New York: Macmillan, 1992).

7. Pember, *Mass Media in America*.

8. Society of Professional Journalists (SPJ), "Code of Ethics," September 6, 2014, https://www.spj.org/ethicscode.asp.

9. See, for example, SPJ, "Code of Ethics"; American Society of News Editors (ASNE), "Ethics," https://www.asne.org/resources-ethics; and International Federation of Journalists (IFJ), "Global Charter of Ethics for Journalists," https://www.ifj.org/who/rules-and-policy/global-charter-of-ethics-for-journalists.html.

10. ASNE, "ASNE Statement of Principles," 2019, https://www.asne.org/asne-principles.

11. Benjamin Mullen, "*New York Times* Cracks Down on Anonymous Sources," Poynter Institute, 2016, https://www.poynter.org/ethics-trust/2016/new-york-times-cracks-down-on-anonymous-sources/.

12. Mullen, "*New York Times* Cracks Down." See also Benjamin Mullen, "The *Intercept* Is Developing Editorial Standards for Using Anonymous Sources," Poynter

Institute, 2015, https://www.poynter.org/reporting-editing/2015/the-intercept-is-developing-new-editorial-standards-for-anonymous-sources/; Shani Hilton, "The *BuzzFeed* News Standards and Ethics Guide," *BuzzFeed*, January 30, 2015, last updated November 2, 2018, https://www.buzzfeednews.com/article/shani/the-buzzfeed-editorial-standards-and-ethics-guide; Jim Romenesko, "AP: No Opinion or Speculation from Anonymous Sources," Poynter Institute, 2011, https://www.poynter.org/reporting-editing/2011/ap-no-opinion-or-speculation-from-anonymous-sources/.

13. Mullen, "*New York Times* Cracks Down."

14. Alexios Mantzarlis and Jane Elizabeth, "Hands-on Fact-Checking: A Short Course," International Fact-Checking Network at the Poynter Institute and the American Press Institute, 2018, https://www.poynter.org/courses/handson-factchecking/lessons/evaluating-sources/topic/reliable-sources/.

15. Jonathan Dube, "Reporter's Privilege Resources," Poynter Institute, 2005, https://www.poynter.org/reporting-editing/2005/reporters-privilege-resources/.

16. Mantzarlis and Elizabeth, "Hands-on Fact-Checking: A Short Course."

17. Garrett Epps, "Does the First Amendment Protect Deliberate Lies?" *Atlantic*, August 16, 2016, https://www.theatlantic.com/politics/archive/2016/08/does-the-first-amendment-protect-deliberate-lies/496004/.

18. Jordyn Holman, Rebecca Greenfield, and Gerry Smith, "Sinclair Employees Say Their Contracts Make It Too Expensive to Quit," *Bloomberg*, April 3, 2018, https://www.bloomberg.com/news/articles/2018-04-03/sinclair-employees-say-their-contracts-make-it-too-expensive-to-quit.

Chapter 17: Wikipedia

1. Wikimedia Foundation, "Wikipedia: Five Pillars," last updated July 31, 2019, https://en.wikipedia.org/wiki/Wikipedia:Five_pillars.

2. Timothy Messer-Kruse, "The 'Undue Weight' of Truth on Wikipedia," *Chronicle of Higher Education*, February 12, 2012, https://www.chronicle.com/article/The-Undue-Weight-of-Truth-on/130704.

Chapter 18: Algorithms, or Digital "Soup" Recipes

1. Robert Booth, "Facebook Reveals News Feed Experiment to Control Emotions," *Guardian*, June 29, 2014, https://www.theguardian.com/technology/2014/jun/29/facebook-users-emotions-news-feeds.

2. Eli Pariser, "Beware Online 'Filter Bubbles,'" filmed March 2011 in Long Beach, CA, TED video, 8:58, https://www.ted.com/talks/eli_pariser_beware_online_filter_bubbles.

3. Zeynep Tufekci, "YouTube, the Great Radicalizer," *New York Times*, March 10, 2018, https://nyti.ms/2GeTMa6.

4. Jose Pagliery, "Man behind 'Carry On' T-Shirts Says Company Is 'Dead,'" *CNN*, March 5, 2013, https://money.cnn.com/2013/03/05/smallbusiness/keep-calm-and-carry-on/index.html.

5. James Bridle, "Something Is Wrong on the Internet," *Medium*, November 6, 2017, https://medium.com/@jamesbridle/something-is-wrong-on-the-internet-c39c471271d2; Anisa Subedar and Will Yates, "The Disturbing YouTube Videos That Are Tricking Children," *BBC Trending*, March 27, 2017, https://www.bbc.com/news/blogs-trending-39381889.

6. John Battelle, *The Search: How Google and Its Rivals Rewrote the Rules of Business and Transformed Our Culture* (New York: Portfolio, 2006).

7. Battelle, *The Search*.

8. Barry Schwartz, "Google Admits It's Using Very Limited Personalization in Search Results," *Search Engine Land*, September 17, 2018, https://searchengineland.com/google-admits-its-using-very-limited-personalization-in-search-results-305469.

9. Greg Sterling, "Survey: People Largely Negative about Google's Personalized Search Results," *Search Engine Land*, February 8, 2012, https://searchengineland.com/survey-people-largely-negative-about-googles-personalized-search-results-110840.

10. James Hu, "A Job Hunter's Guide to Getting Your Resume Past the ATS and into Human Hands," *Muse*, November 4, 2015, https://www.themuse.com/advice/a-job-hunters-guide-to-getting-your-resume-past-the-ats-and-into-human-hands.

11. "Stat Oil," *Economist*, February 9, 2013, https://www.economist.com/finance-and-economics/2013/02/09/stat-oil; Penny Crosman, "This Lender Is Using AI to Make Loans through Social Media," *American Banker*, December 28, 2017, https://www.americanbanker.com/news/this-lender-is-using-ai-to-make-loans-through-social-media.

12. Sharon Silke Carty, "Many Cars Tone Deaf to Women's Voices," AOL Autos, May 11, 2011, https://web.archive.org/web/20110603084904/http://autos.aol.com/article/women-voice-command-systems/

13. wzamen01, "HP Computers Are Racist," YouTube video, 2:15, December 10, 2009, https://youtu.be/t4DT3tQqgRM.

14. Tom Simonite, "Photo Algorithms ID White Men Fine, Black Women Not So Much," *Wired*, February 6, 2018, https://www.wired.com/story/photo-algorithms-id-white-men-fineblack-women-not-so-much/.

15. Clare Garvie and Jonathan Frankle, "Facial Recognition Software Might Have a Racial Bias Problem," *Atlantic*, April 7, 2016, https://www.theatlantic.com/technology/archive/2016/04/the-underlying-bias-of-facial-recognition-systems/476991/.

16. Colin Lechter, "Facebook Drops Targeting Options," *Verge*, March 19, 2019, https://www.theverge.com/2019/3/19/18273018/facebook-housing-ads-jobs-discrimination-settlement.

17. ACLU Tennessee, "Facebook Settle Civil Rights Cases," ACLU Tennessee website, March 19, 2019, https://www.aclu-tn.org/facebook-settles-civil-rights-cases-by-making-sweeping-changes-to-its-online-ad-platform/.

18. Gregory Barber, "San Francisco Bans Agency Use of Facial-Recognition Software," *Wired*, May 14, 2019, https://www.wired.com/story/san-francisco-bans-use-facial-recognition-tech/.

Chapter 19: Beware the Profit Motive

1. Adam Chandler, "The Many Reasons to Dislike Facebook's Mood Manipulation Experiment," *Atlantic*, June 28, 2014, https://www.theatlantic.com/technology/archive/2014/06/the-many-reasons-to-dislike-facebooks-mood-manipulation-experiment/373657/.

2. Don R. Pember, *Mass Media in America* (New York: Macmillan, 1992).

3. Janko Roettgers, "Kardashians in Trouble," *Variety*, August 22, 2016, https://variety.com/2016/digital/news/kardashians-instagram-paid-ads-product-placements-1201842072/.

4. Emil Protalinski, "Google Killed 2.3 Billion 'Bad Ads' in 2018," *VentureBeat*, March 13, 2019, https://venturebeat.com/2019/03/13/google-killed-2-3-billion-bad-ads-in-2018-down-28-from-2017/.

5. Zoey Chong, "Up to 48 Million Twitter Accounts Are Bots, Study Says," *CNET*, March 14, 2017, https://www.cnet.com/news/new-study-says-almost-15-percent-of-twitter-accounts-are-bots/.

6. As I write this, *Network* has been revived on Broadway, starring *Breaking Bad*'s Bryan Cranston. The story is just as relevant today as it was in 1976.

7. Julia Cagé, *Saving the Media: Capitalism, Crowdfunding, and Democracy*, trans. Arthur Goldhammer (Cambridge, MA: Harvard University Press, 2016), excerpted in "News Is a Public Good," *Nieman Reports*, April 7, 2016, https://niemanreports.org/articles/news-is-a-public-good/.

8. Victor Pickard, Josh Stearns, and Craig Aaron, *Saving the News: Toward a National Journalism Strategy* (Washington, DC: FreePress.net, 2012), https://web.archive.org/web/20130605103903/https://www.freepress.net/sites/default/files/fp-legacy/saving_the_news.pdf.

9. Cagé, *Saving the Media*.

10. Janine Jackson and Peter Hart, "'The Profit Motive': CounterSpin Interview with Laurie Garrett," *FAIR: Fairness & Accuracy in Reporting*, July 1, 2005, https://fair.org/extra/8220the-profit-motive8221/.

11. Maureen Ryan, "David Simon Talks about His Career in Journalism and the Final Chapter of 'The Wire.'" *Chicago Tribune*, January 10, 2008, https://web.archive.org/web/20080203054141/http://featuresblogs.chicagotribune.com/entertainment_tv/2008/01/david-simon-tal.html.

12. Bill Carter, "ABC Shelves Report on Parent Disney," *New York Times*, October 15, 1998, https://www.nytimes.com/1998/10/15/us/abc-shelves-report-on-parent-disney.html.

13. Janine Jackson, "11th Annual Fear & Favor Report," *FAIR: Fairness & Accuracy in Reporting*, March 1, 2011. https://fair.org/extra/11th-annual-fear-amp-favor-report/.

14. Janine Jackson, "FAIR Report: 13th Annual Fear & Favor Report," *FAIR: Fairness & Accuracy in Reporting*, February 1, 2013, https://fair.org/extra/fair-report-13th-annual-fear-favor-review/.

15. Ben H. Bagdikian, *The New Media Monopoly* (Boston: Beacon Press, 2004).

16. Robert W. McChesney, *The Problem of the Media: U.S. Communication Politics in the Twenty-First Century* (New York: Monthly Review Press, 2004).

Chapter 20: Going Forward ...

1. J. David Goodman, "Amazon Is Getting At Least $1.7 Billion to Come to Queens," *New York Times*, November 13, 2018, https://nyti.ms/2DjeWod; Adam Brinktow, "Supervisor Haney Demands Accounting for Twitter Tax Break," *Curbed San Francisco*, March 6, 2019, https://sf.curbed.com/2019/3/6/18253043/matt-haney-twitter-tax-break-hearing-sf-tech.

Index

Passwords
  strength, 108–110
  changing, 106, 107
  overview of, 105, 106
  random, 109
  storing, 110–112, 152
  unique, 107–110
Peer review, 255
Personal brands, 164
Personal experience, 203, 204
Personally identifying information, 86, 89
Perspective, 186, 187
Physical threats, 123, 124
Pictures, sending, 144, 145
Police, 130, 131
Presidential election of 2016, 157
Price, Catherine, 37, 38
Primary-source material, 237, 278
Printing press, 59, 209
Privacy settings, 121
Private browsing, 125, 126, 152
Private keys, 219
Product placement, 312
Professionals
  areas of expertise and, 246, 247
  basic requirements for, 236, 237
  casual communications from, 246
  evaluating information from, 247, 248
  historians, 237–239
  overview of, 233–236
  religious figures, 239–241
  scientists, 241–244
  writing of, 244–248
Profit
  consolidation and, 317–319
  editorial decisions and, 315, 316
  importance of, 307
  on the internet, 59–60, 68–69, 313–315
  news cycle and, 19
  questions to ask regarding, 308, 309
Propaganda, 170–174
Public health campaigns, 173, 174

Public relations, 170, 173, 274
Public versus private spaces, 64
Public wi-fi, 85
Publishing process, 254, 255
Puyo Puyo, 39

Rankings, search engine, 297–301
Ratings, 310
Real name requirements, 89, 222, 223
Recording technologies, 203, 204
Relationships
  account access and, 135–138
  knowing yourself before, 139–141
  online, 143–145
  setting boundaries and, 141, 142
  sharing accounts in, 139, 141, 142
Reliability, 243, 272, 273
Religious figures, 239–241
Religious traditions/groups
  fiction and, 256, 257
  textbooks and, 261
Research
  journalism and, 270–278
  historians and, 234–235, 237–238, 244, 258–261
  science and, 163, 173, 234–235, 241–246, 258–261
  Wikipedia and, 282–283, 285–287
Response, 37
Restraining orders, 123, 124
Résumés, 302
Retweeting, 43
Rewards, 37, 41–44
Rogers, Fred, 13–15
Rogers, Nancy McFeely, 15

Schools, 128–130
Scientists, 241–244
Screen time, limiting, 41
Search
  as exploration, 166–167
  strategies, 124, 217, 226–227, 273, 297–301

Search algorithms, 297–301
Search engine optimization (SEO), 298, 299
Secure text messaging, 131–133
Security, asset assessment and, 79–85
Security measures, 46
Security reports, 115
Security settings, 121
Self-censorship, 62–65
Self-published books, 254
Settings, customizing, 4, 5
Shopping information, 91, 92
Signatures, 204, 205, 210, 211, 219
Sinclair Broadcast Group, 264, 265, 279
Slander, 277
Slot machine effect, 39–41
Small-group interactions, 64, 65–67
Social construction of information, 166
Social media/networking
  algorithm selections and, 293
  breaking cues and, 37, 38
  credit services and, 302
  digital information on, 94, 95
  effects of, 53
  election influence and, 77
  fake accounts on, 130, 225–228
  filter bubbles and, 189, 190
  lack of moderators on, 68–70
  manipulation by, 289, 290
  presidential election of 2016 and, 157, 158
  questions to ask regarding, 54
  "report account" options on, 121
  rewards and, 41, 43, 44
  sharing violent acts on, 22–25
  signs of abuse on, 146–150
  small-group interactions and, 65–67
  tracking with, 125, 126
Social security number (SSN), 87
Socrates, 171–173, 208
Software, constant changes to, 7, 8
Sound, 29
Spelling errors, 92, 93

Spyware, 151, 152
Standardized tests, 260
Standards
  of decency, 61, 62
  for journalists, 268–270
  for professionals, 234–236
Startle reflex, 159, 160
Stereotype threat, 1
Stress, effects of, 13
Surprise sound, 29
SWATing, 123, 124
Systems, trust in, 164–166
Systems of trust, 201

Tails operating system, 131–133
Technology
  bad experiences with, 5–7
  learning about, 2, 10, 11
Technology skills, myths regarding, 1, 2
Telecommunications Act (1996), 317
Testimony, rethinking, 210–212
Textbooks, 258–261, 286
Tor browser, 131–133
Tracker obfuscation tools, 125, 126
Training, 11, 235
Transparency, Wikipedia and, 281–283
Trigger, 37
Trolls, 121, 122
Trust
  in appearance, 162, 164
  development of, 159–161
  disruption of, 161, 162
  importance of, 153
  online sources and, 213–219
  personal experience and, 203, 204
  rebuilding, 166–168, 328
  relationships and, 136–138
  roots of, 157–168
  in systems, 164–166
  systems of, 201
  and the written word, 204–209
Truth in Advertising, 312
Turkle, Sherry, 72

Twitter, 39, 43, 68, 314
    presidential election of 2016 and, 157
Two-factor authentication, 46

Undo function, 114, 115
Updates
    importance of installing, 99–103
    making room for, 104
    older devices and, 104, 105
URL (uniform resource locator), 216
User retention, 46

Validity, 243
Victory gardens, 77–79, 119
Videos, editing of, 211
Violent crimes
    decrease in, 18
    social media sharing and, 22–25
Virtual private network (VPN), 85, 128,
        129, 130
Voice command systems, 303
Voice recognition, 91, 112
Volume, 29
Vulnerabilities, identifying, 139–141

Walled gardens, 322–324
War of the Worlds, 169
Web proxies, 128–130
"White hat" hackers, 100
WHOIS privacy, 123, 124, 217
Wi-fi, security and, 84, 85
Wikipedia, 281–287
Work pressures, 50, 51
Writing, 29, 204–210

Xu, Christina, 45

YouTube, 293, 294, 295

Zero days, 100